BANKING IN NINETEENTH-

for
Hilary

BANKING IN
NINETEENTH-CENTURY IRELAND:
The Belfast Banks, 1825–1914

Philip Ollerenshaw

Manchester
University Press

Copyright © Philip Ollerenshaw 1987

Published by
Manchester University Press
Oxford Road, Manchester M13 9PL, UK
27 South Main Street, Wolfeboro, NH 03894–2069, USA

British Library cataloguing in publication data
Ollerenshaw, Philip
  Banking in nineteenth-century Ireland:
  the Belfast banks, 1825–1914
  1. Banks and banking – Northern Ireland
  – Belfast – History
  I. Title
  332.1'09416'7   HG3000.B42

Library of Congress cataloging in publication data applied for

ISBN 0 7190 2276 2 *hardback*

Photoset in Linotron Times
by Northern Phototypesetting Co, Bolton
Printed and bound in Great Britain by
Biddles Ltd, Guildford and King's Lynn

CONTENTS

		page
	LIST OF FIGURES AND TABLES	vii
	PREFACE	viii
	ABBREVIATIONS	x
	MAP OF IRELAND	xi
	INTRODUCTION	1
1	ORIGINS	5
	1.1 Attorneys and bankers	5
	1.2 Banking reform and the formation of the Northern Banking Company	9
	1.3 Living with the neighbours	17
	1.4 The crisis of 1825–6 and the small note controversy	22
	1.5 The Belfast Banking Company	27
2	COMPETITION, COLLUSION AND CRISES	31
	2.1 Branch expansion	34
	2.2 The Agricultural and Commercial Bank of Ireland and the 1836 crisis	39
	2.3 The Ulster Banking Company	46
	2.4 The depression of 1839–43	52
	2.5 The legislation of 1844–5	56
	2.6 The Famine and the commercial crisis of 1847	65
	2.7 Origins and impact of the 1857 crisis	72
3	ASPECTS OF BANKING BUSINESS IN THE MID-NINETEENTH CENTURY	81
	3.1 Note circulation	82
	3.2 Bill discounts	87
	3.3 Deposits and credit balances	90
	3.4 Advances	94
4	TOWARDS LIMITED LIABILITY	102
	4.1 The agricultural depression, 1859–64	102
	4.2 The linen boom	105
	4.3 The agricultural depression of the late 1870s	114

Contents

	4.4	Inter-bank relations	122
	4.5	The adoption of limited liability	140
5	**INTO THE NEW CENTURY**		152
	5.1	The cartel widened	152
	5.2	Banks and politics	157
	5.3	Aspects of lending before 1914	163
	5.4	Irish banking before 1914	183

CONCLUSION	188
NOTES	203
APPENDIX: TRENDS IN PROFITABILITY	244
BIBLIOGRAPHY	245
INDEX	256

FIGURES AND TABLES

Figures

1	Belfast Bank notes in circulation, 1840–5	page 85
2	Overdrawn accounts at Ulster Bank Head Office, 1838–42	95

Tables

1	Members of the Belfast Chamber of Commerce in 1827	3
2	Average annual circulation of the Belfast Bank, 1812–25	8
3	Northern Bank shareholders in September 1824	12
4	Agencies of the Belfast banks in 1825	14
5	Agents of the Northern Bank in 1825	16
6	Belfast Bank shareholders at 1 August 1827	28
7	Agents of the Belfast Bank in August 1827	29
8	Irish joint-stock banks in January 1840	32
9	Dividends paid by the Belfast banks, 1825–40	35
10	Branch opening dates of the Belfast banks, 1834–40	38
11	Shareholders in the Ulster Bank at 12 April 1836	48
12	Average circulation of Irish banks of issue in the four weeks ending 3 January 1846	62
13	Number per thousand occupied males engaged in farming in Ulster, 1831–1901	65
14	Note circulation in Ireland, 1846–55	67
15	Summary of the Irish grain trade, 1839–48	68
16	Deposits in Irish joint-stock banks, 1840–65	71
17	Movements in rates of interest, April 1857–February 1858	76
18	Deposits withdrawn from branches of the Belfast Bank during the panic from 17 October until 30 November 1857	78
19	Account holders at Ulster Bank Branch in Aughnacloy, c. 1852	82
20	Actual note circulation of Irish banks as % of authorised issue, 1846–52	86
21	Ulster Bank discounts, 1836–53	90
22	Northern Bank deposits and current accounts at 16 August 1859	91
23	Ulster Bank deposits and current accounts at 31 August 1859	92
24	Employment and salaries in the Belfast Bank, 1860–1914	101
25	Deposits and current accounts in credit in three Irish banks, 1859–64	105
26	Dividends and reserve funds, 1859–71	110
27	Deposits and current accounts in credit in the Belfast banks, 1876–81	115
28	Northern Bank branch deposits and credit balances, 1876 and 1881	116–17
29	Bank offices in Ireland, 1850–1913	124
30	Irish joint-stock banks in 1875	133
31	Deposit structure of the Belfast banks, June 1880	141
32	Bank shares on the Dublin stock exchange, 1878–9	146
33	Business at two Belfast city branches, 1896 and 1906	158
34	Religious affiliation of bank directors and clerks, 1881 and 1911	164
35	The Belfast Flax Spinning Company, 1886–97	172
36	Acceptances discounted by the Bank of Ireland for Belfast shipbuilders at 6 January 1909	176
37	Irish joint-stock banks, 1886 and 1912	184
38	Bank offices in the United Kingdom in October 1913	187
39	Bank offices in 1912	187

PREFACE

This book would not have been completed without the active assistance and co-operation of a large number of people. The PhD thesis upon which it is based was accepted by the University of Sheffield in 1982. My supervisors, Dr D. E. Bland and Professor Sidney Pollard, had the arduous task of discussing my ideas in conversation and correspondence over a period of more than five years. My debt to them is enormous and is gratefully acknowledged.

Helpful staff at the Goldsmiths' Library (University of London), Institute of Bankers in Dublin, Linen Hall Library and Queen's University in Belfast and Ulster Polytechnic ensured that research was made as problem-free as possible. At the Public Record Office of Northern Ireland, Valerie Adams, Bill Crawford, Andrew Harrison, Trevor Parkhill, Gerry Slater and Brian Trainor were of invaluable assistance in facilitating access to bank and business archives, catalogued and uncatalogued. Without them this book would not have been written. Friends and colleagues who have contributed through their much-appreciated comments and suggestions include Michael Collins, Cyril Ehrlich, Robert Gavin, Edwin Green, Keith Jeffery, David Johnson, Liam Kennedy, Tony Morris, Charles Munn and Leslie Pressnell. In the banking world I would like to thank the following for their assistance: Mr D. E. Harvey and Mr A. St J. Lambkin (Allied Irish Banks); Mr J. A. Henigan and Ms Sarah Ward Perkins (Bank of Ireland); Mr N. C. Beattie, Mr J. F. McIlmoyle and Mr J. N. Simpson (Northern Bank); Mr H. Burrowes, Mr C. Colthurst and Sir Robin Kinahan (Ulster Bank); Mr R. J. Pounder (Northern Ireland Bankers' Association).

Research was financed by an SSRC studentship (1976–8) and during the year 1978–9 by my tenure of a Junior Research Fellowship in The Institute of Irish Studies at the Queen's University of Belfast. The late Director of that Institute, Professor Rodney Green, gave unstinting guidance and was always willing to share his immense knowledge of Irish economic history. His sudden death in 1981 deprived the world of Irish history of one of its shrewdest and most likeable practitioners. Since 1979 my research

Preface

has been generously funded by the Ulster Polytechnic and the University of Ulster.

A number of long-suffering typists, Virginia King, Pauline Knox, Janet Campbell and Jackie Darrah, found time to translate a semi-legible manuscript without audible complaint; Ian Alexander drew the graphs and the map.

My wife, Hilary, has been a constant support and helped me through the inevitable crises which accompany any project such as this. Dedication of this book to her is undoubtedly inadequate recompense for such a vital contribution.

Finally, I would like to thank the Northern Ireland Bankers' Association for their encouragement and financial support.

ABBREVIATIONS

BBSM	Belfast Bank Board of Superintendence Minutes
NBCM	Northern Bank Committee Minutes
PBCM	Provincial Bank Court Minutes
PBHO	Provincial Bank Head Office
PRONI	Public Record Office of Northern Ireland
SC	Select Committee
UBB	Ulster Bank Branch
UBCM	Ulster Bank Committee Minutes
UBHO	Ulster Bank Head Office

INTRODUCTION

The aim of this book is to throw some new light on the growth and role of joint-stock banks in Ireland with special reference to the three banks based in Belfast. Banks often receive relatively little treatment in history and economic history textbooks; indeed, two recent surveys of British economic history manage virtually to ignore them altogether.[1] As far as Ireland is concerned there have been some valuable contributions to the study of banking institutions[2] but rarely do these contain discussion of the links between banks and economy in which they functioned. Moreover, Ireland does not feature in either volume of seminal essays on banking collected by Rondo Cameron,[3] or in Kindleberger's recent *Financial History of Western Europe*.[4] The justification for this work, then, is simply that there is little published work in the area.

In the early nineteenth century visitors to Belfast were clearly aware that the town differed from other parts of the country and that rapid population growth was under way. As H. D. Inglis remarked in the 1830s,

> Belfast has little or nothing in common with the rest of Ireland.... The present town of Belfast is but of twenty years standing. At least one third of the town has been built within the last fifteen years, and no town of the United Kingdom has had so rapid an increase in population.[5]

Other commentators wrote along similar lines. One called Belfast 'at once the Liverpool and Manchester of Ireland',[6] another described it as 'the only manufacturing town' in Ireland.[7] The industrial development of the Belfast region, though modest enough by British or European standards, was unique in Ireland. The population of Belfast itself, a mere 37,000 in 1821, had doubled twenty years later and increased fivefold between 1841 and the First World War, by which time 400,000 people (a quarter of the total Ulster population) lived in the city.[8] Apart from the Great Famine of the late 1840s, the rise of industrial Belfast has been described as 'certainly the most dramatic event in Irish economic history since 1800'.[9]

The emergence of Belfast as an industrial centre was preceded, and subsequently paralleled, by vigorous commercial development, most obviously in the export of linen. Irish exports of linen cloth, for example, rose from about two million yards in 1715 to more than forty million by the 1790s. In the second half of the eighteenth century linen exports were increasingly channelled through Belfast rather than Dublin. Indeed, Dublin's share in this trade declined from eighty-five per cent in the early eighteenth century to under fifty per cent in the last quarter of that century.[10] Northern bleachers and drapers began successfully to wrest control of this lucrative and expanding trade from Dublin merchants, and this bid for independence was symbolised in the construction of a White Linen Hall in Belfast in the mid-1780s. The extent of commercial independence enjoyed by Belfast became greater during the next few decades and was virtually complete by the 1820s.

As Belfast's direct connections with Britain strengthened, so the influence of Dublin on the pace and direction of northern commercial life waned. It has recently been suggested that, because Belfast lacked a resident gentry, the temptation of the town's merchants to invest in land to emulate landlords was diminished. Money was instead diverted more into industry and trade and in the late eighteenth century an industrial sector – including cotton spinning and weaving, shipbuilding, ironfounding and glassmaking – developed alongside the flourishing export trade in linen and provisions.[11]

The Belfast region in the nineteenth century constituted something of an 'enclave' economy based on textiles (linen and, in the early nineteenth century, cotton) and, especially after 1850, increasingly important engineering, shipbuilding, food processing, distilling and tobacco industries. In the nineteenth and twentieth centuries the region has been heavily dependent on imports of raw materials – cotton, flax, coal and iron for example – and relied for its growth on the exploitation of cross-channel and overseas markets. More particularly, Belfast developed strong and enduring commercial links with Merseyside and the west of Scotland, links far more important than those between north-east Ulster and the rest of Ireland.[12] The integration of Belfast with the British economy resulted in a pattern of economic fluctuations which was for the

Introduction

most part remarkably similar. Acknowledged depression years in Britain – 1826, 1842, 1859, 1886 and 1908, for example – were also bad years in north-east Ulster.

The Belfast business community found institutional expression in the Chamber of Commerce established in 1783. Energetic and vociferous, the Chamber campaigned to promote industrial and mercantile interests. In particular it lobbied for improvements in postal communication within Ireland and with Britain, for improvements in internal and cross-channel communications, and frequently joined forces with similar groups in Britain and Ireland to lobby various government departments on all manner of issues. The Belfast Chamber was the largest and most influential organisation of businessmen in Ulster before 1914. Table 1 shows that in the 1820s its members were drawn from a large number of different occupational groups, and membership of the Chamber did reflect fairly accurately the business structure of the town. In the 1820s the most prominent groups, predictably, were textile manufacturers and merchants and provision traders, but the professional service sector was quite well represented. This study is concerned essentially with the development of one part of that service sector between the 1820s and the First World War.

Table 1 *Members of the Belfast Chamber of Commerce in 1827*

Accountant	1	Sadlers ironmonger	1
Baker	1	Salt manufacturer	1
Bankers	4	Ship chandler	1
Brokers	2	Shipowner	1
Cotton spinners	8	Shipbuilders	2
Distiller	1	Tanner	1
Engineer	1	Timber merchants	2
General/provision merchants	12	Tobacconist	1
Grocer/tea dealers	3	Wheelwright	1
Insurance agents/brokers	5	Wine and spirit merchants	4
Linen merchants/bleachers	9	Wool drapers	3
Lighterman	1	Others	3
Muslin manufacturer	1		
Printers	2		
Publicans	2		
Rope, sail and canvas manufacturers	2		
		Total	76

Source. Belfast Chamber of Commerce Papers PRONI D.1857/1. Occupations taken from *Pigot's Directory* 1824, pp. 358–62.

If the establishment of the White Linen Hall and the Chamber of Commerce symbolised Belfast's determination to declare commercial independence from Dublin, such determination was also reflected in the way in which the financial sector in Belfast emerged from the later eighteenth century. Cullen has shown that before 1750 Irish banking developed primarily to meet the need of landlords to transfer rents either from the provinces to Dublin, or from Dublin to London. The 'landed dimension' was therefore obvious in Ireland as in Scotland where banking developed in Edinburgh before Glasgow. In the later eighteenth century banking business in Ireland was dominated by the activities of landlords and rent remitters.

As far as Ulster was concerned, the gentry had close ties with Dublin and London bankers but Presbyterian merchants in the Belfast region were increasingly anxious to break their financial dependence on predominantly Anglican Dublin.[13] Local Belfast financial initiatives included the formation of a bank in 1784 and a Discount Office in 1793. Both were relatively short-lived. The bank's capital, totalling £40,000, was contributed by four Belfast men in equal amounts of £10,000. This venture was undoubtedly small-scale: note issue never exceeded £30,000 and no country offices were opened. The bank ceased business about the time of the 1798 rebellion, while the Discount Office closed around 1807.[14]

At the time of the Act of Union between Great Britain and Ireland, which came into force in January 1801, Belfast possessed no formal banking facilities. The town continued its industrial and commercial development, however, and within a few years three private banks had been established. In addition, it is clear that credit was provided by a number of non-bank financial intermediaries. As explained later, there was a flourishing local capital market in which attorneys played a key role. It has also been established that many northern merchants by the early nineteenth century engaged in the provision of credit, not least by way of long-term mortgages on local estates. Lending money on landed security was commonplace, often involving sums in excess of £10,000.[15] In the early nineteenth century all the basic requirements existed for the emergence of a banking sector in Belfast. It is one of the aims of this book to examine the development of formal banking in this regional capital and to consider the role of the banks in the area in which they operated.

CHAPTER ONE

ORIGINS

1.1 Attorneys and bankers

The rapidly growing manufacturing base of early nineteenth-century Belfast required a corresponding growth in the service sector, and according to *Pigot's Directory* of 1824 the town supported sixteen attorneys, six accountants, three private banks, eight brokers, sixteen fire and life assurance offices and six public notaries. Of particular interest to us are the attorneys and the banks. It is clear that the attorney's role in early nineteenth-century Ireland went far beyond the provision of legal services.

Recent research into the activities of English attorneys in the eighteenth and early nineteenth centuries has shown them to be key figures in the supply of capital for industry and commerce. The importance of the attorney in an economic context derived from two related sources. First, the legal profession had been rising in status for well over a century, and the attorney's position in society approached that of a landed gentleman. Second, legal services were required for most financial transactions such as trust administration, estate purchase and sales, and public investment of any kind.[1] For these reasons, the attorney was one of the few people able to act as an intermediary between lenders and borrowers who were unknown to each other. The pivotal position of attorneys in the provision of capital in England has only recently begun to be fully appreciated by economic historians, and little is known of their activities in early nineteenth-century Ireland. Some idea of the role of the attorney as financial intermediary can be gathered from newspaper notices advertising funds from lenders and for borrowers. Several attorneys had premises in both Belfast and Dublin; others had premises in a provincial town as well as in Belfast and/or Dublin.[2] They were thus in a position to find 'urban' borrowers for 'rural' lenders or vice versa, and so reduce the problems posed by the need to supply funds to a rapidly growing industrial town like Belfast from a number of dispersed sources.

On the supply side, the size of sums offered through attorneys in Belfast in the 1820s ranged from as little as £30 to over £30,000, and even £80,000 on one occasion.[3] Very often the larger sums were divisible into smaller individual lots. A typical such notice[4] read:

MONEY
£10,000 to be lent on mortgage at 5% in one sum or in sums not less than £1,000.

Mr Darcus, Solicitor, Larne
or 55 Dorset Street, Belfast.

The security required, when specified at all, was usually unencumbered land, and the rate of interest varied from four and a half to six per cent. Money was also offered by the Belfast Annuity Company and by public notaries.[5] Advertisements seldom mentioned the term of loans, but some were explicitly offered on a long-term basis.[6] Indeed it is not at all improbable that medium and long-term loans were more typical than short-term. It is also worth noting that London-based attorneys advertised funds in Belfast from the mid-1820s.[7] Thus, potential borrowers in Belfast had a large number of diverse sources from which to obtain funds. On the demand side, the largest individual sums required were smaller than those offered, only rarely exceeding £10,000.[8] The security tendered was diverse: unencumbered land seems to have been the most common, but others included valuable leaseholds and turnpike tolls.[9] It seems clear then that the local capital market in Belfast was an active one, and that the attorney was a key figure in this market.

As well as the sixteen attorneys listed in *Pigot's Directory* for 1824, Belfast had three private banks: Batt, Houston and Batt, commonly known as Batt's or the Belfast Bank; Orr, McCance, Montgomery and McNeile, known as Montgomery's or the Northern Bank; and Tennent, Callwell, Luke and Thomson, known as Tennent's or the Commercial Bank. The first of these opened on 1 August 1808, the last two opened on the same day: 1 June 1809.[10] When these banks were established they were, of course, obliged to operate within the prevailing framework of banking legislation which may be briefly summarised. An Act of the Irish Parliament of 1756 required the names of all partners to be written on all notes and receipts, and prohibited any person from engaging in banking business who also undertook 'trade or traffick

Origins

as merchants in goods or merchandises imported or exported'.[11] This last clause effectively prevented the emergence of the overseas trader-banker in Ireland, and had no parallel in British law.

Another Act of 1760[12] contained a clause which prohibited any banker giving 'any note, negotiable receipt or accountable receipt with any promise or engagment therein contained for the payment of interest'. It will be shown below that this Act led to some confusion as to whether it was legal to pay interest on deposits. The third, and perhaps the most significant, Act was that of 1782[13] which granted a royal charter to the new Bank of Ireland with a capital of £600,000, and stipulated that no body other than the Bank of Ireland could 'borrow, owe or take up any sum or sums of money on their bills or notes payable at demand for any less period than six months'. The practical effect of this was to limit all Irish banks, with the exception of the Bank of Ireland, to a maximum of six partners. The limitation of a maximum number of partners did not mean that all the banks operated with the maximum. The Belfast Bank started with four partners in 1808, but was down to three by 1825; the Commercial Bank began with five partners in 1809, but had only three by 1825; the Northern Bank operated with four partners between 1809 and 1822.[14]

Relatively little is known about the business of these three private banks. When they were established, Ireland was mid-way through the so-called restriction period (1797–1821) when cash payments were suspended in Britain and Ireland.[15] During this period there was a proliferation of private banks in Ireland, particularly in the south. In Ulster in 1804 there were no more than two banks: Ferguson's in Derry and possibly also Malcolmson's in Lurgan.[16] In addition to the three banks in Belfast opened in 1808–9 another bank, Moore, Foxalle and McCann, opened for a short time in Newry during the restriction period, as did Hanington's bank in Dungannon.[17]

In the ten years or so after the suspension of cash payments gold largely ceased to circulate in most parts of Ireland, but continued to circulate in Ulster apparently because landlords and their agents demanded it for rent payments.[18] When the private banks were established in Belfast in 1808–9, however, their notes quickly superseded gold.[19] One contemporary estimate put the circulation of Malcolmson's Bank in Lurgan at £170,000 in the summer of 1808, and the 'average circulation' of the three banks in Belfast in 1810 at

£225,000.[20] Although there is no way to check these figures it is very likely that they are an underestimate. The 'average circulation' of the Belfast Bank alone was £249,000 in 1811, and Table 2 shows corresponding figures for the same bank to 1825. Notes of the Belfast Bank were payable by Solomon Watson, its Dublin agent. All three banks in Belfast pushed notes into circulation by the use of agents who discounted bills at linen and other markets. By the early 1820s, notes of the Belfast banks circulated mainly in counties Antrim, Down and Londonderry, but also in Armagh, Cavan, Monaghan and Tyrone.[21]

Table 2 *Average annual circulation of the Belfast Bank, 1812–25 (£000)*

Year	£	Year	£
1812	354	1819	412
1813	396	1820	300
1814	378	1821	310
1815	313	1822	268
1816	239	1823	297
1817	271	1824	300
1818	389	1825	351

Source. *S.C. of the House of Lords . . . on promissory notes . . .*, BPP 1826–7, VI, p. 25.

Although it has recently been suggested that private banks in Belfast did not lend on mortgage,[22] there were exceptions to this. In 1810 the Commercial Bank lent £5,000 (Irish) on mortgage to John McCracken, a leading cotton spinner of Belfast.[23] The dearth of private bank records makes it impossible to say how typical such loans were, but when more research has been undertaken into solicitors' and business records it may well be that they were far more common than has hitherto been thought.

During the restriction period, the structure of the Irish banking system, with one large chartered bank and many small private banks, was similar to that existing in England and Wales where the Bank of England was the only bank with more than six partners. In Scotland, however, the banking system was very different, not least because there was no bank with special privileges comparable to those enjoyed by the Bank of England and Bank of Ireland, and so virtually all banks in Scotland had many more than six partners.[24] These basic differences between Scotland and other parts of the United Kingdom lay at the heart of demands for banking reform in

Origins

England, Wales and Ireland after the Napoleonic Wars. In Ireland, the Act of 1756 which, as noted above, had no parallel in British law, was also a specific target for reform.

1.2 Banking reform and the formation of the Northern Banking Company

While it is difficult to be precise about the number of private banks operating in Ireland at any one point in the restriction period it is likely that there were about eleven in 1800, forty by 1804, and twenty by 1820.[25] In England and Wales too the twenty years or so after 1797 were a 'fertile breeding ground for swarms of new banks',[26] and the number increased from around 230 in 1797 to more than 800 by 1810.[27] All these banks were essentially local concerns and limited to a maximum of six partners. Herein lay their greatest potential weakness, which became obvious during the deflation which followed the end of the Napoleonic Wars. Deflationary pressures, which were particularly great in the south of Ireland, put an intolerable strain on many private banks and culminated in the crisis of 1820. In the two weeks following 25 May 1820, seven of the fourteen banks in the south of Ireland failed.[28] Apart from the loss sustained by depositors, these failures had serious implications for traders and the business community in general since in many areas by June 1820 there was 'no circulating medium, and no means of barter or carrying on trade'.[29]

The crisis of 1820, serious though it was in parts of the south, would certainly have been more severe if the Bank of Ireland had not stepped in to support all the private banks in Dublin as well as Montgomery's (the Northern Bank) in Belfast.[30] This was neither the first time, nor the last, that the Bank of Ireland provided assistance to Irish banks in time of severe pressure in the nineteenth century.[31] In Ulster, Malcolmson's Bank in Lugan quietly passed away, so too did the bank in Newry, but the three banks in Belfast survived. Although Montgomery's received a total of £35,000 in assistance from the Bank of Ireland in June 1820, which undoubtedly helped to see it through the crisis, the other two banks in Belfast do not appear to have received any similar assistance. Confidence in all the Belfast banks was also preserved by the publication of several manifestos from hundreds of landowners, merchants and manufacturers in Belfast, Coleraine, Dundalk and Newry to demonstrate their faith in the banks by 'voluntarily' pledging themselves 'to accept of their notes in all our transactions of whatever kind'.[32]

The 1820 crisis, while falling short of a national disaster, resulted in unprecedented demands for reform of the Irish banking system. Reformers concentrated their efforts in two particular directions: removal of the offending clauses in the 1756 Act, and modification or even abolition of the Bank of Ireland's special privileges. Critics of private banks in England, Wales and Ireland were impressed with the stability of the vast majority of Scottish banks after 1815, and it was generally believed that such stability derived from the absence of legislation in Scotland confining banks to a maximum number of six partners.[33]

Before banks of more than six partners could be established in Ireland, the Bank of Ireland's charter needed to be modified. This was done by an Act of 1821[34] under which the Bank of Ireland's monopoly as a bank of issue with more than six partners was restricted to a radius of fifty Irish miles(sixty-five statute miles) from Dublin. The same Act went on to specify that partners in any new bank established under it had to be resident in Ireland. The 1821 Act, innovative though it was, was likely to remain a dead letter unless the two clauses of the Act of 1756 (requiring the names of all partners to be written on all notes and receipts and preventing merchants engaged in overseas trade from becoming partners) were repealed. The initiative for removing these two clauses came from 'several wealthy and respectable merchants and bankers of Belfast', and their case was advocated in the House of Commons by Sir Henry Parnell in March 1824.[35] The petitioners proposed that partners' names, instead of appearing on all notes and receipts, should be registered in the Court of Chancery or with the clerk of the peace. On behalf of the petitioners, Parnell remarked of the 1756 Act that 'no system could be more ingeniously devised to prevent opulent and respectable persons from establishing themselves as bankers in Ireland'.[36]

The clauses of which Parnell and the Belfast petitioners complained were removed by the Irish Banking Act 1824 which became law on 17 June.[37] A week later it was announced in Belfast that a joint-stock bank would be formed as soon as possible to take over Montgomery's as a going concern. The deed of co-partnership of the new bank, styled The Northern Banking Company, was dated 1 August 1824 and so the Northern was the first joint-stock bank in Ireland.[38] The question arises as to why the partners in Montgomery's made the first move into joint-stock banking. One reason was almost certainly that the rapid development of Belfast was outstripping the capacity of private banks.[39] A second reason may also be valid, namely the need to make the private bank more secure. The collapse of so many private banks in Ireland in 1820 cannot have been forgotten by the partners in Montgomery's, and Montgomery's itself had to apply for assistance to the Bank of Ireland during the 1820 crisis. This last fact may well explain why it was Montgomery's, rather than either of its two neighbours, that made the move into joint-stock banking.

The capital of the Northern was fixed at £500,000, in 5,000 shares of £100 each. The first issue was oversubscribed and not all those (264 persons) who signed the deed subsequently became shareholders. By 18 September 1824 there were 221 shareholders[40] and their geographical distribution is shown in Table 3. Shareholders came overwhelmingly from the Belfast area and were drawn almost exclusively from the professional, manufacturing and mercantile classes. Until 1824 Irish investors had never been given the opportunity to take shares in a firmly established, successful bank. This opportunity, together with the fact that the 1820 crisis had not destroyed confidence in the Belfast banks, combined to make the Northern's task of finding local shareholders an easy one. Conversion of a successful private bank into a joint-stock concern had its advantages. One of the most significant of these was that the partners of the old bank could retain a decisive control over the new, so that its local reputation was undiminished.[41] Such conversions were common in England and Wales after 1826, but in Ireland few banks apart from those in Belfast followed this pattern.

Montgomery's had four partners and when the bank was floated as a joint-stock concern three of them became directors. James Orr, the Senior Partner in Montgomery's, was paid a salary of £1,000, John McNeile and Hugh Montgomery were paid £900 each and all three were appointed for life.[42] All of them agreed to retire from business on their own account, and devote their whole time to the bank. At least two directors had to attend the bank during all hours of business, and there were financial penalties for absence.[43] The deed also specified that no director 'shall be engaged or concerned in any other business whatsoever, under pain of forfeiting his office'. This particular clause was very unusual since most directors

Table 3 *Northern Bank shareholders in September 1824*

County	Number	Remarks
Antrim and Down	193	(of which 119 Belfast)
Londonderry	8	
Armagh	10	
Tyrone	3	
Monaghan	1	
Total Ulster	215	
Scotland	2	(both Edinburgh)
England	4	(1 Manchester, 1 Bath, 2 Liverpool)
Total	221	(201 male, 20 female)

Source. List of Proprietors of the Northern Banking Company, 24 September 1824 (printed)

Original members of the Advisory Committee

John McCance	Linen merchant and bleacher (Chairman)
Andrew Alexander	Tallow chandler
John Ferguson	Linen merchant and bleacher
Cunningham Gregg	Vitriol manufacturer
John McKenzie	Distiller
George Mitchell	?
John McConnell	General merchant

Sources. NBCM and *Pigot's Directory*, 1824.

in Scottish and English joint-stock banks in the nineteenth century had other business interests.[44]

Full-time directorships (later also features of the Belfast Bank and the Ulster Bank) were to be advocated by J. W. Gilbart in his influential *Treatise on Banking* (1849). Gilbart argued that retired businessmen were 'unquestionably' the most appropriate candidates for directorships because they were 'not apt to be contemplated with the suspicion, jealousy and distrust which tradesmen sometimes exercise towards such directors of a bank who are likewise engaged in trade'.[45] If part-time directors were typical in British banks, they were not without their critics. In the first half of the nineteenth century the inexperience of part-time directors attracted criticism since it was sometimes seen to lead to a highly unpredictable supply of credit: too rapid an expansion when money was abundant, too abrupt a contraction when money was tight.[46] The banks in Belfast were not only aware that their full-time directorships were highly unusual; they believed them to be superior and later argued that the public would object strongly to the part-time system 'for a man cannot be a banker for a year and cease for a year

Origins

and then come again into the bank'.[47]

The three directors were assisted by an advisory committee of seven, including a chairman. Members of the committee had to hold at least twenty shares in the bank, the chairman at least thirty. The original chairman, John McCance (a linen merchant and bleacher from the Suffolk area of Belfast) was appointed for life at a salary of £500. McCance, a former partner in Montgomery's, chaired the committee until his death in 1835, but from this date onwards chairmen were elected annually.[48] Other members of the committee were elected annually from the start, provided that at least two new members were elected every year. The committee met every second Monday during the year, with a quorum of three. Its duties were to inspect and audit the accounts, strike the dividend, prepare the yearly report and advise the directors on any point which the latter 'may think proper to submit to them for their opinion'. The original members of the committee are set out in Table 3, and they were paid £1 for each attendance.[49]

The business of the bank was outlined in the object clause of the deed, which ran:

> That the business of the company shall consist of issuing notes of hand or bank notes, lending money on cash accounts, or real or personal security, bills of exchange or letters of credit, borrowing or taking up money on receipts, bills, promissory notes, or other obligations, purchases or investments in the government or public funds of Great Britain and Ireland, exchequer or navy bills, or other securities of the government of the country, dealing in annuities, shares of the stock of this company, or of the stock of the banks of England, Ireland, or chartered banks of Scotland, or on deposits of goods, wares and merchandises, and all other businesses whatsoever, usual in banking establishments for carrying on banking in all its branches, but for no other adventure, trade, merchandise, or business whatsoever, except what is herein provided, and what is usual in banking establishments.[50]

The Northern's ability to lend money on cash accounts on real or personal security was a clear reference to the adoption of the Scottish cash credit technique. The cash credit was a type of advance pioneered by the Royal Bank of Scotland in 1728 and subsequently adopted by other Scottish banks.[51] A bond was signed by the borrower and normally two guarantors without the necessity of any other security. A maximum limit was set, but interest was charged only on the amount drawn. James Orr told a parliamentary enquiry in 1826 that the Northern Bank granted cash credits 'occasionally' at six per cent, one per cent more than minimum discount rate because bill business was considered to be 'safer and more profitable'.[52] The bond signed by the borrower and two or more guarantors may have been typical, but could be modified. Thus in October 1827 the Northern opened a cash account with Charles Brownlow of Lurgan 'accepting as collateral security against advances the Bond of Lord Darnley to Mr Brownlow for £10,000'.[53] Evidently, then, one guarantor only was necessary in this instance. Whatever the permutations, the Northern Bank was the first bank in Ireland explicitly to adopt the cash credit.

Table 4 *Agencies of the Belfast banks in 1825*

Location	Bank
Armagh	Northern, Batt's, Commercial
Ballymena	Northern, Batt's
Banbridge	Northern, Batt's, Commercial
Coleraine	Northern, Batt's, Commercial
Cootehill	Commercial
Cookstown	Commercial
Derry	Northern, Batt's
Downpatrick	Northern, Batt's
Dungannon	Northern, Batt's Commercial
Dundalk	Batt's
Lurgan	Northern[(a)], Commercial
Monaghan	Northern, Commercial
Magherafelt	Northern
Newry	Northern, Batt's, Commercial
Tandragee	Northern, Commercial

Source. S.C. *of the House of Commons on Promissory Notes 1826*, pp. 252–3.
Note. [(a)] The Lurgan Agent attended Lurgan, Tandragee, Banbridge and Portadown; NBCM, 15 November 1824.

When the Northern opened in January 1825 it had one office and a number of agents in country towns. Table 4 shows the distribution of agents for the Northern Bank and its two private bank neighbours in 1825. The function of such agents was to promote note circulation through bill discounts. They had no power to accept deposits, and this could only be done at the Belfast offices. As noted earlier, the Act of 1760 had prevented bankers from promising to pay interest on 'any note, negotiable receipt or accountable receipt'. By 1820, however, all the banks in Belfast paid interest.[54] James Orr explained how and why the Northern paid interest on deposits:

Origins

Do you pay interest on deposits? Yes.
Do you give accountable receipts to persons that deposit money with you? We do, or enter the amount to the credit of the depositors in pass books, if they have running accounts.
Do you, upon the face of those receipts, express that interest is payable upon those deposits? We do not.
Then what remedy has the depositor to recover interest if you think fit to refuse it to him? I do not think he could compel us to pay interest; but if we committed a breach of faith, by refusing it after promising, people would cease to deal with us.
Why do you not express that in the receipt? Because there is an old law which states that a banker's receipt with a promise to pay is void.[55]

Orr's view, then, was that it was legal to pay interest, but illegal to make a written promise to pay.

When the Northern opened in 1825, its only full time employees were at the Belfast office. The Northern's agents were not salaried, but paid on commission. Although the bank's deed of co-partnership permitted the establishment of branches with salaried managers, no such branches were opened until 1835. At a special meeting of the committee and directors in November 1824, the terms on which agents acted were set out.[56] Initially commission of one quarter per cent was allowed on Dublin and Belfast bills, one half per cent on English bills and one tenth per cent on cash transactions. Each agent had to give security (his/their own or that of a guarantor) and initially the level of security was as follows:

Agency location	Security payment (£)
Derry	10,000
Newry	10,000
Armagh	5,000
Ballymena	5,000
Coleraine	5,000
Dungannon	5,000
Lurgan	5,000
Monaghan	5,000
Magherafelt	3,000

At the same meeting it was further decided that when the new bank opened 'the same rate of interest shall be charged in the country as in Belfast'. The levels of security payment outlined above were maxima and in some cases a smaller sum was accepted by the bank,[57] although the scale of security was evidently related to the directors' estimate of the expected business at the agency in question.

In two instances, Armagh and Lurgan, the Northern accepted offers of the services of agents who had previously acted on behalf of the Belfast Bank and the Commercial Bank respectively. The Armagh agent, Leonard Dobbin, had been agent for the Belfast Bank for over fifteen years when he offered his services to the Northern in December 1824. He attended Armagh's public markets in which the total weekly note circulation was about £20,000 in 1826, and contributed about a fifth of this through bill discounts. Agents of the Belfast Bank and the Commercial attended the same markets at this date, the former supplying about £3,000 of notes through discounts and the two agents of the latter a total of £2,500 in the same way.[58]

Agents of the Northern combined their banking transactions with other business interests. Table 5 lists the other interests of the Northern's early agents, and it is clear that the range of occupations from which agents were drawn was broad. A long and successful business career was the main criterion used by the Northern in its selection of agents, and virtually all of them dated from the private bank era. The one known exception was Downpatrick where Hugh Wallace was appointed agent in March 1825. Wallace was an attorney and therefore likely to have wide-ranging financial

Table 5 *Agents of the Northern Bank in 1825*

Name	Occupation	Location
Thomas Hall	Notary public (formerly Commercial Bank agent)	Lurgan
John and Hugh Boyd	General merchants	Newry
Thomas Harvey	Merchant	Derry
John Johnston	'Gentleman'	Monaghan
Leonard Dobbin	Land agent (formerly Belfast Bank agent)	Armagh
John Walker	Linen buyer	Magherafelt
William Swan	Linen bleacher	Ballymena
Hugh Wallace	Attorney	Downpatrick
J. and R. Young	Musical instrument maker/watchmaker	Ballymena
Thomas Bennett	Linen merchant and bleacher	Coleraine
Messrs Peebles and Kinley	Insurance agents/ general merchants	Dungannon

Sources. NBCM and *Pigot's Directory*, 1824.

connections. He was Law Agent for the Northern Bank, and subsequently manager of the bank's Downpatrick branch for twenty years after 1835, and described as 'a person of great influence' in County Down.[59]

The formation of the Northern Bank as a joint-stock concern was thus in some respects a complete break with the past, and in others little more than a continuation of its long-established style of business. The most obvious innovations were the joint-stock form and lending by way of cash credits. Management of the Northern was still entrusted to the former partners of Montgomery's, and there were still no branches run by salaried managers. The Northern, however, certainly perceived itself as a new-style bank, and at the first annual meeting shareholders were informed that 'the success of this Bank fully equals the expectations formed of the first Bank established on principles which have proved so eminently successful in Scotland'.[60] For more than two years the Northern was the only joint-stock bank based in Belfast. The remaining two private banks subsequently merged as the Belfast Banking Company in 1827. Prior to this merger, however, branches of two other banks, the Provincial and the Bank of Ireland opened in the town. The next section explores this development, and considers relations between the various banks to 1828.

1.3 Living with the neighbours
In July 1825 the Bank of Ireland opened a branch in Belfast, followed by the Provincial Bank of Ireland in March 1826. The Provincial had been established after an Act of Parliament of 1825[61] which, *inter alia,* made it absolutely clear that partners in Irish banks did not have to be resident in Ireland. The Provincial was the brainchild of Thomas Joplin who pointed to the stability of Scottish 'joint-stock' banks and their contribution to the economic development of Scotland through extensive branch systems, cash credits, note-issue and payment of interest on deposits.[62] Joplin opined that such a model would be highly beneficial to Ireland, and the original plan for the Provincial was drawn up by James Marshall, an accountant from Edinburgh.[63] The capital was set at £2 million in £100 shares, and the bank promised to set up 'establishments for business in the principal towns of Ireland which are above fifty miles from Dublin'.[64]

Each branch had a manager, an accountant, and a number of

'inferior officers' appropriate to the scale of business. The managers were advised by a board of between three and five local directors whose task was to meet daily with the manager 'to judge of the bills presented for discount, and of all applications for credit'.[65] The main board of the Provincial which sat in London, kept a fairly tight rein on the scale of credit facilities at each branch. In 1826, all applications for credit over £1,000 had to be sent to London for approval.[66]

The Provincial's explicit intention to set up branches all over Ireland outside the Bank of Ireland's monopoly area, meant that it was faced with an urgent need to find staff to run them. In a country like Ireland with no established banking tradition outside a very few towns it was evident that correspondingly few trained bank officers were on hand to supply the needs of branch expansion. There were basically three options open to any bank which wanted to find staff to operate a large branch network from a base of nought: importation from outside the country, attraction from other occupations within Ireland, or 'poaching' from other banks. The dearth of ready-made staff was a general one extending from clerks to managers and inspectors. Admittedly the problem was not peculiar to Ireland, but common to many parts of Britain.[67] The Northern Bank sidestepped the problem by its reliance on part-time agents. The Provincial, on the other hand, opted for recruitment of trained staff at modest salaries mainly from Scotland, and virtually all of its early staff were Scots.[68] This was the first migration of Scottish bank staff and expertise into Ireland. In the later 1820s it was relatively easy for the Provincial to recruit staff in this way; in the mid 1830s, when joint-stock bank promotion in Britain was proceeding apace and competition in the labour market for bank staff reached unprecedented heights, it may well have proved a much more difficult task.

The novelty and dynamism of the Provincial with regard to branch expansion contrasted strongly with the Bank of Ireland which, although established in 1783, had resolutely refused to open any branches despite numerous requests from Irish towns to do so.[69] There is little doubt that the arrival of the Provincial and the prospect of further joint-stock bank promotion forced the Bank of Ireland to reconsider its policy towards branch banking.[70] In January 1825 a special committee of Bank of Ireland directors resolved to establish branches 'in some of the Provincial Outports

Origins

and other considerable cities and towns in Ireland'.[71] Many observers poured scorn on this apparently enforced *volte face*. Prominent here was the *Dublin Evening Post* which criticised the Bank of Ireland for acting:

> in anything but a manly and respectable manner. . . . We can tell the Bank the time has gone by, they have lost the opportunity of doing a public service when *they alone* could have effected it, and they can only proceed with a certainty of defeat and a loss of character as the wisdom of His Majesty's Government and the spirit of the times are opposed to *monopoly* in every shape.[72]

In view of the Bank of Ireland's refusal to move outside Dublin for over forty years, such a comment was understandable; but however much the Bank's opponents openly despised the belated conversion to the idea of branch banking it cannot be seen as anything other than a positive step. At the least it would help to promote a more competitive environment in Irish banking, and promote the use of Bank of Ireland notes which had always been highly acceptable wherever they circulated. Indeed, even if the Provincial's intention to open a nationwide branch network was the main reason for the Bank of Ireland's change of policy, it remains valid to point out that the latter opened branches in many towns before the former and there were fundamental differences in the staffing and operation of branches of both banks.

While the Provincial opted mainly for Scottish staff, the Bank of Ireland preferred to appoint persons 'of commercial knowledge with local experience'.[73] Several early Bank of Ireland managers had formerly been private bankers but their number cannot have been great. Further, the Bank of Ireland demanded that its branch managers had to deposit as security at least £10,000 in government or Bank stock together with an additional £10,000. Sometimes twice this sum was required.[74] It is hardly surprising that the Bank occasionally had trouble finding men able to meet these stringent requirements. In Belfast, for example, several men were interviewed for the post of manager, but rejected. Eventually in June 1825, James Goddard, an agent for the British and Irish Fire Insurance Company, and Thomas Lyle, a merchant, were appointed.[75] Bank of Ireland managers were permitted to discount bills and accept deposits but prevented from granting overdrafts. They were salaried and also paid commission on discounted bills. The Bank of Ireland did not pay interest on deposits until 1864 and until that date believed such payments were against the law, nor did the court of the Bank give official approval to the provision of overdraft facilities before 1855.[76]

The Provincial Bank, by contrast, paid interest at all its branches, and lent on cash account from the outset. Moreover, the level of security payment required of a Provincial manager was generally much lower than that demanded by the Bank of Ireland. Theoretically, up to £10,000 could be required of a Provincial manager, but in practice this bank 'found £5,000 a more commandable sum . . . within the reach of the description of parties who are aspirants to these offices'.[77] A willingness to import staff from Scotland, an immediately realistic level of security payment from managers together with its offer of cash credits and payment of interest on deposits explain why the Provincial was able to build up rapidly from nothing in 1825 to thirty-three branches with a national coverage ten years later.[78] As early as April 1825 the Provincial invited 'sealed Tenders from persons having Houses suitable for Banking establishments' in nine Irish towns including Belfast.[79] The Belfast branch opened on 1 March 1826 with a Scottish manager James Duncan, and a Scottish accountant William Moncrieff. The local directors were all Belfast businessmen: Thomas Hughes (merchant), John Sinclair (linen merchant), John Sloane (a former partner in Montgomery's Bank) and Alexander Stewart (a grocer and tea dealer).[80]

Between the Provincial Bank's announcement of its intention to establish a branch in Belfast and the actual opening of the branch, the Belfast-based banks raised their rate on deposits from two to three per cent, presumably in an effort to attract deposits which might soon go to the Provincial. This was the first sign that competition for deposits was beginning to develop. Indeed, when the Provincial opened in Belfast it was forced to follow the new local rate of three per cent even though the rate at all its other branches was two per cent.[81] This differential continued until November 1825 when a deputation from the Provincial met the Northern Bank directors and 'stated their wish to be on friendly terms and to co-operate on all matters likely to produce general benefit'.[82] At this meeting it was decided to reduce deposit rates to two per cent, the Northern's directors considering it 'in the interest of this bank to take a lead in this matter'. Clearly then the Provincial was anxious not to be over-aggressive in the search for deposit business, and the Northern

Origins

reciprocated by duly lowering its deposit rate. The Bank of Ireland, since it did not pay interest on deposits, was not, of course, party to this mutual reduction of deposit rate. However, there does seem to have been multilateral discussion between all banks operating in Belfast with a view to equalising discount rates in December 1825.[83]

If relations between the Northern and the Provincial appear to have been cordial, the same cannot be said of relations between the Northern and its two private bank neighbours in Belfast. Between 1825 and 1826 there were three controversies. The first arose in October 1825 when the Northern complained to partners in both private banks that country agents of the latter, 'despite frequent remonstrations' of the Northern, had advanced money to linen buyers and others *before* receiving bills. The Northern considered this practice 'discreditable to banking establishments', all the more so since it contravened an earlier agreement that no agent of any of the three banks would act in this way, and warned that however reluctant it was to enter into a 'system of warfare' it would certainly do so unless both private banks stopped the practice.[84] The second source of friction concerned the design of the new notes of the Commercial Bank. In January 1826 the Northern considered these to be so similar to its own that it was almost impossible to distinguish between them. The Commercial was told to alter its note design forthwith.[85] These two sources of friction suggest that the private banks may have felt disadvantaged by the size of their new joint-stock neighbour, the Northern. Advancing money prior to the receipt of bills can be interpreted as a method of attracting business away from the Northern (and indeed the Bank of Ireland whose branch was open by that time), while the Commercial's issue of almost identical notes was a way of imitating its joint-stock rival.[86]

The third, and possibly most serious, controversy involved the Commercial's gold supply in October 1826. The Northern's directors had suspected 'for a long time past' that the Commercial was depending on the Northern for its supply of gold which was 'withdrawn through the agency of private individuals'. Thus suspicion was confirmed when the Commercial was unable to meet a demand for £2,000 and the Northern had to lend it 1,000 sovereigns. In an attempt to prevent such a loss of gold in the future the Northern's committee resolved to suspend the note exchange with its neighbour and insist that 'payment of such Commercial notes as may be received here shall be required daily and no notes of the Commercial Bank shall be taken in the office of this company after 3 o'clock'.[87] Only after a categorical assurance from the Commercial Bank's partners that no future attempt would be made to obtain gold in this manner was the exchange of notes resumed.[88]

The two private banks in Belfast must have become increasingly uneasy with the formation of the Northern as a joint-stock bank and the arrival in Belfast of branches of the Bank of Ireland and the Provincial. It is plausible to suggest that their possibly perceived disadvantage was a motive for their amalgamation and joint promotion of the Belfast Banking Company in 1827.

1.4 The crisis of 1825–6 and the small note controversy

Close trading links between Belfast and Britain meant that the depression in Britain was likely to affect Belfast adversely. This almost inescapable link became apparent in 1826. In Britain from the end of 1824 there were signs of increased economic activity, share speculation, a rise in domestic prices and imports accompanied by an adverse balance of payments.[89] The details need not concern us; it is enough to point out that pressure intensified well into 1825. By autumn of that year share prices in new companies fell sharply, as did prices of foreign loan stocks. Many English bankers were 'loaded up' with long-dated bills. On 1 December there was a huge demand for discounts at the Bank of England, a demand likened to that 'for the pit of a theatre on the night of a popular performance'.[90] The crisis of 1825–6 brought down about seventy banks in England and Wales, but very few in Scotland[91] and none in Ireland. Part of the blame for crisis rested with the Bank of England which had not tailored its discount policy to fit the state of the exchanges.[92] The collapse of the speculative boom and ensuing depression in England began to affect Belfast early in 1826.[93] The cotton industry was hit particularly hard.[94] The Northern Bank told its shareholders that 1826 had been a year of 'unexampled distress',[95] but the banks generally do not seem to have been under any great strain.

In England and Wales the crisis was the first to show that convertibility of note issue was not its own safeguard and in the post-mortem critics of the banking system focused on the country banks as well as on the Bank of England. The charter of the Bank of England was

Origins

modified in 1826 so as to enable the formation of joint-stock banks of issue provided they operated outside a sixty-five-mile radius from London.[96] In England and Wales, then, just as in Ireland six years previously, it took a major crisis to bring about banking reform. Although banking legislation applied only to England and Wales, one aspect of the post-crisis debate was relevant to all parts of the United Kingdom. This was the criticism of unlimited note issue. It was a widely-held belief in government circles that an important contributory factor to the crisis was irresponsible issue of banknotes, particularly those in denominations of less than £5. These so-called 'small' notes, it was alleged, were likely to be held by poor, ignorant people with a high propensity to panic in a crisis.[97] If such notes were replaced by coin, the argument ran, then over-issue was by definition impossible, so too was a run to convert notes in a period of panic. An Act to abolish small notes in England and Wales was duly passed,[98] and there was a good deal of talk about extending abolition throughout the UK. Two parliamentary enquiries, one of the House of Commons, the other of the Lords, were set up in 1826 to consider evidence from Scottish and Irish witnesses on the question of small notes.[99] The Scots were unanimous in their opposition to any plan to extend abolition of small notes to their country, pointing out convincingly that there was no necessary link between small notes and 'unsound' banking.[100]

In Ireland, the campaign against abolition of small notes, while not nearly so organised as in Scotland, was nevertheless sustained. Indeed, at no other time in the nineteenth century did Irish banks of issue show such a high degree of unanimity in their hostility to a government proposal. As will become clear, such hostility was neither irrational nor misconceived; it was the most appropriate response of those who wished to preserve and promote the satisfactory operation of the exchange mechanism in Ireland. The suitability of small notes as an acceptable medium of exchange in any area depended on several factors. Given that the population was not averse to the use of paper money the most important determinant of the appropriate note denomination was the size of daily transactions in markets and fairs. If transactions were typically small, that is, less than £5 each, then small notes would be appropriate. The government's view, however, was that a metallic currency was equally appropriate. For this to have been the case the local population would have to be willing to substitute coin for notes and also be sure of being able to obtain a supply of coin as and when it was required. In order to capture some of the flavour of this major controversy in Ulster it is necessary to review evidence from the bankers and traders most affected by it.

Modern textbooks on money usually identify five essential properties of an acceptable medium of exchange; divisibility, durability, stability, homogeneity and portability.[101] To these we might add a sixth property which was very relevant to Ulster in the 1820s: procurability. By comparing the attributes of small notes with coin under these various headings it will be possible to arrive at a reasonable judgement on the relative merits of the one over the other as far as consumers were concerned.

First, banknotes were highly divisible. The Belfast Bank, for example, issued notes of £1, £1 5s, £1 10s, £1 15s, £2, one guinea, one guinea and a half, two guineas and 'a very few over'.[102] Gold, silver and copper coin was, of course, even more divisible down to a farthing. Second, small notes had only a limited life span and became 'fairly worn out in fourteen or fifteen months if they are continually in circulation',[103] but were very cheap to replace. Coin could circulate for many years, depending on velocity, without the need for replacement. Third, as the post-1815 period had shown, the value of Irish private bank notes could be highly unstable. Although the formation of banks along joint-stock lines tended to make them more secure, there was still no guarantee that notes would retain their value since no effective check to overissue existed. However, as an author in the *Belfast Commercial Chronicle* pointed out in 1826, notes of the Belfast banks had always retained their value and he felt confident that they would continue to do so.[104] The value of coin was inherently more stable than paper, unless undermined by a sudden large increase in supply or increased by a sudden speculative demand.

Fourth, banknotes were homogeneous but were susceptible to forgery. On the other hand coin, especially gold coin, could be 'light' or debased. The advantage of, and hence preference for, paper in this respect was succinctly stated by a Northern Bank agent in 1826: '. . . if a man should lose notes, or a house be robbed or if there is a forgery, it would be much easier to trace the notes than it would gold . . . guineas became light and troublesome to the people; when standing beam there was a shilling charged, and when lighter than standing beam, two shillings and sixpence'.[105] Fifth, it

Origins

goes without saying that notes are more portable than coin. As one Ulster bleacher argued, the abolition of small notes would be a retrograde step because it 'would bring us back to such times as many of us would recollect; riding on horseback ten or twenty miles on a wet morning with from one to ten pounds weight of gold dangling in our pockets. (I almost feel my thighs ache at the recollection).'[106] Finally, while the supply of banknotes was extremely elastic, the same cannot be said of coin. Several witnesses before the parliamentary enquiries of 1826 had very serious doubts whether they would be able to obtain a supply of coin adequate for their requirements.[107]

Thus there was both a strong positive preference for small notes as well as real fears for the operation of markets if such notes were withdrawn. Bank agents in country towns were especially worried by the prospect of abolition of small notes. In Derry, for example, the vast majority of linen webs changed hands between £1 and £4; butter between 30s and two guineas per firkin; flax between £2 and £20 per bundle; pigs between £1 and £5; grain in 'small quantities', the farmer typically brought in two or three sacks of oats which changed hands for a total £2 or £3.[108] In Armagh a similar price system prevailed.[109] The small size of transactions in Ulster markets enabled witnesses from Ulster to reject decisively the suggestion that the exchange mechanism could operate in a similar way to Lancashire where, in the mid-1820s, the main currency was bills.[110]

As far as bank directors were concerned, there was a strong link between note issue, profitability and the provision of credit. In this respect evidence from Ulster was very similar to that of Scottish witnesses before the parliamentary enquiries of 1826.[111] Bank profits in the mid-1820s were crucially dependent on notes issue, and small notes accounted for the bulk of the issue of the Belfast banks. From this it follows that abolition of small notes would strike a body blow to bank profits which might threaten the very existence of the banks themselves. J. H. Houston of the Belfast Bank considered that if small notes were withdrawn 'we would probably discontinue the bank immediately . . . our business has been profitable in consequence of the circulation'.[112] James Orr of the Northern did not go quite so far as Houston, but still thought most or 'perhaps all' of his bank's agencies would be withdrawn.[113] There was general agreement then that abolition of small notes would result in a severe contraction of banking services in most country towns.

Several Scottish witnesses to the parliamentary enquiries of 1826 were convinced that the cash credit system would be unworkable without small notes.[114] In Ireland this point was made most clearly by the Provincial Bank which explained that even the prospect of small notes being withdrawn had caused the bank to cut back the provision of cash credits, and all applications for new credits had been 'peremptorily' refused.[115] Leonard Dobbin, Armagh agent for the Northern Bank, could remember that before the introduction of banknotes, discount rates had been about twice the level of 1820. If both the Usury Laws and small notes were abolished 'the bankers and gentlemen who have money might ruin the country by charging such discounts and interest as they thought proper'.[116]

The tenor of the evidence outlined above was that abolition of small notes would be unambiguously detrimental. There were, however, some who failed to come out strongly against abolition. A town meeting organised by the Belfast Chamber of Commerce[117] to consider the question could not reach agreement and discussion quickly broadened into a debate on the merits of joint-stock *vis-à-vis* private banks and a metallic *vis-à-vis* a paper currency. Discussants were in favour of a secure currency, but were unsure of how best to achieve it. In general they were happy to 'place their reliance on the wisdom of His Majesty's Government (provided) that no measure will be extended to this country which will have the effect of altering that system of banking under which the town and neighbourhood of Belfast has continued to improve'.[118] Failure to reach any definite conclusion was also a feature of the two parliamentary reports. Both parliamentary enquiries devoted far more time to Scotland than to Ireland, and the reports on Ireland each ran to little more than a single page of text. Neither report made specific recommendations, although the 'impression' of the Commons report was that it would not be advantageous to abolish small notes immediately, but advisable to 'fix a definite, though not an early period at which the circulation in Ireland of all notes below five pounds shall cease'.[119] Apart from this imprecise statement, little else came out of the two parliamentary reports. As it turned out, the issue of small notes continued to be permitted throughout the nineteenth century although the vague threat issued by the reports of 1826–7 was not finally withdrawn until 1845.

For Irish banks of issue the threat to small notes was a serious one from which they were perhaps rather lucky to escape. There can be

Origins

little doubt that abolition of small notes would have resulted in extreme difficulties in country markets, raised discount rates, slashed bank profits and deprived the growing economy of northeast Ireland of its preferred medium of exchange. The Belfast banks were able to tell the parliamentary enquiries that there had been no abnormal pressure in the crisis of 1825–6.[120] We do not know whether the government would have been more willing to abolish small notes if there had been a large number of failures in Ireland during 1825–6, but it seems likely. The fact that there were no such failures may well have been important in blunting the criticism of small notes. The link between small notes, financial crises and bank failures was never unequivocal. Certainly there were dangers in overissue of notes not backed by gold, but confidence in Irish banknotes in the period 1825 to 1914 remained for the most part intact. As far as the Belfast banks were concerned, on only one occasion (1857) did confidence crumble temporarily.[121]

1.5 The Belfast Banking Company

The Northern Bank, and branches of the Bank of Ireland and the Provincial Bank had been established before the parliamentary enquiries into small notes had begun. The two private banks in Belfast remained. In the summer of 1827, partners of the private banks, on the initiative of the Commercial, proposed the dissolution of both banks and the formation of a joint-stock concern styled the Belfast Banking Company. The deed of co-partnership was dated 2 July 1827[122] and submitted to the public for signatures the following day.[123] As noted earlier, it may well be true that partners in the private banks felt increasingly disadvantaged by the new joint-stock banks and so decided to adopt the joint-stock form themselves. They probably also felt that the developing economy of the Belfast region was fully able to support another joint-stock bank. In addition, the actual timing of the formation of the Belfast Bank may not have been purely accidental. The Lords' Committee on small notes published its report on 6 April 1827, almost a year after the Commons' report. It is plausible to suggest that partners of both private banks were waiting to see whether small notes would be abolished or not. After all, it had been J. H. Houston, a partner in Batt's, who had argued that if small notes were abolished his bank would probably go out of business. It may be speculated then that the outcome of the parliamentary enquiries on small notes, a fear of being overshadowed by the new joint-stock banks, together with reasonably optimistic 'expectations of the future' were all instrumental in the decision to form the joint-stock concern.

The historian of the Belfast Bank has suggested that partners of both private banks canvassed customers and country agents to take shares in the new bank.[124] Although there is no direct evidence, this seems highly likely. Shares were offered to the public on 3 July 1827 and the geographical distribution of shareholders at that date is shown in Table 6. In every important respect the Belfast Bank's deed of co-partnership was very similar and often identical to that of the Northern.[125] A capital of £500,000 was divided into 5,000 shares of £100 each. Three calls on shares were made within exactly two years of the bank's opening: £10 on 1 August 1827, £10 on 1 August the following year and £5 on 1 August 1829.[126] There were no more additions to capital until the 1860s. Of the four original directors two were drawn from each of the private banks and were appointed for life.[127] Like the Northern, the Belfast Bank had an advisory committee (known as the Board of Superintendence) of seven, including a chairman who was also a life appointee.[128] The object

Table 6 *Belfast Bank shareholders at 1 August 1827*

County	Number	Remarks
Antrim and Down	157	(of which 76 Belfast)
Londonderry	65	
Armagh	39	
Fermanagh	1	
Monaghan	18	
Tyrone	44	
Total Ulster	324	
Dublin	1	
England	3	(all London)
Total	328	(308 male, 20 female)

Source. *List of the Properties of the Belfast Banking Company*, 1 August 1827 (printed)

Original members of the Board of Superintendence

William Tennent	Former private banker
Robert Callwell	Auditor of accounts
George Langtry	Shipowner
Edward Curteis	Linen merchant
Hugh McCalmont	?
Francis McCracken	Rope, sail and canvas manufacturer
Narcissus Batt	Calico printer

Origins

clause was the same as that of the Northern, as was the requirement that directors retire from business on their own account.

The Belfast Bank's deed had empowered directors and the Board of Superintendence to open country branches[129] but, like the Northern, the Belfast Bank did not open any branches with salaried managers until the mid-1830s. There is not a great deal of information available on the original country agents of the Belfast Bank, but their names and locations are given in Table 7. It would appear that agents of the Belfast Bank were drawn predominantly from the linen industry rather than, as with the Northern, from a wider cross-section of the Ulster business community.

After 1827 no private banks remained in Ulster. One effect of this was that there could be no opposition or hostility to joint-stock banks from established private banks as there was in many parts of England from the 1820s.[130] Between 1827 and 1914 there were never more than six registered private banks in Ireland, while the number of joint-stock banks operating at any one time in the same period was always less, usually much less, than twenty.[131] Almost all of the latter were formed between 1824 and 1827, and 1834–6. This was in marked contrast to England and Wales where as late as 1855 there were still one hundred joint-stock banks and just over three hundred private banks.[132] In England and Wales there was thus vast scope for bank amalgamation in the second half of the nineteenth century, whereas in Ireland the small number of both

Table 7 *Agents of the Belfast Bank in August 1827*

Name	Occupation	Location
Robert Boyd	?	Tandragee
J. Miller and Son	Linen merchant/bleacher	Kildrum, Ballymena
J. Acheson Smyth	Linen merchant	Derry
William Kirk	Linen manufacturer	Ann Vale, Armagh
S. R. Magill	?	Cookstown
A. McClelland	Woollen draper/linen and cotton manufacturer	Banbridge
D. and W. Cunningham	Linen merchants/bleachers	Ballymena
J. McFarland	Linen merchant	Coleraine
John Jackson	'Gentleman'	Ballybay
Jonathan Hogg	?	Redford, Armagh
Isaac Glenny[a]	Merchant	Newry

Note. [a] The Newry Agency was on the edge of the Bank of Ireland's monopoly area, and was closed after protest from the Bank of Ireland in October 1827.
Sources. Various Bank Records and *Pigot's Directory*, 1824.

private and joint-stock banks meant that there was no comparable scope at any time.

With the formation of the Belfast Bank the first distinctive phase of joint-stock banks in Ireland came to an end, and there were no new joint-stock banks until 1834. Of the banks established between 1824 and 1827 those based in Belfast, while very similar to each other, differed in at least one important respect from the others: their shareholders were virtually all from Ulster. The Hibernian Bank, a non-issuer based in Dublin and open from 1825, had a substantial English ownership, as did the Provincial.[133] Banks based in Belfast were locally owned and locally run from the start, and continued to be so throughout the nineteenth century. One other feature which distinguished the Northern and the Belfast Bank from the Hibernian and the Provincial Bank until 1828 was that the former's shares, unlike those of the latter, always sold at a premium. Shares in the Northern and the Belfast often changed hands privately, but when they were offered for public sale the selling price was invariably above par. Possibly the first public sale of Northern Bank shares was in August 1826 when ten shares were sold by the bank to liquidate a debt owed by one of its shareholders.[134] The substantial premium at which these were sold afforded, according to the *Belfast Newsletter,* 'strong proof indeed of the high opinion entertained by the public of the stability of this useful establishment and of the integrity and skill with which it is managed'.[135] Throughout 1827 and 1828, shares in the Northern were sold at between £35 and £40 each,[136] that is at premiums of between forty and sixty per cent. Similarly Belfast Bank shares attracted considerable premiums from the start.

The experience of the Hibernian and the Provincial was quite different. By the autumn of 1827, shares of both these banks were at a discount. Over the next year or so Hibernian shares continued at a fairly steady rate of discount, while Provincial shares sold mainly above par until the summer of 1828 when they went below par once again.[137] The volatile, but generally depressed value of Hibernian and Provincial shares was a consequence of the lingering suspicion of banks in the south of Ireland in the later 1820s, a reflection no doubt of widespread private bank failures. The Hibernian had no office outside Dublin, but the Provincial's southern branches were subject to periodic 'runs' in the late 1820s and early 1830s.[138] There was no sign of pressure on either of the Belfast banks in this period.

CHAPTER TWO

COMPETITION, COLLUSION AND CRISES

This chapter attempts to deal with a wide range of influences operating on the growth of the Belfast banks in the formative period of thirty years or so before 1860: the creation of a modern branch network, increased competition from Dublin and London-based banks, the signature of a collusive agreement in 1839 and the introduction of crucial legislation in 1844–5. In addition, comment is made on the impact of the Great Famine and on the effects of economic fluctuations down to 1858.

The first phase of joint-stock bank formation between 1824 and 1827 was followed by a second phase between 1834 and 1836. Between these two phases no joint-stock banks were formed, and after 1836 there were few new banks of any significance except the short-lived Tipperary Joint-Stock Bank established in 1838 and the Munster Bank in 1864. Table 8 shows the name of, and number of shareholders in, each joint-stock bank operating in Ireland at the beginning of 1840. All banks formed in the first phase, and all except one formed in the second, were to be successful. The only casualty was the Agricultural and Commercial, and the brief, interesting and inglorious history of this concern will be given fuller discussion later in this chapter. The banking scene in the north of Ireland was altered considerably and permanently in 1836 by the foundation of an entirely new joint-stock concern: the Ulster Banking Company. The Ulster was the third and last joint-stock bank to be established in Belfast, and after 1836 banking in the north of Ireland was dominated by the three banks with head offices in this town.

In the later 1820s the Belfast banks were faced with an economy which was still largely depressed and showed little indication of rapid improvement. It was clear that the widespread effects of the 1825–6 crisis were not to be overcome either easily or quickly. The banks' reaction to the temporarily depressed state of trade was not,

Table 8 *Irish joint-stock banks in January 1840*

Name	Date of establishment	Number of shareholders	Remarks
Bank of Ireland	1783	not available	
Northern	1824	186	
Provincial	1825	813	
Hibernian	1825	n.a.	Non-issue
Belfast	1827	270	
Agricultural	1834	4,114	Failed 1840
National	1835	1,140	
Ulster	1836	590	
Clonmel National	1836	1,298	Merged with National 1856
Carrick on Suir National	1836	1,254	Merged with National 1856
Royal	1836	360	Non-issue
Tipperary Joint-Stock	1838	50	Issued Bank of Ireland notes; failed 1856

Source. *An Account of Joint-Stock Banks existing in Ireland in January 1840*, BPP, 1844, xxxii, p. 445.

however, purely passive. By mutual consent, the Northern, the Belfast and the Provincial altered interest rates across the board. Interest on current accounts and money lodged for less than three months was suspended. The rate on deposits lodged for more than three months was reduced from three to two and a half per cent and the discount rate on bills with more than three months to run was reduced to five per cent.[1] In addition to this alteration of interest rates, the boards of both the Northern and the Belfast felt the time appropriate to remind shareholders that it was in their own interest to increase note circulation as much as possible. The importance of an extensive circulation was repeatedly impressed upon shareholders at annual meetings, and the Northern strongly recommended 'the proprietors and all their friends to keep this matter in mind when paying away even the smallest sum of money'.[2]

The Belfast believed that by 1828 both imports and exports were 'at the lowest possible prices', and complained about the effect of such low prices on its note circulation.[3] Despite the depressed state of trade the Northern and the Belfast suffered no serious bad debts, and their shares continued to attract a premium whenever they were sold on the open market.[4] Particularly satisfying to the board of the Belfast was the revelation that one gentleman had actually sold out of government stock to buy Belfast Bank shares, but was unable to obtain the requisite number even though he was prepared to pay a £5 premium on each share.[5] While the banks looked forward to any development which would enhance the value of their shares it was clear that these shares were considered to be safe investments as early as the later 1820s. From a shareholder's point of view, however, safety was only one consideration. Any investment decision must depend not only on safety but also on profitability. As far as the banks were concerned, they could not escape the need to determine a dividend policy which was consistent with both their own safety and the desires of their shareholders to whom they had to report annually.

Until the publication of balance sheets in the second half of the nineteenth century, shareholders in the Belfast banks were given only a very limited amount of precise information concerning the volume of, and trends in, business. The Northern's view from the outset was that it was inexpedient to announce such details at a public meeting, and trusted that proprietors, who had 'no right to know' how the bank was managed, would be satisfied with the board's assurance that all was well.[6] Up to 1836 the Northern judged that 'making public the prosperity of one company would have the effect of exciting competition where the circumstances of that prosperity might not be fairly estimated, and that competition thus excited might be carried on to an extent likely to be injurious to old establishments without being beneficial to new ones or to the public'.[7] If fear of competition made the Northern secretive about its prosperity, then this secrecy was to no avail. Prosperity, reflected in sustained dividends and share premiums, spoke for itself. Indeed, even without publication of detailed accounts, the competition which the bank feared had arrived by 1836 in the shape of the Agricultural and Commercial Bank and the Ulster Bank. For this reason the mere prospect of competition was no longer a valid argument for the degree of secrecy which had hitherto been a feature of annual meetings. Consequently the Northern's board, by way of minor concession to its shareholders, decided to print and circulate annual reports at meetings instead of simply reading them.[8]

It was noted in the last chapter that the Belfast banks looked to Scotland for their model and that an early example of Scottish influence was the adoption of the cash credit system. Scottish influence on the Belfast banks again became apparent in the latter's search for an acceptable dividend policy. In determining the level of dividend banks were conscious of the need to maintain, or preferably increase, their share prices. The Northern held that the best way to do this was to imitate successful banks in Scotland: 'In this establishment we may follow the example of the Scotch share banks, declaring a bonus at whatever period it may be considered most desirable. The consequence is their shares have reached very high prices – the more time that has elapsed since the declaration of a bonus, the higher their shares are valued'.[9]

Both the Northern and the Belfast opted for consistency in dividends with an occasional bonus not simply to increase their share prices, but also to enable them to accumulate a reserve or 'surplus' fund to meet bad and doubtful debts, and increase resources without having to make further calls upon shares. On several occasions the Belfast Bank announced to its shareholders that it was preferable to increase dividends slowly rather than be obliged to reduce them when profitability declined. Too high a level of distributed profit, and (its corollary) an inadequate reserve fund in general proved very prejudicial to the interest of joint-stock banks 'and is contrary to those sound principles which should influence the investment of capital in their shares, in making them an object to the public, by being founded on a fixed and permanent basis – instead of their being matter of mere fancy and speculation'.[10]

The Belfast banks' declared policy on dividends is reflected in Table 9. In the late 1820s and 1830s, dividends paid by the Belfast banks put them in the middle order of Irish banks. Between 1825 and 1837, for example, the Hibernian paid a steady four per cent, while the Provincial paid four per cent until 1830, five per cent in 1831 and 1832 and raised this by one per cent in each of the years 1833, 1834 and 1835, and the dividend remained eight per cent for several years.[11]

2.1 Branch expansion

Of the five joint-stock banks established in the first phase, between 1824 and 1827, only the Provincial proceeded immediately to open branches. The only other bank to set up branches in Ireland before 1834 was the Bank of Ireland. The Hibernian opened no branch until 1843, while the Northern and the Belfast relied exclusively on part-time agencies until 1834. The Bank of Ireland's monopoly area

Table 9 *Dividends paid by the Belfast banks, 1825–40*

	Northern		Belfast		Ulster	
Date	Dividend (%)	Bonus	Dividend (%)	Bonus	Dividend (%)	Bonus
1825	5	—				
1826	5	—				
1827	5	5%	5	—		
1828	5	—	5	—		
1829	5	—	5	—		
1830	5	—	5	£2 per share		
1831	5	—	5	—		
1832	5	£4 per share	5	—		
1833	5	—	5	—		
1834	5	—	5	—		
1835	6	—	5	—		
1836	7	—	6	—		
1837	8	—	7	—	5	—
1838	9	—	7	—	6	—
1839	10	—	7	—	6½	—
1840	10	—	7	—	7	—

Sources. NBCM, 1825–40, BBSM, 1828–40, Ulster Bank *Annual Reports*, 1837–40.

forced the Provincial to locate all its branches more than fifty Irish miles from Dublin. Before 1830 the Provincial opened only four branches in Ulster, (Derry, Belfast, Armagh, and Coleraine), but in the early 1830s this pattern changed dramatically and of eighteen branches of the Provincial opened between 1831 and 1835 eleven were in Ulster.[12] The Bank of Ireland opened four branches in Ulster between 1825 and 1827 (Belfast, Derry, Newry and Armagh), but momentum was not sustained and no further branch was opened in the province until 1865.[13] This apparent reluctance of the Bank of Ireland to colonise Ulster cannot be explained by an absence of invitations from provincial towns to establish branches. Between July 1833 and March 1844 twenty-six different Irish towns invited the Bank of Ireland to open branches. Only nine of these were accepted and none was in Ulster, while seven of the seventeen rejected invitations came from Ulster towns.[14] Two possible explanations for the Bank of Ireland's slow expansion can be offered. First, the exceptionally high level of security payment demanded by the bank from its managers may well have been a constraint on expansion, since the bank sometimes found difficulty in recruiting suitable staff who could afford it. Second, the bank's declared preference for appointment of local (Irish) men, with banking experience wherever possible, immediately narrowed the available field of candidates. Unwilling to follow the Provincial's example of recruiting staff in Britain, the Bank of Ireland was forced to search for staff in a country where bank officers were rare. Relaxation of its stringent rules for appointment of managers by either lowering security payments and/or looking to Britain for staff would have gone a considerable way to removing constraints to expansion. The Bank of Ireland, however, failed to do either.[15]

For the Northern and the Belfast, then, the main thrust of competition in the early 1830s came from the Provincial. Just as the Provincial must be given some credit for forcing the Bank of Ireland to open branches, so it must also be given credit for forcing the Belfast banks to convert their part-time agencies to branches. Until the Provincial's rapid expansion into Ulster in the early 1830s, the Belfast and the Northern were content to continue operation of agencies. For the latter, agencies were a cost effective, risk minimising means to increase circulation through bill discounts. They required no specially trained staff, and could be opened or closed with great speed and little expense. Admittedly there were occasional, perhaps inevitable, problems. Since agents of the Belfast and the Northern had no power to grant overdrafts, their debts could be incurred from bill business or the transmission of notes. References to protest accounts are very few, but in two instances early in 1830 the Northern remitted £1,000 to its agent in Derry to help him settle his protest account which was 'upwards of £3,000', and remitted about £1,400 to its agents in Newry who had lost '£4,300 or thereabouts by their transactions'.[16] It would appear that bad debts incurred by agencies were small, and that the advantages of such agencies initially far outweighed their disadvantages.

As far as customers were concerned, agencies offered only a very limited range of facilities. The branches of the Provincial, however, provided a more comprehensive range of banking services, including cash credits, and this bank's rapid expansion in Ulster during the early 1830s forced the Belfast banks to reconsider their position with regard to branches. The decision to open branches was taken simultaneously by the Northern and the Belfast in the late summer of 1834.[17] The Northern justified the move on the grounds that its 'mode of transacting business in the country [was] not calculated to afford the convenience and accommodation now looked for by the Public . . .'[18] From this statement it is clear that the Northern was responding to the demands of customers who might be won over by the erstwhile superior services offered by the Provincial. It is interesting to speculate how long many Ulster towns would have had to wait for branches if the initiative taken by the Provincial, and hence the Belfast banks' reaction to it, had been absent.

The decision by the Belfast banks to open branches was promptly and unequivocally welcomed by the local press. The *Belfast Newsletter,* for example, called on the banks' shareholders 'who generally are all highly respectable mercantile men resident in the province' to support the move since it would lead to an increase in bank profits, and be of substantial benefit to the economy of Ulster.[19] The Belfast banks' move into full branch banking was, however, far from being a leap in the dark. Agencies of both banks, most of which dated from the private bank period, had laid the necessary foundations upon which it was relatively easy to build a branch network. Long-established and successful agencies had at least proved the demand for discount facilities and there was no reason to suppose that the demand for a wider range of banking services was lacking. In any case, if conclusive evidence was needed that such a demand existed, the initial success of all the Provincial's branches in Ulster was enough to prove the point.

The urgent need to counter the Provincial made late 1834 and 1835 a hectic period for the Belfast banks. In the twelve months following September 1834 when the decision to open branches was taken, the Belfast Bank had opened thirteen branches and the Northern eight.[20] Neither bank was to open so many branches in a single year again. Table 10 gives the chronology of early branch expansion by the Belfast banks.[21] Most of the early branches of both the Northern and the Belfast grew out of agencies, a process which undoubtedly hastened expansion. The terms on which managers were employed were diverse. Just as the security given by part-time agents was a function of the level of business, so the salary (or, more precisely, net advantages) received by the manager depended on the bank's assessment of the importance of the branch. Branches of the Northern and the Belfast were either solely or jointly managed, but in the latter case there were never more than two managers and they were paid a joint salary.[22]

The task of finding, and fitting out, a suitable office often fell to

Table 10 *Branch opening dates of the Belfast banks, 1834–40*

Town	Northern	Belfast	Ulster
Antrim			1836
Armagh	1836	1835	1836
Ballymena	1835	1834	1838
Ballymoney		1834	1836
Banbridge		1835	1837
Carrickfergus	1836		
Clones	1840		
Coleraine	1835	1834	
Cookstown		1835	
Cootehill			1837
Derry	1835	1835	1840
Downpatrick	1835		1836
Dungannon		1835	
Enniskillen			1836
Larne		1836	
Letterkenny		1835	
Limavady	1835	1835	
Lisburn	1835		
Lurgan	1835	1834(a)	1836
Magherafelt	1835	1835	
Monaghan		1835	1836(b)
Newtownards		1836	
Portadown		1835	1836
Strabane		1835	
Tandragee		1835	1836(c)

Notes. (a) Converted to agency 1841.
(b) Converted to agency 1837, reopened as branch 1840.
(c) Converted to agency 1837.

Sources. *Northern Bank Company Ltd., Centenary Volume; Belfast Newsletter; Decades of the Ulster Bank.*

the manager(s) concerned, and where this was done, a rent allowance on top of the agreed salary was paid by the bank.[23] The speed with which the two Belfast banks felt it was necessary to set up full branches is demonstrated by the fact that if a suitable office could not be found immediately, the manager was asked to provide one in his home until such time as appropriate premises could be rented or built.[24] The Northern maintained, or at least told its shareholders, that branches had been established to give the public greater facilities, and 'not from the expectation of much increased profit'.[25] The Belfast was rather more candid, and told its shareholders in 1835 that the thirteen branches opened up to then were all doing well and that the annual expense of those branches will not be much greater than that paid to the company's agents, the extra expense will be fully covered by the additional advantages derived from the branches. Already your directors have found the good effects from them; their having very considerably increased the company's circulation and deposits.[26]

Between 1834 and 1836, when the Northern and the Belfast had begun seriously to counter the Provincial in Ulster, two further banks appeared in the province. The origins of each will be considered in turn.

2.2 The Agricultural and Commercial Bank of Ireland and the 1836 crisis

This bank, founded in 1834, suspended payment in 1836, resumed in 1837 and staggered on until 1840. It was the first Irish joint-stock bank to fail, although its intrinsic interest lies not merely in the fact that it failed, but in the way in which failure occurred. Pamphleteers as well as more balanced journals not normally given to crass exaggeration were at one in their condemnation. A good example of the latter was the *Bankers' Magazine,* which declared that 'for an example of unmatched impudence and incompetency, successfully imposing on the confiding ignorance of a people, we may seek in vain for any that can stand a comparison with the Agricultural and Commercial Bank of Ireland'.[27] How accurate was this judgment?

When the scheme was first publicised in June 1834, it was, to say the least, exceptionally ambitious. The Agricultural's nominal capital (5 million) exceeded by £1 million that of the Northern, the Belfast, the Hibernian and the Provincial put together. The nominal value of each share, however, was a mere £5 while that of the above four banks was £100. Not only this but the bank declared its intention to establish 300 branches 'to cover the whole Kingdom' to be governed by the local proprietory in each town.[28] The unprecedentedly low share denomination and large number of shares reflected the explicit intention of the bank's promoters to enable as many people of modest means as possible to buy shares.[29] As a model, the Agricultural took the Northern and Central Bank of England, established in 1834, with small denomination shares (£10).[30] The Northern and Central had opened almost forty branches within a year, and this rate of expansion so impressed the directors of the Agricultural that they considered it to be the most powerful bank in Britain after the Bank of England.[31] It was 'perhaps the most extraordinary instance on record of complete success, yet this bank ranks with its shareholders working artisans, as well as the more wealthy class of traders and shopkeepers'.[32]

In 1835 the apparent success of the Northern and Central was plain for all to see. More generally the obvious prosperity of joint-stock banks in Britain and Ireland, typified in share premiums, was another reason why the Agricultural's low denomination shares attracted so much interest from poor investors. Until the formation of the Agricultural, Irish joint-stock bank shares had all had a nominal value of £100 which was prohibitively high for the 'poor' investor. It was hardly surprising that such investors flocked to this new concern. Apart from a branch at Strabane the Agricultural initially showed little intention of moving into Ulster and concentrated its effort in the scantily-banked south and west.[33] Early in 1836, however, there was a change of direction. In the south and west the Agricultural had to compete with the Bank of Ireland, the Provincial and, from 1835, the National. In these areas it could emphasise that both the Provincial and the National were supported by English capital and directed from London.[34] This tactic was redundant in the north-east since the Belfast banks were, and were known to be, locally owned and locally run. The Agricultural recognised this, but argued that the increasing trade and population of Belfast demanded 'another [bank] of a more ample construction, . . . the shares of which shall be more accessible to the people'.[35]

Potential investors in the Agricultural in Belfast who may have been suspicious of its abnormally low share denomination were given some cause for believing their suspicion was misplaced when the new Ulster Bank declared that *its* shares were to be £10.[36] Another reason why the Agricultural found ready buyers for its shares was that although these shares were said to be attracting a premium of twenty per cent elsewhere, Belfast investors were to be given an opportunity to buy them at par.[37]

The Agricultural was invited to establish a Belfast branch by Arbuthnot Emerson, brother of James Emerson, an MP for Belfast. The operation of this branch and indeed the bank's other Ulster branches seems to have differed from those in other parts of Ireland. They were controlled not by the local directors but by the Dublin board who 'had heard so much of the enormous cash credits

Competition, collusion and crises

and . . . habits of discount'[38] of the Belfast banks that it was felt too dangerous to leave control in the hands of local directors.

The Belfast branch of the Agricultural opened in Donegall Place about the beginning of May 1836.[39] At this date there were some fears in Ireland and England that a speculative boom akin to that of 1824, accompanied by stringency in the money market, were portents of an impending crash.[40] In England, speculative activity focused on railway and bank shares, and was increased by the substantial premiums at which such shares were sold.[41] Even the limited market for shares in Belfast showed intense activity in both railway and bank shares. By the middle of 1836 Belfast investors were offered a wider range of shares than ever before, not only in railways and banks but also in mines, china clay works, steamships and other enterprises.[42] This increase in the range of shares, symptomatic of the speculative boom in joint-stock companies after the summer of 1835, goes far to explain the emergence of the 'stockbroker' in Belfast around this time.[43]

The Agricultural expanded its branch network against this background of speculation without ever questioning either the sources or likely outcome of such speculation. By August 1836 there were ominous signs of serious pressure in the London money market. Bank rate, four per cent since July 1827, was raised to four and a half per cent in July 1836 and to five per cent in September.[44] The Bank of Ireland, however, did not follow the Bank of England, and its discount rate remained four per cent until October. For the first time in its history, the Bank of Ireland discounted at a lower rate than the Bank of England.[45] This differential, and the Bank of England's refusal in August to discount any bills already bearing the name of a joint-stock bank of issue,[46] combined to attract English bills to Ireland.[47] Although not all Irish banks followed the Bank of Ireland,[48] the differential in discount rates was enough to cause a significant drain of gold from Ireland to England.[49]

The Bank of Ireland raised its discount rate abruptly from four to five per cent immediately after publication of the Agricultural's balance sheet in October 1836.[50] Doubts about the solvency of the Agricultural which had been raised for several months past were now seen to be well founded. The bank suspended payment in November, about the same time as the concern upon which it was modelled, the Northern and Central Bank of England, suffered the same fate.[51] The Agricultural's history of almost unbelievable managerial incompetence became plain only in the parliamentary enquiry of the following year, and has been recounted several times since.⁵² For the purposes of this study it is relevant to discuss briefly the operation of the Belfast branch.

The explicit intention to bring bank shares within the reach of 'poor' people was fully realised by the Agricultural in Belfast. Of the 500 or so shareholders in the branch many were from 'the poorer classes' who were induced to subscribe because of the obvious success of other joint-stock banks. George Dundas, the Belfast branch manager of the Agricultural explained that a

> great many of the poorer classes who had money in the savings bank were induced to become subscribers from the success which attended the management of the Northern Bank and the Provincial Bank; for instance there was a coach porter who took 150 guineas out of the savings bank and invested in the stock; a street constable, who had been 30 years engaged in making £300, which he invested likewise; many young men in offices, linen lappers, widow ladies and females seeking a better interest on the faith of the respectibility of the gentlemen who were appointed directors.⁵³

Dundas believed most shareholders incapable of paying further calls on shares, but they were given a personal assurance by the Dublin board that further calls would not be made. The financial status of shareholders was further demonstrated in 1837 when they were unable to pay the fare to Dublin to attend a general meeting. Expenses had to be defrayed by subscription.⁵⁴ The unsatisfactory state of the Belfast branch was not confined to shareholders. The amount of gold held was clearly inadequate. Dundas and the local directors were determined not to commence business with less than £25,000 in gold, but only £15,000 was supplied to the branch when it began operations in summer 1836, and this had dwindled to just 500 sovereigns by early November. Dundas judged that confidence in joint-stock banks in Belfast was so great as to preclude the possibility of panic. For this reason much of the gold from the Belfast branch was sent to bolster the Agricultural's other branches in Ulster.⁵⁵

Publication of the Agricultural's balance sheet was only one contributory factor in the precipitation of a financial panic, which started in Dublin but soon spread to several other parts of Ireland. Another factor was the momentary refusal of the Hibernian to pay the drafts, notes and bills of two Belfast banks (the Belfast and the

Ulster) for which it undertook agency work in Dublin. This refusal was apparently the result of an unprecedented decision by the Bank of Ireland to refuse discount of any bill having more than twenty-one days to run.[56] The hard-pressed Hibernian sent bills to the Bank of Ireland

> of such a class they were as good as any in the world; they had, perhaps, the first rate names in London on them, they had our bank indorsed on them, and they had the northern banks indorsed on them, and all their proprietors, and some of the first characters in Ireland; and most whimsically they turned them back on us . . .[57]

The above version of the Bank of Ireland's conduct was given to the *Select Committee on Joint-Stock Banks* in 1838 by two directors of the Hibernian Bank, who blamed the Bank of Ireland for its 'whimsical' refusal to discount first class bills. It would appear, however, that the Hibernian was at least partly to blame. On 8 November, the latter did not send in bills to the Bank of Ireland until after the close of business. The next day, 'so certain of accommodation being granted', the Hibernian's secretary neglected to check with the Bank of Ireland that the bills would be discounted at the usual time (1.00p.m.). At four o'clock the Hibernian learnt that the bills had been refused. This left the Hibernian so short of funds that it was unable to pay the notes and bills of the Belfast and Ulster, and when this became known alarm was spread 'both in Dublin and other parts of the country'.[58] The Hibernian's impasse certainly contributed to an already deteriorating financial environment, and the Bank of Ireland quickly came to the assistance of six Irish joint-stock banks to the tune of £246,200.[59] All Irish banks except the Agricultural survived the panic and even the latter resumed payment in January 1837,[60] though it never fully recovered and closed a little over three years later.

The failure of the Agricultural and Commercial Bank in 1840 cast a shadow over the whole Irish financial scene and provoked demands for reform. One of the main criticisms of the Agricultural was its low share denomination. Mountifort Longfield expressed this forcibily:

> . . . the effect of small shares is to produce a numerous and ignorant body of shareholders, who will elect as directors the nominees of the men who made themselves most active in getting up the company without any regard whatever to their fitness for office. The natural

effect will be fraud, neglect, confusion and ruin, while an appeal to the shareholders themselves will only make the confusion worse.[61]

While there was no doubt about fraud, neglect, confusion and ruin, it is far less certain that these were the 'natural effect' of small shares as Longfield suggested. The argument against small shares was analogous to that against small notes: they were likely to be held by poor, ill-informed people. The relationship between small notes and financial panic was, however, a tenuous one. Similarly, the verdict must be that correlation between small shares and bank failures was weak.

The Ulster Bank's shares, for example, were very small by the standards of the day, yet no criticism was directed against them and the Ulster went from strength to strength. Indeed by 1836 there was an unambiguous downward trend in the denomination of bank shares, particularly for new banks established in industrial regions.[62] Several early joint-stock banks in England found small shares advantageous since they were taken by local traders who brought in business. Such people held a large proportion of their bank's notes and were thus motivated by self-interest not to panic and demand gold in a crisis.[63] Moreover, smaller shares were possibly more marketable. Furthermore, fraud, neglect, confusion and ruin were no monopoly of banks with small shares, as the British experience was to prove.[64] Significantly, one of the earliest and most detailed examinations of the Agricultural Bank's failure did not mention small denomination shares as a contributory factor. The *Bankers' Magazine* stressed instead a coincidence of four factors which accounted for failure: dishonesty, ignorance and incompetence of directors, lack of managerial experience at branch level, a poor inspectorate and shoddy book-keeping.[65]

Rectification of deficiencies in branch management and book-keeping by legislation was of course extremely difficult to ensure. As a general precautionary measure, both Longfield and Pierce Mahony called for legal changes to protect the interests of shareholders. Longfield argued that the deed of copartnership should be scrutinised by 'some proper attorney' before a bank commenced operations and intimated that it might be better to dispense with the deed altogether and 'let the law declare the rights of the proprietors and the duties of the directors and the remedies in the case of neglect and fraud'.[66]

Mahony, who had been solicitor to the Provincial Bank since

1824, in a valuable survey of Irish banking law[67] considered that shareholders were in a dangerous position because if they selected fraudulent or incompetent directors, they had no control whatsoever if 'those parties seek to resist them, or keep possession of their property' even though they may be dismissed or suspended as directors by a unanimous vote of shareholders.[68] The only recourse was to file a bill in equity, but problems associated with this procedure were so complex that they remind us of the conditions sketched by Charles Dickens in *Bleak House*.

It was legally unnecessary for a partnership to be constituted by deed. The partnership agreement could simply be oral and any person who found his name registered and any person 'recovering a judgement is entitled to issue his execution without the risk of an action being brought against him because there is no *male fides* on his part; he finds the part registered, and he takes the remedy the law provides'.[69]

Although the failure of the Agricultural Bank highlighted defects in company law, it was the affair of the Southern Bank of Ireland which added weight to the critics' case. The Southern was formed in Cork early in 1837 by three former employees of the Agricultural: William Mitchell, a sacked general manager, John MacKenzie, an accountant, and William Bennett, a manager.[70] For Mahony, the Southern was the quintessence of everything a rotten bank should be.[71] The financial circumstances of shareholders can be deduced from Mahony's comment that if all their names were put on a bill for £500 he did not believe the Bank of Ireland, the Provincial or the National would cash it.[72]

Shortly after the formation of the Southern, the Provident Bank of Ireland (also inspired and led by former employees of the Agricultural) started business. The adverse publicity received by both banks from the start was unique in Irish joint-stock banking history. The prospectus of the Provident arrived in Mahony's hands as he was concluding his *Confidential Letter* and he confessed that it only increased 'his anxiety for an immediate interference by Parliament, to check so ruinous and delusive a system'.[73] Mahony's worst expectations were fulfilled. Unlike the Agricultural, the collapse of the Southern created very little stir. During the few months of the latter's existence its notes had only a limited circulation confined to County Cork. So small was its business that on suspension liabilities were said to be £6,000, assets a mere £1,500.[74]

From this unfortunate series of events two results emerged. First, the debate on how to clarify and impose order on the nebulous and inadequate legal code intensified, although it was to be many decades before all the worst abuses were eradicated. Second, the failure of the Agricultural and Commercial Bank attracted so much adverse publicity that it was believed public support for any new bank in Belfast would be impossible to gain for many years.[75] As far as the Belfast banks were concerned, the collapse of the Agricultural Bank was potentially most serious for the newly-established Ulster Bank.

2.3 The Ulster Banking Company

In one sense, the formation of the Ulster Bank was an accident, and cannot be understood without reference to the National Bank of Ireland. The latter, established in 1835, was organised along highly unusual lines with regard to shareholders and profit distribution.[76] Its deed contained a clause which ran

> that in the Establishment of the Partnership between the Society and any bank with local shareholders the court of directors shall have full power to make such arrangements with the subscribers for shares in such bank in regard to the division of profits of the Bank with local shareholders between the Proprietors of such bank and the proprietors of the society . . . and in regard to the management of such bank and of the affairs and concerns thereof and in regard to the extent of the control of the court of directors over such affairs and concerns and of their interference therein as the court of directors shall in their future discretion, think fit.[77]

The National announced a plan in Belfast in November 1835. The local committee, however, refused to support it since most of the deposits and profits from the branch would be transferred to England.[78] It was generally believed that the developing trade of the Belfast region, together with the success of all Irish joint-stock banks, justified the formation of another bank under the control of resident proprietors. In February 1836 local merchants declared their intention to form the Ulster Banking Company 'with branches throughout the trading towns' of the province.

The Ulster was to be managed by four directors and an advisory committee of seven proprietors. Nominal capital was £1 million denominated into 100,000 shares of £10 each. Initially £2 10s was to be called up, together with one shilling per share for 'the necessary outfit'.[79] The four directors, John Heron, Robert Grimshaw, John

Curell and James Steen, were all prominent local businessmen[80] and all had originally been large shareholders in the Northern Bank.[81]

Heron and Grimshaw were appointed managing directors at a salary of £500 p.a. each. Like the directors of the Northern and Belfast Banks, the Ulster's managing directors were specifically prevented from engaging in any other business 'under pain of forfeiting said office'. Steen and Curell, the assistant directors, were not so prevented but were required to attend daily at head office 'for such a length of time as the business of the company shall require . . .'.[82]

The liberty given to assistant directors to engage in business was more apparent than real since compulsory daily attendance at the bank was a considerable imposition on their time. Indeed Curell resigned his post only a year after the bank had opened because of pressure of other business commitments, while Steen resigned early in 1840.[83] Nevertheless, the evidence suggests that both Steen and Curell did borrow on a large scale from the bank to finance their respective businesses. John Curell and his sons were leading bleachers in Ballymena. Their overdrawn accounts were persistently the largest in the first years of the Ulster Bank's existence. The first half-yearly balance shows John Curell's account to have been £18,579 overdrawn, far more than any other account. Over the next few years the account fluctuated widely but was never in credit. Indeed by February 1842 Curell's overdraft was about £28,000. James Steen was a prominent provision merchant and pork curer in Belfast. Early in February 1837, his account was £11,330 overdrawn, second only to Curell's overdraft in size. Steen's account also fluctuated a great deal but was still overdrawn £7,500 in February 1853.[84] In addition to directors, the Ulster had an annually elected advisory committee. No shareholder was eligible for a directorship or committee membership if he held shares in another Irish bank or (of course) if he became insolvent.[85] The geographical location of original shareholders and occupations of members of the advisory committee are set out in Table 11.

The Ulster opened its doors on 1 July 1836 as financial pressure was becoming apparent in London and anticipated, at least by some, in Dublin. Grimshaw was despatched to Dublin on 6 October to arrange with Solomon Watson, a leading bill broker, to help the Hibernian negotiate English bills. Watson was given 'a sufficient

Table 11 *Shareholders in the Ulster Bank at 12 April 1836*

County	Number	Remarks
Antrim and Down	649	(of which 431 Belfast)
Armagh	125	
Donegal	1	
Fermanagh	30	
Londonderry	9	
Tyrone	13	
Monaghan	7	
Cavan	2	
Total Ulster	836	
Other Irish	24	(5 Drogheda, 14 Dublin, 3 Dundalk, 1 Sligo, 1 Limerick)
Total Irish	860	
English	56	(46 Liverpool, 3 Manchester, 1 Northwich, 1 Huddersfield, 1 Lancaster, 4 London)
Total	916	

Members of Ulster Bank Advisory Committee (12 April 1836)

John Dunville	Wholesale tea, wine and spirit merchant
James Boomer	Flax, tow and cotton spinner
Jonathan Cordukes	Provision merchant
William Hunter	Linen merchant
Thomas Greer	Wholesale warehouseman (woollen and printed calico)
John Sinclair	Linen merchant
Joseph Gillis	Provision merchant

Sources. UBCM; Ulster Bank Share Register.

amount to meet all demands'. By early November, as pressure intensified, the Hibernian expressed serious doubts about its ability to continue to pay the Ulster's drafts and notes. Curell went to Dublin and placed £6,700 with the Hibernian to enable the latter to pay a draft which it had just refused to honour as well as to meet further demands. Despite this, the Hibernian allowed the draft to go unpaid. The drafts of the Belfast Bank also remained unpaid. According to the Ulster, it was the Hibernian's action, coinciding with suspension of the Agricultural which precipitated panic, and the Ulster was forced to pay off £80,000 of its notes within fifteen days.[86] Both the Ulster Bank and the Belfast immediately transferred their agencies from the Hibernian.

Part of the Dublin press, not for the last time in the nineteenth century, exaggerated the effects of panic on the Belfast banks. The response in Belfast to this misrepresentation was predictable and echoed that of 1820. Almost 200 signatures, headed by that of the Marquis of Donegall, were attached to a declaration of public confidence in local banks and cautioned 'all persons holding their notes and other securities against being alarmed by ignorant or designing persons, to take any course likely to injure themselves, or produce inconvenience to the banks and trading community'.[87] The 1836-7 crisis certainly caused a general cutback in accommodation by banks. The Belfast Bank circularised its branches that no account was to be overdrawn without written permission from head office, 'such permission to be precise as to the name or address of the houses that are to be favoured, and the amount'. Managers were held personally responsible for 'any deviation'.[88]

The Ulster Bank survived the trauma of a run on its notes and bad publicity. Over the next three or four years the bank set about consolidating its position. Unlike the Northern and Belfast, the Ulster at the outset announced its intention to establish branches and even before the bank opened Curell and Grimshaw had made preliminary enquiries as to possible locations.[89] Nine branches were in operation before the end of 1836, two more opened in 1837, one in 1838 and one 1840 (see Table 10). With so many banks already operating in the province, the Ulster had much ground to make up. In addition to opening branches in larger towns such as Armagh, Derry and Ballymena, where there were as many as four branches of other banks, the Ulster was quick to exploit the potential of smaller towns like Ballymoney, Banbridge, and Antrim where there was little or no competition.

As rivalry increased, the banks looked forward to securing accounts which would increase business and add to their public prestige. One opportunity to do this occurred in 1838 when it became necessary for the Grand Jurors to appoint banks in which the collectors of the Grand Jury Cess 'would deposit the county money, and through which all the future business of the county would be transacted'.[90] In the counties of Londonderry, Donegal, Down and Monaghan, the Belfast Bank was selected; in Tyrone and Armagh, the Provincial. The Belfast board was clearly pleased with the appointment since it would considerably increase note circulation and 'add to its standing throughout the province'.[91]

It was noted in the last chapter that the Northern, Belfast, Provincial and Bank of Ireland had been in contact with each other from 1825. Such contact, in the form of high-ranking deputations had (for the Northern and the Belfast) been for the purposes of ironing out sources of inter-bank friction, and more generally the four banks had discussions about the level of interest rates. It was hardly surprising that the Ulster should now become party to this liaison, and indeed the first public advertisement for the bank announced that 'from the arrangement already entered into this bank will have that friendly confidence and full co-operation with our other established respectable banking houses which is so essential to the mutual prosperity and welfare of our large and increasing community'.[92]

In the late 1830s the three banks in Belfast developed far closer and more formal relations with each other and by 1837 it was becoming clear that inter-bank collaboration was entering a new phase. The first indication of this concerned assistance to the Liverpool firm of W. and J. Brown. Brown's were prominent financiers of Anglo-American trade, but extreme difficulties in that trade in 1836–7 had put the firm under such pressure that it was forced to apply to the Bank of England for help.[93] The Bank of England offered aid on condition that Brown's could find guarantors, and the firm set about this in late spring 1837.[94]

Naturally enough Brown's campaign focused on England but since the firm acted as correspondents for the Northern Bank the latter took up their cause in Belfast. The Northern decided to contribute up to £20,000 provided its two neighbours did the same.[95] The Belfast and Ulster, however, decided initially to contribute £5,000 and £10,000 respectively. The Ulster, as the youngest and smallest of the three, considered on reflection that its contribution should be below that of its two neighbours.[96] The Northern sent one of its directors to Liverpool to scrutinise Brown's accounts, and on the strength of these, decided to go ahead with its original guarantee of £20,000.

The great importance of Belfast trade with Liverpool and the United States meant of course that it was in the banks' own interest to help prevent a possible collapse of a major finance house involved with the Atlantic trade. On another occasion, more than sixty years later, when the Bank of Liverpool was rocked by public revelations about fraud, the Belfast Bank did what it could to preserve the bank's credit by 'explaining to your friends in the North of Ireland how secure and unassailable your financial position is'.[97] In Brown's case, self-interest may go far to explain the

Competition, collusion and crises

Belfast banks' intervention, but it is also relevant to point out that the Brown family had strong ancestral links with Ulster. The founder of the firm, Alexander Brown, was born in Ballymena and built up a linen export business from Belfast to Liverpool and North America. He left Ulster for Baltimore around 1800 and subsequently developed a major interest in Anglo-American mercantile finance.[98] One of his sons, William Brown, the head of the firm's Liverpool branch, was also an original shareholder in the Ulster Bank.[99] Personal and family connections may thus have played a part in the decision to support Brown's.

The important point about this episode was that the three Belfast banks consulted with each other for the first time even if the result of consultation was not perhaps entirely satisfactory to the Northern. How much purely verbal, and therefore unrecorded, discussion took place between the banks' directors is of course impossible to decide. Informal discussion 'over gins' for the purpose of collusion is as difficult for the economic historian to detect as it has proved to be for modern economists and policymakers.[100] Collusion can take many forms, the most extreme being amalgamation. There are two reasons for believing that the Belfast banks' records are not especially good guides to the extent of collusion. First, although there is no mention in the minutes of any of the three banks during the 1830s and 1840s that amalgamation of two or even all three banks was suggested, it later transpired that such suggestions were in fact made.[101] Second, early in 1839, the Belfast banks signed a formal agreement relating to the canvass of customers and levels of interest rates. Some prior discussion of this highly significant move must have taken place but, again, unfortunately it is not recorded. In fact only the Belfast Bank's minutes spelled out just what this agreement entailed.

At a meeting of the directors of the three Belfast banks held on 18 March 1839 it was unanimously agreed that

> in future no solicitation or canvassing for accounts either of public bodies or private individuals is to be permitted on the part of any director, manager or any other person in the pay or employment of any of the above banking companies, that all applications or proposals emanating from the banks are to be considered as solicitations and discontinued accordingly.[102]

The agreement went on to announce that henceforth a uniform scale of rates was to be observed by the three banks 'until notice is given by the bank wishing to depart from them'. The section of the agreement relating to rates was very comprehensive and included all rates and charges.

This agreement was a formal demonstration of the fact that the Belfast banks had fairly rigid notions about the acceptable level of competition between themselves. It was tantamount to an elimination of price competition as well as 'ungentlemanly' canvassing for accounts. After 1839 non-price competition became the norm. The importance of the 1839 agreement was its longevity; later in the century it was modified more than once, but the Belfast banks worked hard to ensure that the terms of the agreement were strictly adhered to by all their staff.

The need to act in concert was seen as paramount, not only to prevent mutually destructive outbreaks of excessive competition, but also to protect the interests of signatory banks against the encroachments of other banks which were later regarded as 'strangers', 'enemies' or 'outsiders'.[103]

Although the agreement was occasionally to be the source of inter-bank friction there were several reasons why it was not insuperably difficult to maintain. First, there were only three signatory banks. While modern research has indicated that collusive agreements can be maintained where the number of firms is very large,[104] it is probably safe to say that the fewer firms involved, the less chance there is that the agreement will be broken. Second, directors and committee members of the Belfast banks were resident in the same locality and drawn from, or actively engaged in, similar lines of business. Ties of kinship, friendship or even mere acquaintance meant that the actions of any one bank could not easily be disguised from the others and, if problems did arise, they could be ironed out easily and quickly. Third, the signatory banks were of a comparable size and all issued their own notes. The resources at their command were not so dissimilar, nor their operating costs so different, that any one them was able to achieve a dominant position in the market. In short, the temptation to breach the agreement was not great. For these reasons, then, the essentials of the 1839 agreement managed to survive throughout the period with which this study is concerned.

2.4 The depression of 1839–43
The Belfast banks survived the commercial crisis of 1836–7, and

were not affected by the failure of the Southern and Provident banks. Indeed, both the Northern and Belfast Banks commented on the prosperous state of trade in the twelve months before September 1839. The former felt the time appropriate to take the equivalent of £5 per share out of undivided profit, and so increase capital without making a further call on shareholders.[105] This picture of prosperity was, however, soon to change decisively.

From the end of 1839 until the middle of 1843 much of Ulster industry was severely depressed, and this was reflected in the fortunes of the banks. The hectic branch expansion of 1834–6 came to a virtual halt, and very few new branches were opened in the following decade. One of the new branches to be established was that of the Northern in Clones, where the closure of a branch of the Agricultural and Commercial Bank had created a void in banking services. At a public meeting it was decided to approach the Northern whose directors, 'from the respectability of the meeting and deputation, ... although not disposed to extend their branches', agreed to the request.[106]

In addition to a marked reluctance to open new branches, the banks clearly found the financial strain of maintaining existing branches considerable, and looked around for ways of cutting costs. The Belfast Bank, for example, withdrew its full branch at Lurgan in 1841 and substituted an agency. The bank judged that the imminent opening of the Ulster Railway at Lurgan together with the advent of penny postage would enable an agency to provide a comparable service to customers at reduced cost to the bank. Moreover the directors pointed out that 'all the respectable friends' who held accounts at the Lurgan branch had transferred them to the bank's head office in Belfast.[107] Another branch closure around this time was that of the Provincial Bank at Moneymore in County Londonderry from the end of September 1843.[108]

The generally depressed state of the Ulster economy in the late 1830s and early 1840s was a result of both domestic and overseas factors. Deficient harvests for five successive seasons to 1842 stifled home demand and were seen as a principal cause of depression.[109] It must be said that bad harvests *per se* could not paralyse the industrial north-east but could exacerbate the situation if overseas markets, upon which so much of the region's trade depended, collapsed. This was the case in the early 1840s. Financial crisis in the United States in 1839 ushered in four years of depression in

Anglo-American trade, and one result of this was a significant reduction in the demand for Ulster's staple export, linen.[110] The Ulster economy was also adversely affected by the depression in Britain which was certainly one of the most serious of the nineteenth century.[111] It is interesting to note that a Belfast newspaper asked its readers to consider 'whether this depression be the inevitable of causes in constant, or constantly recurring operation, or of the local temporary nature'.[112] This comment suggests that the *Belfast Mercantile Register* was beginning to give thought to the question of whether trade depression was simply a random shock or a predictable periodic phenomenon. In Britain, too, this question was attracting a good deal of attention.[113] On both sides of the Irish Sea, then, the notion of a trade cycle began to gain currency in the late 1830s and early 1840s.

What was the banks' reaction to this depression? From April 1840 until July 1843 the level of interest payment on deposits was rather high: three per cent on deposits remaining three months or more, two per cent on current accounts in credit.[114] The Belfast Bank admitted that such rates were 'higher than warranted by the value of money', but maintained them 'in the hope that an improved trade would create a greater demand for discounts and enable them to dispense with the unpopular step of reducing interest'.[115] This optimism proved misplaced, and interest rates were reduced in July 1843 and again in March 1844.[116]

Both the Belfast and Northern Banks managed to sustain their dividends through the depression at seven and ten per cent respectively, but the Ulster was forced to reduce its dividend from seven per cent in 1841 to six and a half per cent in 1842 and five in 1843.[117] The Ulster, as a relatively young bank, had only a very small reserve fund, and dividends were reduced to built up this fund to 'protect the bank against casualties and ensure a regular and equable dividend'.[118] Stability of dividend payment thus quickly became a policy objective for the Ulster Bank as it already was for the Belfast and the Northern. Indeed this objective was not confined to these banks alone. The directors of the Dublin-based Royal Bank, established in 1836, announced to shareholders in 1840 that it was inadvisable to raise the dividend without first adding to the reserve fund. The directors made it clear that they preferred 'the assurance of that permanency in the dividend which a good Reserve Fund will afford, to the ephemeral approbation which they might have obtained by the premature raising of it'.[119]

Another sign of retrenchment in 1843 was the Ulster's decision to reduce the salaries of all its directors and officials.[120] This unusual move may well have been taken to show shareholders that bank officers were prepared to reduce *their* incomes in the face of depression. Admittedly salaries were restored the following year,[121] but by this time the economic outlook was considerably brighter.

Depression in Britain and the United States, together with deficient harvests, which had such adverse effects on the Ulster economy, were beginning to disappear by early 1843[122] and throughout 1844 and 1845 trade picked up steadily. Despite the improvement in trade there were complaints from bankers and warnings in the financial columns of newspapers. The banks naturally welcomed the upturn but complained that discount rates continued 'much lower than they had formerly been in times of prosperous trade'.[123] The newspapers also welcomed the upturn but spotted inherent dangers in the emergent pattern of investment. Economic recovery in Britain was closely associated with railway promotion and construction, and boosted by abnormally low interest rates which continued to prevail through the upturn.[124]

The Belfast merchant community was 'deeply impressed' with the need to construct a coast-to-coast railway network linking strategic towns such as Armagh, Monaghan and Clones with Newry and Belfast.[125] Particular emphasis was laid on the effects of railway construction on employment and the circulation of money. By keeping the poorer population employed and paid, railways would instil industrious habits and prevent people from 'idling after useless legislation or party politics'.[126] Against the many obvious benefits which railways would apparently confer on the Ulster economy, the press was quick to point out the damaging effects of over-investment in railway shares. An abundance of cheap money would generate irresistible temptation to sink too much in ventures where returns were 'tedious and uncertain'. So great had this temptation become by 1844 that the *Belfast Mercantile Register* forecast that it 'must do temporary injury in the course of two years, to our commercial interests'.[127]

This warning went unheeded as the attraction of railway shares continued and shaded into mania by 1845. The outcome of railway mania will be discussed later in this chapter. All we have to note here is the strategic place of railway investment and construction in the upturn of the British economy in the mid-1840s.

2.5 The legislation of 1844–5

Extraordinary instability in the British and Irish money markets from the 1820s to the 1840s led to searching discussion as to how economic activity could be stabilised and attention focused primarily on the role of money in fluctuations. Debate was perpetuated and confused somewhat by an unwillingness or inability to define 'money', and for this reason consensus was impossible. Even if a universally acceptable definition of money had been arrived at, the relationship between money supply and economic activity was so obscure that the scope for argument was enormous.[128] The major parliamentary inquiries on joint-stock banks (1837–8) and banks of issue (1841) produced an impressive array of conflicting evidence, but little more. In Britain the leading reviews had long held different opinions on key monetary questions,[129] and even within the court of Bank of England there was no consensus on the appropriate role of the Bank.[130]

Convertibility was generally regarded as the primary goal towards which efforts should be directed: the real controversy arose as to the best way to achieve it.[131] The defenders of the status quo – those who argued that as long as the obligation of convertibility was maintained, the 'needs of trade' would control the amount of notes in circulation via conventional channels of competitive banking – acquired the name of 'The Banking School'. Opposing them were those who wanted regulation of note issue by law, so that a mixed currency was made to operate precisely as would a purely metallic currency according to the theory of international gold movements. These writers became known as 'The Currency School' and could be identified as such from the later 1830s. The practical outcome of this classic controversy was the Bank Charter Act of 1844 which embodied the Currency School's ideas. After 1844, the Banking School's cause was lost and rearguard action, typified by the work of Fullarton and John Stuart Mill, its only possible strategy. The Irish contribution to the currency-banking controversy was virtually nil, although in the 1850s there was a belated but minor academic exchange of views.[132] Similarly, none of the major British theorists devoted any attention to the question of Irish banking.[133]

With the exception of two clauses, the 1844 Act applied only to

Competition, collusion and crises

England and Wales, but in 1845 two further Acts were passed dealing with Ireland[134] and Scotland[135] respectively. These three Acts were the most important changes in United Kingdom banking law until the First World War. Sections ten and twelve of the 1844 Act applied to the United Kingdom as a whole. The former prohibited the issue of bank notes by any person other than a banker who had legally been issuing on 6 May 1844; the latter prevented any banker who had ceased to issue from resuming after that date. In other words, no new banks of issue could be formed, and no old banks of issue (such as the Agricultural) were allowed to resume. Thus the Act moulded the future structure of the Irish banking system.

Existing banks of issue were quick to recognise the removal of this 'chief inducement to inordinate competition'.[136] One effect was that price competition, which had already been eliminated by the Belfast banks, was now less likely to be reintroduced by new entrants to the system. If the 1844 Act moulded the future *structure* of Irish banking, that of 1845 resulted in significant changes in banking *policy*, and is worthy of much more detailed examination.

The 1845 Act abolished the Bank of Ireland's fifty-Irish mile monopoly area, and so gave every existing bank equality of territorial opportunity and apparently 'put the Bank of Ireland and all other banks of issue upon exceedingly good terms with one another'.[137] Perhaps the most significant sections of the 1845 Act were concerned with notes. Existing banks of issue were allowed a fiduciary issue equal to the average circulation of the previous twelve months. Beyond that notes had to be backed *pari passu* with bullion. Thus in Ireland, and Scotland, there was no absolute upper limit to individual bank issues. This was in marked contrast to England and Wales where no existing individual bank (except the Bank of England) could issue additional notes under any circumstances.[138]

Scottish and Irish banks were thus left with privileges denied to those in England and Wales. Even so a note issue in excess of the fiduciary limit was expensive since the requisite gold had to be obtained and held. Before looking in some detail at the response of Belfast banks to the legislation of 1844–5 it should also be pointed out that the 1845 Act abolished fractional notes and required each bank to submit to the Stamp Office a weekly return of notes in circulation together with the daily amount of gold and silver held. A four-weekly synopsis of these was published in the *Dublin Gazette* from the beginning of 1846. Notes were deemed to be in circulation from the time of issue to the time they were returned to the banker, 'his servant or agent'. The 1845 Act came into operation on 6 December.

One of the main worries of Irish and Scottish banks before 1844 was the threat to small notes. Ever since the two parliamentary committee reports of 1826–7 had vaguely spoken of suppression, the banks had never felt this crucial aspect of their issue secure. In 1844 however the banks were given an assurance that their power to issue small notes would not be withdrawn. In view of the currency-banking controversy, the legislation of 1844–5 was assured of a mixed reception. Some of the criticism stemmed from the different treatment received by Scotland and Ireland. The *Circular to Bankers,* for example, commenting on the Act of 1844, thought Scottish and Irish banks should be 'dealt with more rigorously than English bankers, when their time comes. The glaring injustice of taking a part of the Kingdom, where the small notes have been suppressed, to commence a course of (alleged) rectification, and letting alone those parts where small notes do circulate, is obvious to all men.'[139]

If the *Circular to Bankers* quite clearly saw the imposition of a uniform system of currency throughout the United Kingdom as a matter of principle, others did not. The *Bankers' Magazine* pointed out the strong attachment to small notes in Ireland and Scotland and, reiterating the arguments of Irish witnesses before the 1826 enquiries, rightly emphasised that their suppression would restrict accommodation, raise interest rates and lead to 'the adoption of other forms of credit for such sums far more objectionable than the notes themselves'.[140] While there was disagreement amongst these two leading banking journals about the idea of a uniform currency, Irish joint-stock banks gave qualified approval to the Act of 1845.

The fiduciary issue of Irish banks was as follows:

	£
Bank of Ireland	3,738,428
Provincial Bank	927,667
National Banks	852,269
Ulster Bank	311,079
Belfast Bank	281,611
Northern Bank	243,440

Competition, collusion and crises

Although the Belfast banks' fiduciary limits were much lower than other banks, they were substantially higher than they would have been if the calculation had been made even one or two years previously. Note circulation had declined sharply in the slump of the early 1840s but began to increase again from 1843. The upturn in trade after 1843 was sustained over the next three or four years, and the Belfast banks were fortunate that their fiduciary limit was calculated during the upturn. The recovery in trade was rapid and sustained into 1845 and for this reason note circulation rose appreciably (see Figure 1). Since the fiduciary limit was calculated over the twelve months before 1 May 1845 it reflected the improved state of trade.[141]

While the banks were no doubt gratified by the timing of the fiduciary calculation they had mixed feelings about other aspects of the 1844–5 legislation. The Belfast banks distrusted the automatism of the Currency Principle embodied in the Bank Charter Act of 1844 and particularly regretted the denial of discretionary power to the Bank of England to protect reserves. The 1844 Act had been passed against a background of improving trade and expanding credit. The Belfast banks recognised that such a background was hardly representative of the possible range of economic conditions and judged that no verdict could be given until the Act had been tested in a crisis. With the railway mania gathering force, the banks expected trouble, but believed it 'impossible to calculate the extent of reaction which must inevitably take place, perhaps at no very distant date, or where its effect may be felt'.[142] The main complaint about the 1844 Act was its apparent rigidity and the banks wondered just how it would operate in an anticipated crisis. They did not have long to wait.

In England critics of the 1844 Act pointed out that the most likely difficulty would arise from exhaustion of the reserve in the banking department while the issue department still had quantities of gold.[143] In Belfast the criticism was the same. Section six of the Act obliged the Bank of England to publish a weekly summary of its position in the *London Gazette,* so reserves held in the banking department were now plain for all to see. The theory behind weekly publication of reserves was that it would influence confidence and what would now be called the precautionary motive for holding cash and so adjust velocity of circulation. This dependence upon an 'information-velocity of circulation'[144] mechanism was the corollary of the Currency School's refusal to accept a lender of last resort role for the Bank of England. Explicit acceptance of such a role would have smacked too much of the discretionary power which the Currency School strove to eliminate.

It is easy to see how the rigid automatism of the 1844 Act could operate to generate alarm. If bankers saw the Bank of England reserve began to decline significantly, they became apprehensive it might quickly be exhausted. The reserve did indeed begin to decline late in 1846. In the absence of discretionary power the possible consequences were clear. For the Belfast banks, 'that was the portion of the Act which appeared . . . to create all the alarm and mischief. We saw the reserve of the Bank [of England] getting less, and we knew that it was impossible for them to give accommodation to the country; they could not give it and there was no one else who could give it.'[145] Bristow made it plain that the Belfast banks had been 'perfectly satisfied' with pre-1844 legislation. Although they reserved judgement on the 1844 Act until it had been tested in a crisis, after the crisis of 1847 when the Act had to be suspended their recommendations were unequivocal. Either the Act should be scrapped altogether thus giving back to Bank directors their responsibility and discretion, or a 'relaxing power' should be granted to guard against a repetition of the panic of 1847.[146]

While the Belfast banks thus expressed grave reservations about the 1844 Act, they were more directly affected by that of 1845, and it is their reaction to the 1845 Act to which we now turn. The main criticism of the latter concerned payment of notes. In Scotland notes were issued and payable only at the head office of each bank, but Irish banks had to pay their notes at the branch where they were issued. Each branch of an Irish bank of issue had therefore to keep a reserve of coin. One problem here was that if any bank exceeded its fiduciary limit, the 1845 Act stipulated that the requisite gold had to be held at four designated 'principal' offices. The banks complained that this number was too restrictive and should be increased especially since they were obliged to pay notes at the branch of issue. They argued that the Irish system of note issue and payment was unnecessarily expensive and burdensome, and pointed to the more efficient system operating in Scotland.[147] Their judgement had indeed much to commend it, and there was no particular reason why the method of note issue and payment in Scotland could not be operated in Ireland.

Competition, collusion and crises

Another aspect of the 1845 Act which caused some alarm was the suppression of fractional notes. We noted before that these notes were highly appropriate for the nature of transactions in Ulster markets and economised considerably in the use of coin. During the parliamentary enquiries of 1826–7 the advantages of fractional notes had been repeatedly emphasised by Irish witnesses as part of their campaign to prevent the suppression of all small notes. The threat to small notes finally disappeared in 1845, but no more fractional notes could be issued after 6 December of that year. Country agents and managers were instructed to withdraw them from the circle and return them to head office for cancellation. Failure to do this would result in a heavy penalty.[148] The evidence strongly suggests that suppression of fractional notes was not so serious as it would have been in the 1820s, especially for the operation of linen markets. In the 1830s and 1840s significant changes had taken place in the organisation of linen markets in Ulster. Most of these changes were the result of the rapid diffusion of power flax spinning after 1830 which meant that spinning mills replaced yarn markets. Some of the larger spinners themselves became manufacturers by giving out yarn to be woven. They themselves then finished and marketed the linen webs or sold large numbers of webs to a merchant. This reorganisation meant that the merchant, 'instead of having as many persons to pay as there were webs to pay for, has comparatively few. The larger class of manufacturers, some of whom will have upwards of a thousand looms at work, bring in large quantities of cloth which they dispose of in their warehouses.'[149]

Thus the *number* of transactions was becoming smaller, the *size* of transactions larger and 'every man in trade nowadays having his banker'[150] cheques replaced cash as the means of payment. Given this change in market organisation in the linen trade, the suppression of fractional notes had little or no detrimental effect.

With agricultural produce, including flax, suppression was expected to create considerable difficulty since transactions were still typically small.[151] While the difficulty was acknowledged there were by 1852 'no complaints, now that the traders have become used to the want of them'.[152] All in all, the suppression of fractional notes was not followed by widespread adverse effects on market mechanisms as some had feared. For the banks, retention of small note issue was far more important. As Table 12 shows, small notes accounted for the larger part of the issue of all Irish banks in 1846 except the Bank of Ireland. The proportion of small notes to total issue was far greater for the Belfast banks than all other banks of issue.[153]

Table 12 *Average circulation of Irish banks of issue in the four weeks ending 3 January 1846*

	Denomination of notes		
	£5 and over	Under £5	Total
Bank of Ireland	2,351,100 (54%)	2,000,100 (46%)	4,352,200 (100%)
Provincial Bank	346,011 (30%)	807,713 (70%)	1,153,725 (100%)
National Banks	251,911 (28%)	645,473 (72%)	897,385 (100%)
Belfast Bank	38,605 (10%)	342,094 (90%)	380,699 (100%)
Northern Bank	24,107 (9%)	252,570 (91%)	276,678 (100%)
Ulster Bank	28,120 (8%)	316,559 (92%)	344,679 (100%)
Total	3,039,854 (41%)	4,364,509 (59%)	7,404,366 (100%)

Source. *Dublin Gazette*, 1846, p. 35.

Two further results of the 1845 Act have yet to be discussed: the change in policy of branch location and note exchange. The imposition of a fiduciary limit meant that it was in each bank's own interest to exceed this limit as little as possible. Since notes were deemed to be in circulation until they were returned to the bank of issue, one way of reducing circulation was to increase the frequency of note exchanges. After the Act was passed, but before it came into operation, the Belfast, Northern, Ulster and Provincial banks agreed to do this by making an extra exchange at Belfast and the branches 'as early *after* the close of business on Saturdays as may be convenient'.[154]

About the same time, moves were being made to effect interbank settlements by opening a clearing house in Dublin along the lines of the long-established one in Edinburgh. The scheme has been attributed to the abolition of legal distinctions between banks of issue and the arrival in Dublin of branches of the National and the Provincial.[155] While this was no doubt true, the need to lower circulation must also have played a part. The clearing house came into operation on 8 December 1845 and seems to have been confined initially to note exchange. Settlements were made by an exchange of Exchequer Bills in Dublin.[156] Since none of the Belfast banks had Dublin branches, they had no choice but to operate the clearing system indirectly through their agents. Since the mid-1830s, Dublin agencies of the Belfast banks experienced mixed fortunes. Until 1835 the Northern's agent was Messrs. Gibbons and Williams who went bankrupt in that year, whereupon the agency was given to Boyle, Low and Pim. Boyle's served the Northern until 1 June 1845 when they were replaced by the Bank of Ireland. The Northern, despite 'great satisfaction' with Boyle's, considered that the prestige of the Bank of Ireland together with its extensive branch network would give 'facilities which their present one (Boyle's) cannot afford which has been their sole reason for changing . . . .'.[157]

The Belfast Bank's agent in Dublin since 1827 was Solomon Watson, but the former appointed the Bank of Ireland in 1847 presumably for the same reason as the Northern.[158] The Ulster Bank initially appointed the Hibernian Bank to undertake its agency work in Dublin but this appointment lasted no more than five months. Great dissatisfaction with the Hibernian's behaviour during the 1836 crisis, when it was blamed for putting the Ulster under severe pressure, led to the agency being transferred temporarily to Boyle's and then to the newly established Royal Bank. The Royal continued as the Ulster's Dublin agent from the end of 1836 until 1862 when the latter opened a branch in Dublin.

Thus the 1845 Act resulted in substantial changes in the frequency and method of note exchange. A further change of policy was in branch location. The main criticism of the Bank of Ireland's fifty-Irish mile monopoly area was that it prevented joint-stock banks of issue from opening branches in 'the seven richest and most fertile counties of Ireland (surrounding Dublin) containing a population of about 1,500,000 souls and within which space only six branches of the Bank of Ireland have been established'.[159] The assumption behind this argument was that abolition of the monopoly area would lead to rapid colonisation of east Leinster and south-east Ulster by branches of joint-stock banks of issue. After abolition in 1845 there was some branch expansion in this region, but it was neither so rapid nor so extensive as was expected. Barrow has argued that this was due partly to the effect of the Famine and partly to the fact that existing joint-stock banks in Dublin were still denied the right of issue.[160] There can indeed be no question of the effect of the Famine on branch expansion.[161] Far more debatable is whether the inability of the Hibernian and Royal to issue notes prevented their expansion. Since the 1820s, when the right of issue had usually been seen as a *sine qua non* of a successful bank,[162] evidence had accumulated to show that this was not the case. In 1837, the Royal intimated that it did 'not contemplate,even supposing the power thrown open, the issuing of notes on demand'.[163] The Royal never showed much inclination to establish a large branch network, but in the later nineteenth century the Hibernian began an aggressive policy of branch expansion and managed to survive without the right of issue. We may conclude then that an inability to issue notes was no effective barrier to expansion, still less to survival.

If the Famine partly accounted for the small number of new branches opened in the late 1840s and 1850s, the Act of 1845 must also be seen as a contributory factor. Prior to this Act bank offices had been located in places which were most likely to maximise circulation. After 1845 this was no longer the case. It was clear that henceforth note circulation was unlikely to make such a vital contribution to the profits of banks of issue as it had formerly done. For this reason, exhortations to shareholders at general meetings no longer emphasised the need to increase circulation but to increase deposits.[164]

This change of emphasis was bound to affect branch location, including expansion into the erstwhile prohibited area of the Bank of Ireland monopoly.[165] It was natural that the Belfast banks should receive invitations from this under-banked area after the abolition of the Bank of Ireland's territorial monopoly in 1845. As the following comment illustrates, their response to such invitations was determined by the need to increase deposits. After a suggestion from a merchant in Armagh that it open two branches in south Ulster, the Northern replied:

> We may think of Ballybay provided it was likely to afford any amount of deposits. As the law is likely to stand, increased circulation will not be an object unless accompanied by deposits. I have nothing to suggest as to Newry. The Provincial will certainly go there, probably the Belfast or Ulster also. We do not contemplate it for the reason above given – unless the prospects were much better than we suppose.[166]

Thus the legislation of 1844–5 had considerable significance for the structure of Irish banking and banking policy. The banks had no alternative but to wait and see how the 1844 Act would work in a

Competition, collusion and crises

crisis. As we shall show, their pessimism on this score was well founded, as was their prediction that such a crisis was not far away. In so far as the banks were able to make a positive response to the 1845 Act, they did so. Particularly important was the effect of this Act in forcing the banks to search for deposits rather than to maximise circulation, and the implications of this for branch location and expansion.

2.6 The Famine and the commercial crisis of 1847

The remarkable industrial development of the Belfast region could not obscure the fact that in 1841 a majority of the Ulster population was engaged in farming. As Table 13 demonstrates, however, the four north-east counties of Antrim, Down, Armagh and Londonderry were relatively less dependent on farming than all other parts of Ulster. This dichotomy persisted throughout the nineteenth century.

Table 13 *Number per thousand occupied males engaged in farming in Ulster, 1831–1901*

County	1831	1841	1851	1861	1871	1881	1891	1901
Antrim	533	483	391	384	358	330	284	207
Armagh	677	597	552	561	568	583	553	586
Cavan	843	809	817	786	809	818	804	831
Donegal	818	817	817	805	807	812	802	813
Down	621	575	558	529	526	534	469	545
Fermanagh	826	804	813	777	794	790	778	790
Londonderry	700	652	628	634	622	623	590	567
Monaghan	796	781	795	773	788	795	789	790
Tyrone	741	722	728	744	766	759	741	745
Ulster	712	676	643	627	620	610	568	534

Source. Census of Ireland General Reports, summarised in David Fitzpatrick, 'The disappearance of the Irish agricultural labourer 1841–1912', *Irish Economic and Social History*, VII, 1980, p. 87.

As we have seen, the banks recognised the importance of a healthy agricultural sector as a prop to their prosperity. Ulster agriculture had emerged from a run of bad harvests in 1838–42 and the harvest of 1845 was expected to be exceptionally abundant.[167] This optimistic picture changed quite suddenly during September 1845, with the discovery that the potato crop was likely to be defective.[168] The crop had indeed partially failed, but in the following year failure was almost total and this turn was followed by three years of partial failure accompanied by disease. The last great subsistence crisis in Western Europe had arrived. In its efforts to grasp the dimensions of the catastrophe the government in London was able to draw on the expertise of Irish banks in the late 1840s rather as it had drawn on the Post Office in the eighteenth century for information about economic conditions in different parts of Britain.[169] The Provincial Bank was better placed than most banks to supply intelligence since it had a network of thirty-eight branches throughout Ireland and a head office in London. The bank received routine annual reports concerning local economic conditions, especially the state of crops, from all its branches. At the request of Peel's government these reports began to be sent to the Chancellor of the Exchequer, Henry Goulburn, from the first week in October 1845. Further reports, often from peripatetic branch inspectors, were sent to the Treasury in subsequent years.[170]

The Famine was most serious in southern and western districts where dependence on the potato was greatest.[171] Ulster as a whole was less affected than other provinces, and north-east Ulster was probably less affected than any other part of Ireland. In 1845, none of the Belfast banks had offices outside Ulster, and the vast majority (thirty-five out of forty-five) of these was located in the north-east of the province. This spatial distribution of offices helps to explain why the records of the Belfast banks make far fewer references to the Famine than one might a priori expect. Throughout the later 1840s the Belfast banks were much more concerned with the operation of the Bank Acts of 1844–5 and the outcome of railway mania than they were with the Famine.

In addition to their fortuitous geographical position, another important reason why the Belfast banks were not especially perturbed by the Famine was that the Great Hunger had its greatest impact on the lower strata of Irish society: small farmers, cottiers and labourers.[172] To the trivial extent that such people held bank accounts, they would undoubtedly have been the savings banks rather than joint-stock banks. As James Bristow of the Northern put it in 1848, 'The working people do not keep banking accounts with us'.[173] Savings banks in Ireland date from 1816 and on the eve of the Famine had accumulated nearly £3 million in deposits. Commenting on the early success of savings banks in encouraging thrift, 'assiduity and regularity of conduct' amongst working people, the *Northern Whig* declared in 1826 with unconscious prescience: 'What a vast resource is here, should any unforeseen

Competition, collusion and crises

disaster reach the dwellings of the poor!'.[174] Twenty years later the unforeseen disaster had begun and the vast resource dwindled rapidly. Between 1846 and 1849 deposits in Irish savings banks fell by more than half and recovery was both slow and faltering. The Cork Savings Bank, for example, had deposits of nearly £500,000 in 1846 but during the following two years suffered withdrawals of no less than £372,000. Deposits in this bank reached their lowest point in 1849 and did not approach their pre-Famine peak until the late 1860s.[175] Many other savings banks must have gone through a similar experience. As far as joint-stock banks deposits are concerned Table 16 puts the Famine period into perspective, and it is clear that both the short-term impact and longer-term trends were very different from those of savings banks.

If a comparison of trends in savings and joint-stock banks helps to emphasise the fact that the Famine struck the poorer sections of society hardest, another pointer in the same direction is the trend in note circulation. From Table 14 it is obvious that this decline was especially marked in the case of 'small' notes of less than £5, and in no year was this more apparent than 'black '47'. As one banker remarked, this drastic fall was a result of the fact that there was 'absolutely comparatively nothing to sell or be represented by bank notes'.[176]

Table 14 *Note circulation in Ireland, 1846–55*

Date	Notes £5 and over	Notes under £5	Total
3 January 1846	3,019,298	4,256,609	7,275,647
2 January 1847	3,168,945	4,290,571	7,459,516
1 January 1848	2,496,235	2,655,117	5,151,352
6 January 1849	2,323,090	2,397,528	4,720,618
5 January 1850	2,190,142	2,471,301	4,661,443
4 January 1851	2,167,589	2,626,067	4,793,657
3 January 1852	2,038,513	2,625,577	4,664,092
2 January 1853	2,396,045	3,238,582	5,634,627
7 January 1854	2,791,172	3,664,406	6,455,578
6 January 1855	3,060,652	3,725,896	6,786,548

Source. *Select Committee on the Bank Acts*, BPP, 1857, X, Appendix 18.

One important factor which carried the Belfast banks through the 'Famine years' was the prosperity of the linen trade. Linen had climbed out of the depression of the early 1840s, and recovery was sustained into the early 1850s, punctuated only by the commercial crisis of 1847–8.[177] In Belfast, trade was 'in a reasonable compass and a sound state' until April 1847 when it was feared that the harvest would be deficient again and as a result of this the Belfast banks 'began to be very cautious'.[178] Throughout the summer of 1847 fears about the state of the harvest were seen to be well-founded. The magnitude of grain imports into the UK to compensate for harvest deficiencies was bound to create balance of payments problems, particularly in 1847 when such imports were at a peak. Some relevant figures for the Irish grain trade are given in Table 15.

Table 15 *Summary of the Irish grain trade, 1839–48*

	All grains		Net grain
Date	Export	Import	flow outward
1839	333	40	+293
1840	339	45	+294
1841	416	39	+377
1842	369	56	+313
1843	480	15	+465
1844	424	30	+394
1845	513	28	+485
1846	284	197	+87
1847	146	889	−743
1848	314	439	−125

Note. All figures are in thousands of tons of grain equivalent.
Source. P. M. A. Bourke, 'The Irish grain trade, 1839–48', *Irish Historical Studies*, XX, 1979, p. 168.

Grain markets in the later 1840s were characterised by wide price fluctuations. Rising prices throughout 1846 and early 1847 resulted in heavy futures buying. Massive grain imports in the early part of 1847 caused an outflow of gold which the Bank of England was unable to stem despite twice raising Bank rate.[179] Prices plummeted and the speculative boom was brought to a shuddering halt with widespread failures in the corn trade. In Britain and Ireland there was general agreement that these failures were responsible for touching off commercial crisis. In Ulster, the most serious bad debt arising from speculation in corn seems to have been incurred by the Derry branch of the Belfast Bank where speculation was 'aggravated by the manager not having attended to the instructions he received, and which caused his dismissal as an example to others as well as to prevent a similar occurrence in future'.[180] The unexpectedly high elasticity of grain supply created problems for all those holding large grain stocks. The true dimensions of the extent to which some grain merchants had financed their operations with bank credit had been concealed from Irish banks since some merchants had received credit from bankers in London. The Provincial Bank summed up the banks' dilemma: 'The facilities of a Bank account in London enable parties in Ireland to keep many of their operations from the knowledge of the managers of the branches with which they transact their business and this has . . . been to some extent the case during the late corn speculations.'[181] Anxiety about the creditworthiness of many merchants involved in the grain trade was clearly widespread by the summer of 1847. To the acute problems of the grain trade was added 'near total annihilation' of the provisions trade in 1847 and 1848 and a slow recovery thereafter.[182] Both contributed to the decline in note circulation and to the decline in discount business (see Chapter Three).

The view in Belfast was that the crisis of 1847–8 surpassed all previous crises, even that of 1825–6. The most visible effect of depression was that construction of new factories was halted, those partially constructed were left unfinished, and some which had been built were not fitted with machinery.[183] Even so, the evidence suggests that Belfast was less affected than many British industrial towns, especially in Lancashire and Clydeside where financial crisis was compounded by a coincidental depression in cotton textiles.[184] Contemporaries noted with relief that there had been little speculation in railway stock in Belfast, and also that the American markets for Ulster linen had held up 'tolerably well' throughout the crisis.[185]

For banks, the most worrying thing about the onset of crisis was the operation of the Bank Charter Act. If Bank of England reserves became exhausted, a logical consequence of the Act was that advances and discounts would have to be refused. In the third quarter of 1847, reserves fell to a post-1844 low and this resulted in a predictably sharp rise in liquidity preference. At this point, banks expected the credit system to be shaken to its foundations. By September 1847 the Northern had no doubts as to where the blame for this lay, judging that while the Bank Charter Act 'has totally failed in guaranteeing the country against rash and extensive speculation, or against the natural effects of an export of gold, it has been too efficient in seriously aggravating all the bad effects necessarily resulting from a bad harvest and depressed trade'.[186]

The automatism of the 1844 Act had failed, and for this reason the government had little choice but to change course. A letter from the Treasury to the Bank of England on 25 October 1847 authorised the latter to grant further loans at a minimum rate of eight per cent. If this involved a breach of the 1844 Act, the Bank of England was indemnified against such a breach.[187] The effect of the 'Treasury Letter' was both immediate and remarkable. The scramble for cash abated, confidence began to be restored and in fact the Act was not breached. Publication of the letter made the Belfast banks 'feel perfectly at ease',[188] although in common with several British economists and bankers they called in vain for modification or repeal of the Act.

Before we leave the troubled 1840s, it is necessary to comment further on the movement of bank deposits outlined in Table 16. It is sometimes suggested that the aggregate deposit series is a 'sensitive barometer' of agricultural incomes,[189] and sharp rises or declines in the series taken as a reflection of prosperity or depression in the agricultural sector. One basic problem with this hypothesis is that it is impossible to test on the basis of aggregate figures. The essential requirement would be disaggregated data not only for each bank but for each branch. Such data are hard come by, but when they become more available in the later nineteenth century we will discuss this hypothesis in much greater detail. Even at this stage, however, it is possible to offer a preliminary critique. It should be recognised that the level of bank deposits at any one time is a function of many variables. Among these we might include the number, income and wealth of bank customers and the relative attractiveness of bank deposits *vis-à-vis* other financial and real assets. The asset portfolio of any individual should reflect the degree of his/her risk aversion and the returns (actual and expected) offered by the available number of assets of which a bank deposit is merely one.[190]

How then can we explain the volume of Irish bank deposits in the later 1840s? The evidence suggests that the decline in 1847 reflected a rise in both the transactions and speculative demand for cash. The Northern's deposits, for example, began to decline as early as January 1847 and were reduced by about a fifth during the next year. The bank explained that:

> deposits were withdrawn partly for the purpose of lending that money on higher rates to some railways; and with us there have been for some

time local improvements which we have been carrying on in the harbour and town, and pipe water, and part of our deposits was taken out and lent upon the security of those works, but still a good many small deposits have been drawn out from the necessities of people obliging them to have their money.[191]

Table 16 *Deposits in Irish joint-stock banks, 1840–65 (£)*

Year	Amount	Increase	Decrease
1840	5,567,851	—	—
1841	6,022,573	454,722	—
1842	6,416,795	394,222	—
1843	6,965,681	548,886	—
1844	7,601,421	635,740	—
1845	8,031,044	429,623	—
1846	8,442,133	411,089	—
1847	6,493,124	—	1,949,009
1848	7,071,122	577,998	—
1849	7,469,675	398,553	—
1850	8,268,838	799,163	—
1851	8,263,091	—	5,747
1852	10,773,324	2,510,233	—
1853	10,915,022	141,698	—
1854	11,665,739	750,717	—
1855	12,285,822	620,083	—
1856	13,753,149	1,467,327	—
1857	13,113,136	—	640,013
1858	15,131,252	2,018,116	—
1859	16,042,140	910,888	—
1860	15,609,237	—	432,903
1861	15,005,065	—	604,172
1862	14,388,725	—	616,340
1863	12,966,731	—	1,421,994
1864	14,422,176	1,455,445	—
1865	17,050,552	2,628,376	—

Source. W. Neilson Hancock, *Report on Deposits in Joint-Stock Banks in Ireland 1840–65*, Dublin, 1866. (All figures at 31 December.)

The point here is that although bank deposits fell in the worst famine year (1847), at least some of this fall was accounted for by a move out of bank deposits into other financial assets. This diversification of asset portfolio supports our earlier contention that the volume of deposits was not a simple function of agricultural incomes and cannot therefore be regarded as a sensitive barometer of them. Of course, deposits in the Belfast banks may have been relatively hard hit by such diversification.

Depositors in the south and west of Ireland were probably less aware of diversification opportunities and in any case as one moved further west such opportunities were fewer. In short, one would not expect a switch into other financial assets to have been very significant as an explanation for the decline in deposits as it was in the north and east. Since the Famine struck hardest in the south and west, banks which operated in these areas were more likely to suffer a decline in deposits as a result of agricultural distress. Nonetheless there was one factor which helped to stem the decline of deposits in 1847. This was dehoarding. During the Famine there was a marked increase in food riots and theft in many parts of Ireland[192] and contemporaries sometimes noted that fear of robbery caused a transfer of cash from house to bank. A writer in the *Bankers' Magazine* in 1847 considered that this fear was so great that it had 'more than doubled the lodgements' in many of the country branches.[193] It is clear then that fluctuations in bank deposits lend themselves to more than one explanation and we should not regard aggregate deposit data as barometers of agricultural incomes.

2.7 Origins and impact of the 1857 crisis

One reflection of the pressing problems which faced Belfast banks in the 1840s was a sharp decline in the number of new branches, although virtually all those open by 1840 managed to stay open.[194] Once recovery was under way, there was a limited revival of interest in branch expansion, and we can see the beginnings of a trend in expansion which was to become increasingly important in the second half of the nineteenth century. Before 1850, all the Belfast banks' offices were in Ulster; after 1850 the banks for the first time showed an interest in moving outside the province. The Belfast Bank, which of the three subsequently showed itself to be the most 'Ulstercentric' made the first move into Leinster by opening in Dundalk, Drogheda and Navan in 1851. This completed the Belfast's 'chain of branches connecting the principal market towns of the North'.[195] Although expansion outside Ulster had thus begun, it did not become rapid until the last thirty years of the century and by 1875 the three Belfast banks had a total of only twenty-four branches outside the province.[196] Even within Ulster the Belfast banks showed only a minor interest in expansion. Reluctance to move into new territory was a marked feature of all Irish banks in mid-century.[197] As far as the Belfast banks were concerned, this general reluctance helped to preserve their dominance in the north-east. In 1854, for example, shareholders in the National urged their board to look into the possibility of opening in Belfast. The board, however, decided against the move since 'it appeared to them quite obvious, from all the information they could collect in the best channels on the spot and otherwise that Belfast already possessed ample banking accommodation'.[198]

If there was somewhat of a pause in branch expansion, there were signs of recovery from the commercial crisis around 1850, although the banks often complained of the difficulty in keeping their funds 'fully and profitably employed' until 1852.[199] Interest rates throughout the United Kingdom plunged after the crisis of 1847–8 and the downward trend continued until the beginning of 1853. For almost eight months following April 1852 the key Bank rate was two per cent. This was the lowest rate ever charged by the Bank of England, and the length of time it remained in force was surpassed only twice before 1914.[200] As the Ulster Bank put it in 1852 there was both 'an abundance of money and a reduction in the rates of interest unparalleled in our experience'.[201] In the same year the Belfast Bank complained that the exceptionally low discount rates and 'the scarcity of bills even at these reduced rates have made themselves very sensibly felt on banking profits'.[202]

As interest rates fell to their lowest levels in the summer of 1852, attempts were made to ensure that clients whose cash accounts had a satisfactory turnover were charged less for their advances than those who used such accounts as 'dead' loans. Giving notice of the reduction in overdraft rates from 1 July 1852, the Ulster Bank's general manager, John Taylor, informed branch managers that:

> From and after this date the rate of interest charged on the Dr. balances for current accounts will be 5% per annum. But this reduction applies only to those accounts which are actively and beneficially operated on and does not extend to those accounts which are inoperative and the balance thereon having become permanent may be considered *Dead Loans* on which the rate of interest will continue to be 6% per annum.[203]

Recovery in the economy of the north-east was under way from about 1850, led by flax-spinning and linen manufacture.[204] Other factors which compensated the banks for abnormally low interest rates included a rapid increase in deposits: those in the Belfast Bank doubled between 1848 and 1854,[205] while during the same period deposits in the Ulster Bank increased 'in a more than ordinary ratio'.[206] In addition, the 1850s saw considerable railway construction in Ulster and many other parts of Ireland.[207] Given the abundance of cheap money the early 1850s was certainly a favourable time for railway companies to seek credit and to receive a sympathetic and positive response from the banks. Some examples of bank finance in this area are provided in Chapter Three. Towards the end of the 1850s, however, the banks had to endure another commercial crisis and the Belfast banks were reminded of the ease with which confidence in them could quickly deteriorate as a result of a sudden wave of public doubt about the banking system in general.

The influence of the United States on the economies of Britain and Ulster has already been stressed. Between 1837 and 1842, a slump in the United States exacerbated commercial difficulties and the effects of bad harvests in the UK to produce a depression of great, possibly unprecedented, dimensions. On the other hand in the later 1840s a buoyant US demand for Ulster linen helped to carry the Belfast region through the troubled Famine years, even if this region did not entirely escape the commercial crisis of 1847–8. In the crisis of 1857 the influence of the United States was again obvious, directly because of its effect on the demand for linen and indirectly because of its effect on financial and trading concerns in Britain.

A brief account of the crisis in America and its repercussions in Britain will provide the necessary background against which to discuss its effects on Ulster.[208] Bearish activity on railway stock in New York sent prices tumbling and triggered off a series of bankruptcies in mid to late September. The pressure on banks became unbearable. In October no less than 1,415 American banks failed and business came to a virtual standstill along the eastern seaboard. Transatlantic repercussions were quickly felt in Britain and Europe. Indeed business in South America, Australia and the Far East was also adversely affected. For this reason the crisis of 1857 can be seen, with much justification, as the first world-wide commercial crisis.

Predictably those areas of the UK with closest economic links with the USA were the first to feel the strain. The demand for Ulster linen declined sharply, but initially Liverpool and Glasgow were most affected.[209] This was reflected in the failure of, *inter alia*, the Borough Bank of Liverpool on 27 October 1857 and the Western Bank of Scotland a fortnight later. The latter was especially alarming since the Western was not only Glasgow's foremost bank but by far the largest bank failure Scotland had ever seen. The Scottish banking system, hitherto the most stable in the United Kingdom and the subject of almost universal praise, was thus seen to be fallible after all. The consensus of opinion was that bank failures in Britain were responsible for causing alarm and panic in Belfast and other parts of Ireland.[210] Ulster was the only province in Ireland with close transatlantic trading links, so the crisis in the USA had very little impact in Munster, Leinster and Connaught. Even in Belfast there was no alarm until the failure of the Western Bank.[211]

Banks began to exercise caution from the middle of October. On 16 October, for example, the Provincial advised its managers that 'the serious condition of monetary affairs in America' required the greatest caution in lending, and the avoidance of any transaction 'not strictly in the legitimate way of business, and with parties known to be good for the amounts'.[212] The day after the Western Bank stopped payment the Provincial made every effort to protect itself by ordering that no new overdrafts be granted without express permission from the directors, existing advances should be kept to (or brought within) authorised limits, and security should be found for unsecured advances. Finally, as a general precaution managers were told *not* to accept

> any new accounts which may be brought to you from other banks with a view of receiving accommodation which their establishments may find it inconvenient or inexpedient to afford; and you cannot too carefully, or too strictly, guard against the admission of any stray or unusual transactions that may present themselves, for while the Directors will approve of all reasonable facilities and support given in the regular way of business to the ordinary good and safe customers of the bank they will not sanction any departure from that prudent watchfulness and caution which is so particularly necessary at the present time.[213]

The most satisfactory indicator of the build-up and subsidence of pressure in money markets in 1857 and 1858 is the trend in interest rates. The key rates are set out in Table 17, from which it is evident that pressure began to build up in the second week of October, when the number of bank failures in America approached its peak, and continued to intensify over the next six weeks or so. As usual minimum discount rates in Belfast moved very closely with those of the Bank of England, rising a full four points in the four weeks following 10 October. In both Belfast and London, discount rates peaked on 9 November (the same day that the Western Bank stopped payment) and the punitive rate of ten per cent was maintained for a full six weeks.

Table 17 *Movements in rates of interest, April 1857–February 1858*

Date	(1) Dr. Current	(2) English Bills @ 3 months or less	(3) Bank Rate
3.4.1857		6½	
4.4.57	7		
14.6.57	6½	6	
18.6.57			6
16.7.57			5½
17.7.57	6	5½	
8.10.57			6
10.10.57	6½	6	
12.10.57			7
13.10.57	7½	7	
19.10.57			8
20.10.57	8½	8	
5.11.57			9
7.11.57	9½	9	
9.11.57		10	10
10.11.57	10		
24.11.57	10½		
24.12.57			8
26.12.57		8	
28.12.57	8½		
7.1.1858		6	6
8.1.58	6		
14.1.58			5
15.1.58		5	
28.1.58			4
29.1.58	5	4	
4.2.58			3½
10.2.58	4½	3½	
11.2.58			3

Sources. (1) and (2): Ulster Bank *Circulars to Branches*.
(3) Sir John Clapham, *The Bank of England 1797–1914*, Appendix B.

So severe was the pressure in London that on 11 November it was decided to suspend the Bank Act for the second time since 1844.[214] As in 1847 the Bank of England was promised indemnity if its fiduciary issue was exceeded during the crisis. As was mentioned earlier in this chapter, in 1847 the 'Treasury Letter' promising indemnity had a magical effect on the restoration of confidence in Belfast and Britain. In 1857 no such restoration of confidence occurred because, in Clapham's words, 'things were much too far gone',[215] and the crisis persisted.

The nature of the 1857 crisis in Belfast differed in two important respects from that of 1847. First, it was neither preceded nor accompanied by bad harvests.[216] Second, and much more important, 1857 was the first occasion that the Belfast banks experienced a simultaneous run on their notes.[217] Prior to this date, with one small exception (in 1836), noteholders had complete confidence in the Belfast banks even if depositors had occasionally made abnormal demands. Long-standing confidence on the part of noteholders had sometimes been cited by the Belfast banks as part of their campaign to retain their right to issue small notes whenever this right was under review. When J. W. Bristow of the Northern Bank was asked by the *Select Committee on the Bank Acts* in 1858 if he believed holders of small notes 'were more in the habit of running upon banks than the holders of large notes or depositors' he answered quite firmly that 'We never knew what a run upon the bank as respects notes was until now; we never had such a thing since the joint-stock banks in Belfast were formed as a run in the case of their notes until last November.'[218] Evidence with which to illustrate the impact of the 1857 crisis is not comprehensive but Table 18 gives some idea of the extent of deposit withdrawal from the Belfast Bank during the crisis period, defined by this bank as 17 October to 30 November 1857. Table 18 suggests that the geographical impact of deposit withdrawal was very unevenly spread over the branch system. Unfortunately there no figures for the level of branch deposits at the very start of the panic, but it is possible to offer some observations on the geographical distribution of deposit withdrawal. It seems clear that while there was no consistent ratio between withdrawals and remaining deposits, the ratio was greater in the south and south-west sections of the branch system than in the north-east. Castleblayney, Drogheda, Dundalk, Dungannon and Navan lost a much greater proportion of their deposits than Ballymoney, Magherafelt and Limavady. Even within the south-west section the impact was far from uniform. Monaghan and Enniskillen, for example, were considerably less affected than either Dungannon or Castleblayney. In general, however, the north-east/south-west dichotomy was real. How can we account for this?

Perhaps the most satisfactory explanation lies in the fact that the

Table 18 *Deposits withdrawn from branches of the Belfast Bank during the panic from 17 October until 30 November 1857*

Branch	Total withdrawn (£)	Deposits at 24 October 1857 (£)
Armagh	8,328	112,876
Ballymena	4,351	39,815
Ballymoney	1,223	40,660
Cookstown	535	18,331
Castleblayney	9,668	37,098
Coleraine	8,540	88,874
Derry	17,547	158,696
Drogheda	17,579	60,868
Dundalk	17,304	54,131
Dungannon	11,174	58,304
Enniskillen	2,602	28,409
Larne	6,294	83,818
Letterkenny	4,337	58,347
Limavady	1,650	75,864
Lurgan	852	6,931
Magherafelt	2,542	43,611
Monaghan	4,259	49,006
Navan	9,418	48,400
Newry	16,818	109,123
Newtownards	7,196	84,968
Portadown	3,751	48,603
Strabane	16,250	146,517
Tandragee	3,098	29,310
Branch Total	175,136	1,482,566

Source. Belfast Bank Miscellaneous Papers.

north-east had never experienced anything like the number of bank failures and hence the same degree of distrust in banks as the south-east. After the Napoleonic Wars private bank failures were characteristic of many parts of Ireland except the north-east. The failure of the Agricultural and Commercial Bank in 1840 affected the south-west most since the majority of its branches were located there. Finally in 1856 came the failure of the Tipperary Joint-Stock Bank which sent a 'cry of wrath and pain that rang through Munster'.[219] This last bank had been founded in Tipperary in 1838 with three directors, one of whom was James Sadleir. Certainly the Tipperary Bank played an active role in an under-banked area.[220] The main problem was that James Sadleir lent a substantial proportion of the bank's funds to his brother John, an MP and for a brief period after 1852 a junior Lord of the Treasury, and John Sadleir used these funds for speculative activity, particularly in England and

Competition, collusion and crises

Europe. So well known and wide-ranging was his railway speculation that 'for a moment he became a veritable little Hudson'.[221]

Just as railways ruined George Hudson, so they ruined John Sadleir and the Tipperary Joint-Stock Bank. At any rate, the failure of the Tipperary Bank in February 1856 administered a further shock to the Irish banking system outside the north-east. According to the Governor of the Bank of Ireland:

> The panic of 1857 was entirely caused as an internal panic; that is to say, that seeing the failure of banks in other parts of the kingdom, the Newcastle Bank, the Western Bank of Scotland, and other banks, and having before them the failure of the Tipperary Bank induced parties to have a disquiet about all banks of deposit.[222]

It is extremely plausible, then, to suggest that the relatively large withdrawal of deposits from the Belfast Bank's south-western branches in 1857 reflected the memory of bank failures in and beyond this region over the previous forty years or so.

As mentioned above, the 1857 crisis was unprecedented in that it spread to noteholders as well as depositors. The evidence indicates that the run on notes was extensive. A footnote to the memorandum on withdrawals from the Belfast Bank summarised in Table 18 shows that during the seven-week panic £195,000 was paid in gold for notes. This represented about thirty-eight per cent of the bank's total circulation (£515,000), and so note circulation declined sharply at a period of the year when it would normally have increased.[223] If the panic of 1857 affected both the notes and deposits of the Belfast banks, they were not the only ones to suffer in these respects. The National Bank, for example, considered that between October and December 1857 the run on deposits was 'pretty heavy' but that the run on notes was greater than at any previous time. The National's circulation during this period declined from £1,300,000 to 'within a few thousand pounds' of its fiduciary limit of £852,000[224] It would appear then that the National suffered a decline of thirty per cent or more in its circulation, which was not very different from that suffered by the Belfast Bank.

Although Irish banks were under severe pressure late in 1857 there were no bank failures. This was in marked contrast to England and Scotland, where there were several such failures and temporary suspensions. The runs on notes and deposits made uniquely heavy demands on the banks' gold reserves, but under the terms of the 1845 Bank Act, they had more than enough gold to meet all demands. Indeed the *Parliamentary Report on the Bank Acts* of 1858 noted that the amount of gold held under the 1845 Act had been 'a source of strength' during the crisis.[225]

The Belfast banks were well satisfied with their stability during the crisis, and were quick to point this out to shareholders.[226] There were bound to be bad debts, and in February 1859 the Belfast Bank directors reported to the Board of Superintendence that during the previous twelve months £20,000 had been deducted from the reserve fund to meet such debts, which included '£5,000 supposed loss by the Council'. As far as this bank was concerned the crisis strengthened its long-established resolve to add to reserves. In August 1859 the reserve fund amounted to £135,000 invested in government stock and the directors recommended that this sum be increased still further.[227]

1857 is significant for the Belfast banks since it was the first and last time that they suffered from a simultaneous run on both deposits and notes. That they emerged from this ordeal must have been a great relief, not least because each commercial crisis successfully endured contributed to the banks' reputation. They had proved their ability not only to survive but to grow during a tough period of adolescence. As we will show, the rapid economic expansion of the mid-1860s caused the banks to add to their capital and build up reserves to new heights, and this provided them with additional financial strength to meet future difficulties.

With hindsight it can be argued that because there were no further simultaneous runs on deposits and notes after 1857, and because the purely fortuitous boom of the mid-1860s helped very considerably in the task of building up contingency funds, the chances of bank failure declined from this period onwards. Before we discuss the development of the Belfast banks after 1860, however, it is necessary to turn to an examination of the major features of their business up to this point.

CHAPTER THREE

ASPECTS OF BANKING BUSINESS IN THE MID-NINETEENTH CENTURY

The aim of the previous two chapters was to describe the origins and to analyse the early development of the Belfast banks and to say something about the economic background in which they operated. The present brief chapter builds on the earlier two with a view to sketching important features of banking business in the mid-nineteenth century. Sources available for this are neither copious nor continuous, but enough have survived to permit some general observations.

The most obvious feature of banking business was its predominantly seasonal nature, a reflection of the agricultural base of the economy and the fact that some important industries such as linen and brewing and distilling were agriculture-related. On behalf of the three Belfast-based banks J. W. Bristow of the Northern explained in 1848:

> Our business is almost entirely at one season of the year from the time of the harvest to the month of May. The principal business that we have for which money is required is business in butter, provisions and flax, which began to come to market then and such articles are almost always sold for cash, and the spinners require to lay in a stock of materials to last them for the whole year, and we frequently make advances to those people to be repaid to us in the summer, when their stock begins to diminish.[1]

Major aspects of banking business subject to seasonal rhythms include note circulation, bill discounts and advances to customers in certain key industries. Seasonality in banking was of course not confined to Ulster but was evident throughout the country.[2]

Those who held bank accounts in Ireland before 1914 were predominantly farmers, professional people and those 'in trade'. There is little precise information on the relative weight of these various groups, but one extant list of account holders at a country branch in mid-Ulster c.1852 indicates the importance of the farming community. The list relates to the Ulster Bank's branch at Aughnacloy in County Tyrone, and is analysed in Table 19. This village had a population of less than 2,000 at the time of the 1851 census and had only one bank office. The nearest towns providing alternative banking facilities were Dungannon and Monaghan,[3] both some ten miles away, and so it may be presumed that the Ulster Bank in Aughnacloy catered for a substantial proportion of the bank-using population in the village and surrounding area. Table 19 shows that half the account holders were farmers and many of the remainder were retailers and those in the professions. Even if we should not generalise on the evidence of one branch, literary evidence supports our argument about the predominance of farmers as account holders[4] and the evidence of customers' occupations in Table 19 has the further merit of helping to explain the seasonal nature of banking in provincial Ireland.

Table 19 *Account holders at Ulster Bank branch in Aughnacloy, c. 1852*

Attorney/solicitor	4	'Lieutenant'	1
Auctioneer	1	Linen manufacturer	1
Baker	3	Mechanic	1
Brewer/distiller	1	MD	2
Bridewell keeper	1	Millwright	1
Builder	1	Policeman	2
'Butcher, postmaster and leather dealer'	1	Postmaster	1
		'Private gentleman'	11
Butter dealer	6	Retired captain	1
Carrier	1	Road contractor	1
Clergyman	11	Saddler	1
Cornmiller	2	Shopkeeper	2
Draper	1	Spade manufacturer	2
Farmer	121	Spirit dealer	4
Flax dealer	1	Traveller	1
Grocer	16	Woollen draper	5
Haberdasher	4		
Innkeeper/publican	7		
Land agent	3	Not in business	4
Leather seller	1	Unknown	12
		Total	239

Source. Ulster Bank Aughnacloy Branch Records.

3.1 Note circulation

Perhaps the most striking reflection of seasonal rhythms in the Irish economy was the annual cycle of note circulation. In mid-nineteenth century Ireland the lowest point in the cycle was normally August or September, the highest in January or February. To a considerable extent the amplitude of the cycle was a result of the demand for, and, supply of, agricultural produce and the cycle itself was 'as regular as clockwork in ordinary circumstances'.[5]

On the supply side the state of the harvest (used here as a proxy for the amount of agricultural produce coming to market) was crucial. The relationship between harvests and economic activity in primarily agricultural regions has long interested historians and has generated a considerable literature.[6] In Ireland the link between harvests, economic activity and banknote circulation was appreciated in particular by J. W. Gilbart, a leading commentator on banking who had spent over six years in the country as a branch manager of the Provincial Bank.[7] On the demand side Gilbart recognised that the price and quantity of agricultural imports and exports would affect note circulation, as would the size of population and rate of emigration.[8]

An illustration of the pattern of note circulation is provided in Figure 1 which graphs the note issue of the Belfast Bank between 1840 and 1845. Bearing in mind both demand and supply factors, the trend in circulation becomes readily explicable. Poor harvests, a weak demand for flax, depression in Britain and in the United States coincided to depress trade and reduce circulation in Ulster in the late 1830s and early 1840s.[9] The upturn from 1843 was triggered and sustained by better harvests and a much stronger demand for flax and linen goods. By late 1844 there was 'full employment' in all parts of the linen trade[10] and it was noted with relief that 'all classes are emerging from their straitened condition in which four or five seasons of agricultural scarcity and deranged commerce had involved them'.[11]

If the general pattern of circulation was clear enough, Figure 1 shows that there were variations in the timing of seasonal peaks and troughs. The explanation for this lies in the general state of trade in the year in question. Seasonal peaks occurred earlier when trade was relatively depressed because 'in seasons of distress the crops are brought earlier to market'.[12] In other words, if sellers did not have much to bring to market then the seasonal peak of market activity was reached in November rather than in January or February. Thus in our illustration the seasonal peak of note circulation in 1840/1 and 1841/2 was noticeably earlier than in 1843/4 and 1844/5 when economic recovery was under way. A relatively early peak in circulation, reflecting problems in the rural economy, was also observed during the Famine years after 1845.[13] The general impact of the Famine years (which include the commercial crisis and slump of 1847–8) on the seasonal circulation of Irish banks of issue is outlined in Table 20.

The predictable increase in circulation at certain times of the year meant that under the terms of the 1845 Act the banks had to secure gold to cover issues in excess of fiduciary limits. The Belfast banks normally imported the necessary gold from England rather than from the Bank of Ireland. Their opinion was that the Bank of Ireland was under no obligation to provide them with adequate gold and so they considered the Bank of England a more reliable source. In addition, some of the banks believed they could secure gold at a cheaper rate from England than they could from Dublin.[14] The almost ritual expense of shipping and insuring gold to satisfy the terms of the 1845 Act must often have seemed an unnecessary waste,[15] although there was always the chance – as in the 1857 crisis – that banks would have cause to be grateful for their gold stocks.

The impact of the harvest on note circulation was important throughout the nineteenth century, but the harvest also had an impact on the circulation of coin. The evidence suggests that silver coin in particular often proved difficult or even impossible to obtain when required. Thus in October 1844 The Provincial Bank pointed out to the Treasury the great inconvenience caused by the scarcity of silver coin 'occasioned by the activity of the markets for country produce being much greater than usual, owing to the abundance of the recent harvest and also the demands occasioned by the increased military force at present maintained in Ireland'. Taking into account the abundant harvest and increased military demands together with the demands occasioned by public works programmes, the Provincial believed that it alone would need between £20,000 and £30,000 in silver coin. It had applied to the Bank of England for a few thousand pounds 'for the present emergency' but had been told that the Bank of England 'could not spare even one hundred pounds'.[16] In view of this shortage of silver coin it was fortunate that small and fractional notes circulated in the pre-Famine period. Indeed it was estimated in March 1845 that notes of 20*s*, 30*s* and 60*s* together with silver coin comprised two-thirds of the total currency of Ireland.[17] Even though fractional notes were abolished in 1845 the small (£1) note survived

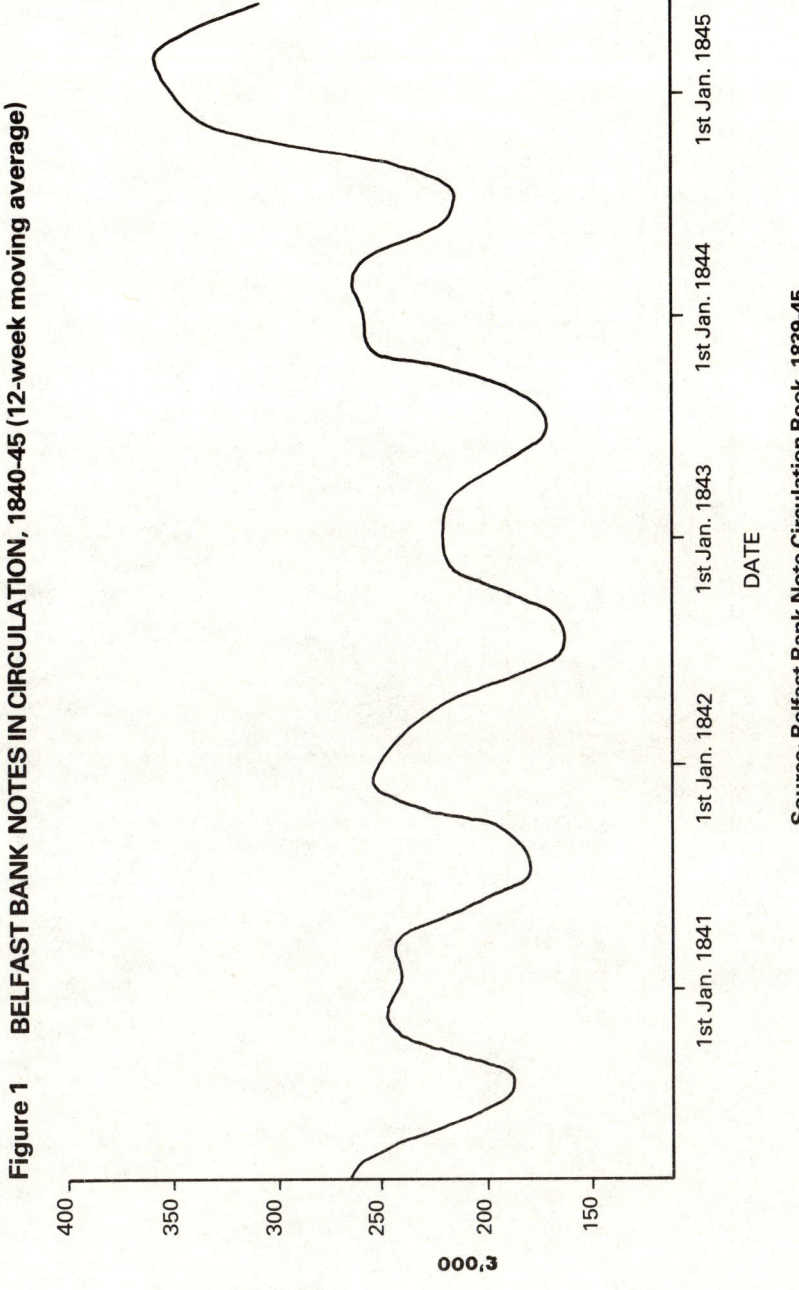

Figure 1 BELFAST BANK NOTES IN CIRCULATION, 1840-45 (12-week moving average)

Source: Belfast Bank Note Circulation Book, 1839-45.

Table 20 Actual note circulation of Irish banks as % of authorised issue, 1846–52

Name of bank	1846		1847		1848		1849		1850		1851		1852	
	Jan.	Aug.	Jan.	Aug.	Jan.	Aug.	Jan.	Aug.	Jan.	Aug.	Jan.	Aug.	Jan.	Aug.
All the banks	116.4	101.9	118.3	80.2	81.8	67.9	73.6	60.3	73.5	64.2	75.3	62.6	73.7	69.2
Bank of Ireland	116.3	103.7	112.7	83.1	82.6	70.6	72.7	62.6	72.0	65.3	70.8	61.7	66.5	66.9
Provincial Bank	124.4	111.3	129.3	83.1	86.8	69.5	77.7	59.2	72.4	61.4	74.1	58.6	71.8	65.8
National Banks	105.2	95.9	127.7	81.6	76.5	62.5	70.7	57.0	74.7	65.8	81.6	64.8	81.6	74.4
Belfast banks	119.8	90.2	121.7	62.7	77.7	59.4	75.8	54.7	80.2	60.7	90.1	69.0	99.8	77.9

Source. J. W. Gilbart, 'On the laws of the currency in Ireland', *Journal of the Statistical Society*, XVI, 1852, p. 325.

Aspects of banking business

and continued to play a strategic role in everyday transactions.

So problematic was the supply of silver coin that banks made sure they paid out as little as possible over the counter and the jealousy with which banks guarded their stock of coin is frequently alluded to. The Provincial, for example, gave particular instructions to its branch managers 'to take strict care that none is drawn from you for supplying the customers of other banks'.[18]

3.2 Bill discounts

Banks discounted bills both for inland and overseas trade and the volume of discount business was determined by a number of considerations. Bills were categorised according to where they were payable. Thus 'English' bills originated in Ireland but were drawn on London or some other town in England (or, more precisely, Britain). It is important to note that discount rates were not uniform for all categories of bill, nor were published rates necessarily the same as those actually charged since published rates tended to be minimum rates. In Ireland as elsewhere in the United Kingdom the lowest discount rates tended to apply to first-class trade bills of three months' date. More often than not English bills were discounted at lower rates than Irish bills, certainly before the 1850s.[19] The Bank of Ireland explained this differential on the grounds that English bills were more likely to 'represent real transactions than the inland bills of Ireland'.[20] The Belfast banks adopted the same policy. All bills presented for discount were examined thoroughly and Irish bills were scrutinised exceptionally closely in the late 1840s. The suspicion surrounding Irish bills can be illustrated by this instruction from the Belfast Bank to its branch managers in 1848:

> . . . no Irish bills to be taken from any part not having previously an account open at the Branch, except same having been sent to the Head Office for approval; otherwise to be upon the personal responsibility of the manager or managers for which he or they shall be held liable to the Bank.[21]

The difficulty of distinguishing between 'promiscuous bills generally discounted at country branches'[22] and accommodation bills meant that in practice the treatment of both was much the same. Accommodation bills, whenever they could be detected, were 'to be avoided as much as possible' but if discounted the rate was usually at least one per cent higher than for 'regular' trade bills.[23] Banks could alter the supply of credit by varying the tenor of bills.

The shorter the drawing date or the longer the discount date, the cheaper the cost of borrowing.[24] Not surprisingly the preferred tenor of bills shortened as the extent of pressure in money markets increased.

The Belfast banks discounted six-month bills 'in easy times' but actively discouraged long-dated bills during periods of pressure or crisis, such as autumn 1847. At all times, however, the banks acted 'upon their own discretion more than according to any rule'.[25] Thus in 1848, although it had been the practice to draw Dublin bills and letters of credit at seven days date, if competition was great the Belfast bank allowed them to be drawn at sight 'to accommodate the friends and customers at the bank, although such transactions are unprofitable'. Similar flexibility was exercised in the case of British bills and letters of credit, to oblige customers.[26]

Although the lowest rates of discount generally applied to three-month first-class trade bills, an important exception to this, which has particular relevance to the province of Ulster, were bills relating to the linen industry. The Provincial Bank directors, for example, were prepared to sanction the discount of four-month bills – provided they were *bona fide* business bills of first class character' – at minimum rates 'when that is the usual credit in the trade in which they arise'.[27] How many 'trades' typically used four-month bills is not at all clear, but linen was certainly one. As we will show in the next chapter, the Provincial Bank was closely involved in the finance of the linen industry and it held some of the larger accounts. As far as discounts were concerned four-month bills were common. Thus in September 1846 Robert Hayes of William Hayes and Son, a pioneering firm of flax spinners and weavers at Seapatrick in County Down, requested the Provincial to 'discount their 4 month bills on English parties at 4 instead of 5 per cent as heretofore'. The branch manager at Banbridge, where the account was held, was permitted to accede to the request.[28]

Sometimes a customer preferred to 'renew', rather than pay, a bill at the nominal maturity date. Bill renewals of were, of course, a method of extending the period of credit and required the agreement of all parties to the bill. A renewal did not require the issue of a new bill, rather the extension of an existing one, and the practice of renewing bills was common in UK banking in the nineteenth century.[29] Renewed bills, like accommodation bills, were charged more than regular trade bills. No bill was renewed by the

Belfast Bank unless the original sum was reduced by a 'reasonable partial payment' or another name was put on as additional security. If neither of these was forthcoming, branch managers were ordered to decline renewal unless given 'express sanction' to do otherwise by head office. To distinguish renewed bills from others they were marked in ink 'R.1.', 'R.2.', and so on, depending on the frequency of renewal.[30]

The point here is that even if banks were generally obliged to discount at rates set by the Bank of Ireland, they could and did exercise control over the volume of discount business. Such control applied to all categories of bill but could be exercised with particular strictness if circumstances demanded. In the agricultural depression of 1859–64 and the late 1870s for example, both farmers' and shopkeepers' bills were treated with unusual stringency.[31] The general suspicion surrounding many local bills has already been mentioned and during the Famine period this suspicion became more obvious. Thus in April 1847 the Provincial Bank's directors issued instructions that 'the amount of local bills under discount at the branches should be reduced'.[32] In the short term, however, the stipulated reduction did not materialise. On 29 January 1848 the amount of local bills discounted by the Provincial totalled £666,194, but this had risen to no less than £714,297 by 11 March.[33] In this period of exceptional distress, then, it did not prove immediately possible to carry out the directors' instructions.

The trend in discount business of the Ulster Bank from its formation in 1836 until 1853 is shown in Table 21. The outstanding feature is the volatility of discount business, particularly of English bills. In addition, English and Belfast bills exhibit greater seasonal fluctuations than the other categories. To a large extent the trend in English bills reflects the seasonal nature of the Irish provisions trade, and discounts were normally much higher in August than in February. Depression, of course, led to a noticeable decline in discount business. In the context of the late 1840s, the decline in the volume of English bills is particularly evident, a result of famine in Ireland and slump in Britain.

Sharp decline in the Ulster Bank's discount business in late 1847–8 applied to all the major categories of bill. Recovery did not properly get under way until 1849 and was generally sustained for the next five years. The experience of the Ulster Bank with English bills in the crisis of 1847–8 was clearly not unique. The Provincial,

Table 21 *Ulster Bank discounts, 1836–53*

Date	Belfast bills	English bills	Dublin bills	Branch[a] bills	Bills with agents
31.8.36	105,500	84,428	37,823		
28.2.37	120,549	43,386	89,587		
31.8.37	97,821	57,876	68,228		
28.2.38	133,027	44,647	113,316		
1.9.38	141,918	73,271	124,927		
28.2.39	161,860	56,505	114,944		
31.8.39	153,165	85,255	111,997		
29.2.40	170,902	49,097	110,849		
31.8.40	110,040	112,783	34,263		
27.2.41	133,665	95,134	42,073	61,048	6,932
31.8.41	103,139	188,218	29,843	51,879	8,457
28.2.42	137,863	121,513	52,975	62,468	7,216
31.8.42	84,210	98,747	37,138	58,941	6,170
28.2.43	106,569	101,757	28,354	51,514	3,789
31.8.43	95,540	128,408	34,720	56,035	6,435
29.2.44	119,885	136,434	51,599	59,150	6,394
31.8.44	90,917	153,148	44,223	69,780	10,426
28.2.45	162,396	151,730	88,119	82,349	11,899
31.8.45	108,721	193,908	66,811	103,913	11,971
28.2.46	140,336	118,954	60,860	99,487	12,293
31.8.46	116,092	139,860	63,267	106,705	10,163
27.2.47	157,157	116,518	71,824	115,811	8,343
31.8.47	96,050	118,789	45,928	80,874	11,665
29.2.48	113,140	77,993	44,411	67,205	8,870
31.8.48	106,915	114,857	37,595	70,422	7,231
28.2.49	153,615	71,696	50,833	80,067	6,120
31.8.49	132,121	94,032	38,468	77,938	9,006
28.2.50	184,836	99,284	55,075	85,440	8,974
31.8.50	156,237	133,408	51,617	87,023	10,382
28.2.51	229,955	134,464	60,636	108,755	11,225
31.8.51	221,828	85,293	59,604	128,766	7,828
28.2.52	236,554	96,805	71,390	137,485	6,200
31.8.52	209,276	125,686	64,292	124,816	8,166
28.2.53	250,396	179,414	70,702	129,878	6,258
31.8.53	292,638	226,958	77,909	138,595	8,829

Note [a] Inland Bills discounted and payable at branches.
Source. Ulster Bank Half-yearly Balances, 1836–53.

for example, noted that 'the magnitude of the crisis was such that it almost instantly diminished transactions with England, and bills of exchange in a great measure disappeared'.[34]

3.3 Deposits and credit balances

The Belfast banks accepted deposits on identical terms, although there was some flexibility with respect to interest paid and ease of

Aspects of banking business

withdrawal. As Bristow of the Northern Bank explained in 1858:

> We require a deposit to be three months in our hands before it is entitled to interest at all; and we require in the case of deposits of £500 and upwards, a notice of ten days for repayment, but we do not in general insist upon that; that, however is part of our arrangement.[35]

This divergence of practice from theory must have been due to a desire to make the bank deposit as attractive and accessible as possible to depositors large and small, and was consistent with the need to maximise the level of deposits, especially after 1845. It is evident from this that the distinction between a 'deposit' and a credit balance on current account was blurred, although for accounting purposes the banks did distinguish the two.

Tables 22 and 23 provide information on the branch distribution of deposits, credit balances and overdrafts in the Northern and the Ulster Bank in August 1859. From the data it is clear, if unsurprising, that head office was easily the most important in each system, although the *relative* importance of head office within each system was very different. Forty-three per cent of the Northern Bank's total deposits were held at head office; in the case of the Ulster Bank the corresponding figure was fourteen per cent. How do we explain

Table 22 *Northern Bank deposits and current accounts at 16 August 1859 (£000)*

Branch	Deposits	Current Accounts	
		Cr.	Dr.
Armagh	29·9	3·4	15·9
Ballymena	77·0	0·8	13·1
Ballynahinch Agency	4·7	—	—
Carrickfergus	59·8	1·6	2·1
Castlewellan	24·6	2·1	5·0
Clones	60·7	3·4	20·5
Coleraine	60·5	4·8	12·0
Derry	106·5	29·4	81·1
Downpatrick	139·7	21·1	49·0
Limavady	49·1	5·8	7·5
Lisburn	93·8	9·3	6·5
Lurgan	42·9	2·5	6·2
Magherafelt	32·9	3·4	6·3
Branch Total	782·1	87·6	225·2
Head Office	592·6	368·4	862·2
Total	1374·7	456·0	1087·4

Source. Northern Bank Abstract of Branch Balances.

Table 23 *Ulster Bank deposits and current accounts at 31 August 1859 (£000)*

Branch	Deposits	Current accounts	
		Cr.	Dr.
Antrim	61·0	5·2	3·1
Armagh	32·9	5·1	21·0
Aughnacloy	44·3	6·4	6·9
Ballymena	67·1	5·9	21·5
Ballymoney	57·8	6·9	17·8
Banbridge	73·4	6·6	8·2
Cavan	75·6	5·1	7·3
Cookstown	71·7	4·0	26·5
Cootehill	33·2	3·5	5·4
Derry	47·3	10·3	12·2
Donegal	44·3	2·2	2·4
Downpatrick	80·0	4·2	9·5
Enniskillen	99·3	15·6	8·7
Lurgan	42·9	6·1	11·6
Maghera	23·2	1·5	1·7
Monaghan	57·7	3·2	12·6
Omagh	73·2	3·4	8·1
Portadown	26·4	3·9	7·5
Branch Total	1,011·3	99·1	192·0
Head Office	169·0	49·5	209·0
Total	1,180·3	148·6	401·0

Source. Ulster Bank Branch Balances.

this major difference? Perhaps the simplest and most plausible answer is that the Ulster Bank was a latecomer to banking in Belfast and when it opened there were already five other banks in the town. One of these, the Agricultural and Commercial, failed in 1840 but the others (the Northern, the Belfast, the Provincial and the Bank of Ireland) continued. When the Ulster Bank opened on 1 July 1836, head office deposits stood at £3,780, rising elevenfold two years later and reaching £61,298 by August 1842.[36] This rate of increase was not, however, sustained and by August 1859 the total was only £169,000. Given that the Ulster paid the same deposit rates as the Northern and the Belfast, and given the Bank of Ireland paid no interest for deposits, the Ulster cannot be described as uncompetitive. It is difficult to explain the huge difference between the head-office deposits of the Northern and the Ulster in any way other than by the chronology of opening dates.

If Belfast was not a particularly promising source of deposits for the Ulster Bank, the bank certainly showed itself willing and able to colonise 'underbanked' towns throughout the province and by 1859 had established a branch network which existed westward well beyond that of the Northern. After 1845 deposit-gathering had become a more important objective than before and on this score the Ulster Bank had gone far to compensate for its late start in Belfast. By August 1859 the Ulster had opened six more branches than the Northern and (excluding head office) had accumulated twenty-three per cent more deposits.

Turning to the ratio of deposits to current accounts in credit it can be seen that in one important respect the two banks were the same: the ratios were lowest at head office in Belfast. Of the branches Derry has the lowest ratio in both cases. Beyond that it is difficult to see any pattern in the ratios, either within each system or between banks. How these figures compare to other Irish or British banks is hard to say because of the present lack of evidence, since most banks did not distinguish deposits and credit balances. Recent pioneering work in this area has been undertaken by Collins who shows, from a sample of six banks in the Midlands, north and west of England and Wales, that the average ratio of current accounts to deposits between 1850 and 1859 was sixty-three per cent. This figure remained virtually unchanged when the sample was increased to ten banks from a wider geographical area for the next two decades (1860–9, 1870–9).[37] Our data indicate that the corresponding figures were twenty-five per cent for the Northern and a mere eleven per cent for the Ulster. As far as the Northern was concerned the decadal figure for 1873–82 was eighteen per cent,[38] although there was a noticeable increase in the period 1879–82 as deposits fell sharply for several reasons, including agricultural depression. Collins acknowledges that there may have been considerable regional variations in the distribution of deposits and our evidence certainly supports this view.

Perhaps the predominance of deposits in Ulster reflects the importance of the farming community in nineteenth-century Ulster compared with more industrial regions served by the banks in Collins's sample. The relative importance of current accounts at Belfast is more consistent with Collins's findings and suggests that the need for assured and immediate access to funds on a regular basis was a good deal greater in major industrial/commercial areas than it was in the countryside.

3.4 Advances

The seasonal nature of banking typified in patterns of note circulation and, to some extent, bill discounts was obvious too in much of the overdraft business. Indeed there is obviously a considerable degree of inter-dependence between these aspects of banking business. Belfast was again easily the most important office as far as overdrafts were concerned, although it does not necessarily follow that these sums were lent to customers in the immmediate vicinity of the branch concerned. Linen firms, for example, sometimes had a mill in the country and an office or warehouse in Belfast, but used a Belfast bank office to provide credit for their mill operations.[39]

Early evidence on seasonality in lending is provided by the weekly overdrawn balances at the Ulster Bank head office between 1838 and 1842, outlined in Figure 2. On behalf of the three Belfast banks, J. W. Bristow, in a comment noted earlier in this chapter, stressed the seasonal pattern of lending. Figure 2 is a demonstration of this. Bristow specifically mentioned that flaxspinners required advances for purchases of flax in the winter months which were repaid to the bank in the spring and summer.[40] This is analogous to the position in West Yorkshire in the second quarter of the nineteenth century where wool traders required advances during the wool-buying season.[41] Some firms employed a specialist buyer to travel to attend different flax markets and an extensive bank branch system could facilitate this task. Thus in August 1867, just before the flax-buying season began, the secretary of the Blackstaff Flax Spinning Company asked the Provincial Bank's Belfast manager to arrange for branch managers in several towns to honour the cheques of their flax buyer 'to the extent of £500 to £600 weekly on each market day until further notice, and you are hereby authorised to charge same to debit of our account'.[42]

In Ulster the seasonality of advances to spinners was paralleled in the case of the provisions trade. The best surviving evidence with which to illustrate this point are the half-yearly balances of the Ulster Bank, struck at the end of February and August.[43] Those engaged in the provisions trade who were dependent on bank credit may have been expected to be more overdrawn in February than August, and this is confirmed by the evidence.[44] February balances invariably show provision merchants amongst the largest overdrawn accounts, but the August balances do not. For example, in

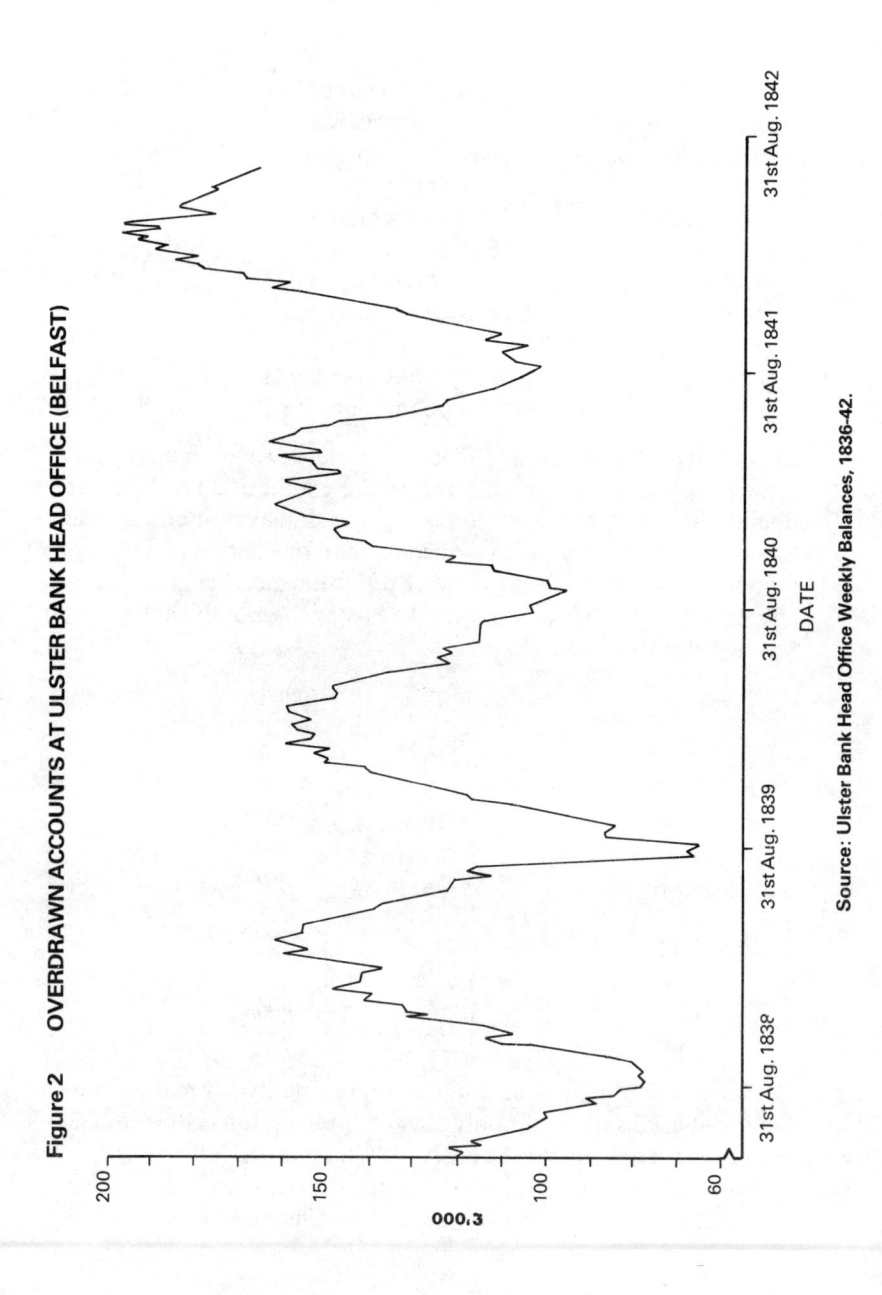

Figure 2   OVERDRAWN ACCOUNTS AT ULSTER BANK HEAD OFFICE (BELFAST)

Source: Ulster Bank Head Office Weekly Balances, 1836-42.

February 1837 the ten largest overdrawn accounts at the Ulster Bank in Belfast were as follows:

		£
J. & D. Curell	(Linen merchants/ bleachers	13,999
James Steen and Co.	(Provisions merchant)	11,331
Alexander Hunter	(Grocer, soap/candle manufacturer)	6,833
J. & T. Sinclair	(Provisions merchant)	6,233
Charles Duffin	(Flax merchant)	5,635
D. & W. J. Shaw	(Provisions merchant)	5,288
Henry Steen	(Provisions merchant	4,849
Hugh Kidd	(?)	3,252
Samuel Gibson	(Provisions merchant)	3,213
Jonathan Cordukes	(Provisions merchant)	2,502

In August of the same year almost all of these provision merchants were either in credit or overdrawn to the extent of a few hundred pounds. This pattern is repeated every year. It may be useful here to trace the account of one provision merchant for a period of ten years (1854–63). W. and J. Campbell were provision merchants in Belfast and the state of their account with the Ulster Bank at the half yearly balances in this period was thus:

	February £	*August* £
1854	− 10,266	− 50
1855	− 8,661	+ 2,377
1856	− 3,116	− 89
1857	− 5,139	− 162
1858	+ 54	+ 1,176
1859	− 7,340	+ 669
1860	− 5,995	+ 1,052
1861	− 3,809	+ 932
1862	− 4,268	+ 409
1863	− 3,223	+ 1,207

Campbell's account can be taken as representative of many others in the provisions trade, the only obvious interruption in the seasonal pattern occurring during the crisis and slump of 1857–8.

While many important accounts fluctuated with the seasons, others did not. For example, the Belfast Chemical Works ran an

Aspects of banking business

overdraft which fluctuated between £3,000 and £6,000 throughout the 1850s and early 1860s, but with no recognisably seasonal pattern. A similar case can be made for James Combe's Falls Foundry. Combe was a Scot who came to Belfast in 1845. His account was opened with the Ulster Bank in that year with a credit balance of £1,320. By February 1846 this had dwindled to just £129 and in August of that year Combe was overdrawn £3,623. Combe was overdrawn at each half-yearly balance for the next fifteen years to the extent of £4,000 to over £10,000. Other examples of accounts which were persistently overdrawn include the Monkstown Spinning Company, whose account fluctuated between £5,000 and £21,000 throughout the 1840s and well into the 1850s.

If the linen industry and provisions trade figure largely in the surviving records, there is also substantial evidence of the banks' involvement in developing the transport network. The Provincial, for example, provided several advances to the Newry Navigation Company. In August 1851 the bank's directors were 'inclined to entertain' a proposal, subject to the provision of personal security by the Newry Navigation's directors, for a loan of £5,000 for five years. This was in addition to two existing advances for £5,000 and £3,000.[45] Far more common than advances to navigation companies, however, were those to railway companies.

The extent, type and purpose of bank finance for railways varied a great deal. At one level, the banks contributed to the legal and other expenses incurred in the projection of a line. Thus the Northern Bank in 1852 subscribed £100 to the preliminary expenses of a projected line from Armagh to Cavan, considering the scheme 'so desirable for the trade of this town'.[46] Such subscriptions, although small, could be of strategic importance at the initial stages of a venture. Certainly not all plans progressed further than the drawing board, but equally certainly no venture could proceed in the absence of sufficient initial resources.[47] Of course, the contribution of any bank could amount to no more than a single small sum, but there is ample evidence to prove that this was not their typical contribution.

At a more significant level the banks provided cash credits and overdrafts to railway contractors and railway companies and two of the Belfast banks invested directly in railway companies in the 1850s. In November 1853 the Provincial Bank awarded a cash credit to Moore Brothers and Killen, a firm of railway contractors then engaged in constructing part of the Dundalk and Enniskillen Railway. The credit limit was £40,000, with interest at six per cent.[48] Professor Lee has shown that all Irish banks supplied working capital to railway companies before 1853.[49] The Northern made frequent loans to the Ulster Railway on the security of calls on shares and advanced a third of the fixed capital of the Belfast and Ballymena. Lee's conclusion, however, is that 'unless the banks were prepared to adopt the unBritish concept of investment banking they could not be expected to take gambles on the fortunes of many companies'.[50] Such a view tends to lose sight of the fact that the banks had long regarded construction of a railway network as potentially beneficial to the Ulster economy. Since the branches of the Belfast banks were almost all in Ulster it follows that the economic health of this province was of crucial significance in determining bank profitability. In addition, improvement of internal transport would facilitate communications between head office and the branches. There was, in other words, usually an element of self-interest.

A good example of extensive overdraft facilities in the 1850s is that provided by the Belfast bank to the Belfast and Ballymena railway. The account was opened in January 1855 with a limit of £20,000 and a further £10,000 until the opening of the Cookstown branch. Interest was fixed at five per cent and no repayment date set, 'either party giving six months notice of a change as to £20,000'.[51] Again in February 1863 the directors of the Belfast, Holywood and Bangor Railway, then trying to finance the construction of the line from Holywood to Bangor, applied for, and received, an overdraft facility of £10,000 from the Provincial Bank in Belfast, secured by the fully paid-up shares of the company together with the directors' promissory note.[52]

If the provision of overdraft facilities on real or personal security was a perfectly ordinary part of banking business the same cannot be said of direct investment in ordinary, preference or debenture stock. The 'legality' of direct investment depended upon the object clause of the deed of co-partnership. In the case of the Belfast banks, such clauses were almost identical. Strictly speaking, all the Belfast banks were precluded from direct investment in railway or other companies unless such investment was 'usual in banking establishments'. However, it soon became clear that this portion of the object clause was open to different interpretation. In the 1850s,

Aspects of banking business

both the Belfast and the Ulster Bank undertook direct investment in railway companies in Ireland. In 1852 the Belfast Bank subscribed £5,000 (£2,500 paid up) in the proposed line from Omagh to Clones, 'this in consideration that the bank be appointed bankers to the said company'.[53] Six months later the directors of the same bank were empowered to subscribe up to £5,000 in the stock of the same railway following the decision to extend the line to Cavan.[54] Between these two decisions, the bank took £1,000 of stock in the Ballymena, Ballymoney, Coleraine and Portrush Junction Railway, and the Ulster Bank subscribed an identical sum.[55]

Neither the Belfast nor the Ulster Bank questioned the legality of their various direct investments. The Northern Bank, however, took a different view. This divergence of attitude towards direct investments can best be illustrated with reference to a projected line from Derry to Letterkenny. In 1859 the directors of this railway company invited both the Belfast and the Northern Bank to buy shares. The Belfast, in keeping with its former policy, agreed to buy up to 200 £10 shares.[56] The Northern, despite assurances from the railway company that the Belfast Bank had agreed to buy, declined because after the object clause was read it was decided that 'this bank is precluded by the terms of that clause from taking any shares in any undertaking whatever except the business of banking'.[57] It is clear then that the object clause was sufficiently imprecise to permit entirely different conclusions as to a bank's ability to undertake investment of any kind. Another relevant point here is that although investment banking may have been, as Lee has put it, an 'unBritish concept' this did not prevent the Belfast and the Ulster Bank from investing directly in railway companies, and this aspect of bank finance certainly deserves more emphasis than Professor Lee has given it.

The numerous examples of financial assistance to railways already cited should not give the impression that this was provided indiscriminately. Although instances of refusal are few, one such instance from 1857 points to an aspect of bank policy not hitherto discussed. In August of that year the Belfast Bank's directors were asked to take shares in a line to Banbridge but the Board of Superintendence opined that 'we should decline, the line being quite a local one'.[58] This refusal suggests that the bank showed a strong preference to invest in main lines between major market towns, rather than in feeder lines, of which this was one.

The evidence on advances assembled in this section suggests a strongly seasonal element superimposed on a rump of longer-term advances. Unfortunately the terms on which overdrafts were granted before the mid-nineteenth century have not survived in abundance, but it is clear that unsecured advances were made, and a diverse range of collateral held as security: banks shares,[59] deeds to properties and life-assurance policies, for example.[60] It is possible that most overdrafts were recallable at a few months' notice, but in practice were allowed if necessary to become instruments of medium and long-term credit provided that the accounts were 'active', not 'dead'. As noted in the last chapter the Ulster Bank penalised those overdrawn accounts which did not have a satisfactory turn-over, though there does not appear to have been any precise definition of 'active' and 'dead'. The Provincial Bank adopted the same policy. Thus in July 1856 the Provincial announced a reduction in some of its rates, including 'undoubtedly well secured and actively and beneficially used cash credit accounts and advances on overdraft authorised by the Court'. The reduction in rate did not, however, apply to 'inactive accounts, however well secured'.[61]

The marked seasonal nature of many of the largest overdrafts leads us into a methodological issue, namely the use of balance sheets as accurate indicators of lending. Before 1860, none of the Belfast banks published balance sheets. When publication began (in the 1860s for the Ulster Bank and the 1880s for the Belfast and the Northern) balances were struck either in July or August, that is when seasonal advances tended to be at their lowest. From this is follows that balance sheets struck in midsummer tend to understate annual lending. One problem faced by economists and business historians to the present day in the interpretation of bank credit statistics, whether derived from bank balance sheets or company balance sheets, is that all balance sheets are snapshot pictures at a single date and certainly cannot be relied upon to reflect the position at any other point in the financial year.[62] Our brief discussion of the accounts of flaxspinners and provision merchants underlines the dangers of using balance sheets derived in the summer months. Banking in Ireland was to a very considerable extent a seasonal activity, and the slackest period of the year was that at which bankers preferred to draw up their annual balance sheet precisely because they had more time to spare to strike the balance.

Aspects of banking business

A final point on banking business, already touched on, is worth re-emphasis. This is that head office was by far the most important office for the Belfast banks. Data on deposits and overdrafts show this and it can be further illustrated by employment statistics. These are available for the Belfast Bank from 1860 and may be usefully summarised here both to show the position around mid-century and how employment (and salaries) at head office and the branches increase during the period with which the remainder of this book is concerned (see Table 24).

Table 24 *Employment and salaries in the Belfast Bank, 1860–1914*

	Head office				Branches		
Date	Officers	Salaries (a)	(£) (b)	Number	Officers	Salaries (c)	(£) (d)
1860	47	5535	118	23	85	9560	112
1865	48	4620	96	25	95	10800	114
1870	55	5595	102	31	117	12560	107
1875	62	6990	113	35	138	15535	113
1880	60	8440	141	37	133	17505	132
1885	65	9145	141	35	129	17665	137
1890	62	9615	155	36	129	19660	152
1895	67	12495	186	38	151	24400	162
1900	75	13475	180	44	181	27020	149
1905	76	14115	186	45	193	28115	146
1910	75	15760	210	46	210	30885	147
1914	77	16763	218	49	227	36300	160

Note. (*a*) Head office total salaries.
  (*b*) Average head office salary.
  (*c*) Total salaries at branches.
  (*d*) Average branch salary.
Source. Belfast Bank Miscellaneous Papers.

CHAPTER FOUR

TOWARDS LIMITED LIABILITY

In his pioneering survey of the development of legislation to limit shareholders' liability H. A. Shannon noted that 'law and economics were mutually interacting'.[1] For this reason it is useful to discuss in considerable detail the economic background to the Belfast banks' decision to adopt limited liability in the early 1880s. Not all the economic changes were instrumental in influencing this decision but some account of them is essential to understand the business of banking in the later nineteenth century. As far as most Irish banks were concerned, key developments in the period 1858–83 included a major agricultural depression between 1859 and 1864, a boom in the linen industry in the mid-1860s and another serious depression in agriculture in the late 1870s. In addition to these particular pressures competition in Irish banking became fiercer, and this had significant effects on inter-bank relations and on the pattern and rate of branch expansion.

4.1 The agricultural depression, 1859–64

The Irish agricultural depression of 1859–64 has been rescued from relative obscurity by James Donnelly who argues that it was more acute than the more famous downturn of the late 1870s which helped to provoke the Land War. Donnelly suggests that the former depression made the least impact on Ulster (with the important exception of Donegal) since the massive extension of flax cultivation to meet the demand for linen goods supported agricultural incomes in the north-east. Flax acreage in Ireland rose from 91,600 in 1858 to 301,700 by 1864.[2] Ulster accounted for some ninety per cent of this increase which was concentrated in the years 1862–4, a response to abnormally profitable conditions for linen during the 'Cotton Famine'. As far as the impact of the agricultural depression on banks is concerned it is important to recognise the importance of linen in the north-east and remember that for the first three years of depression linen still suffered from considerable excess capacity. The effects of the linen boom are discussed in the next section.

In May 1860 the Provincial Bank commented that the past year had been less profitable for the agricultural classes than the previous few years.[3] Three months later the Ulster Bank head office advised its managers to exercise '*great* caution' in the discount of bills on farmers and country traders, avoiding both bill renewals and accommodation bills as much as possible.[4] About the same time the National Bank suffered losses of £66,500 arising from failures in the leather trade and the chairman believed 'many others' had suffered from similar failures.[5]

If credit restrictions to the agricultural sector began to be implemented in the summer of 1860, they were imposed with increasing severity during the next three years. The Ulster Bank, with branches throughout the province, including the hard-pressed west, had reached the point by September 1861 where managers were not permitted to renew farmers' bills for the full amount without extra security or express permission from the directors. Interest charged on such bills was to be at least that for overdrafts and the minimum charge for small bills was half-a-crown.[6] By the next summer Ulster Bank branch managers were instructed 'to abstain from discounting farmers' bills at present'[7] and Provincial Bank managers were asked to be very guarded about extending credit to millers, corn merchants and provision traders.[8]

By the winter of 1862–3 prospects for agriculture appeared very bleak indeed. Donnelly has shown that in County Cork contemporaries sometimes compared the early 1860s to the Famine period of the late 1840s.[9] In the north of Ireland a similar comparison was made. Thus in January 1863 a profoundly pessimistic Ulster Bank circular again drew managers' attention to the state of the country:

> In our opinion it has not been in so critical a condition since the year 1847. Three successive bad harvests have reduced the farmers –particularly the smaller class – to a very low ebb. The country shopkeepers, who are dependent upon the farming and labouring population cannot collect the money due to them, while the traders carrying on business with small provision dealers in Lancashire and the North of England, must have been doing a very unprofitable trade. Under these circumstances we must act with extreme caution and we rely on you to use your best exertions to keep down the advances at your branch whether on bills or open accounts to the lowest possible limit. . . . We look to you confidently to carry out these instructions firmly but with discretion.[10]

Restriction of bank credit to agriculture had thus become stringent by 1863 and it reflected the banks' perception of depression and their acute awareness of the obvious interdependence of rural society. A similar reaction was evident in the late 1870s.

Another indicator of agricultural depression in the early 1860s to which attention has been drawn is the decline in Irish bank deposits from £16 million in 1859 to £13 million in 1863. This fall, it is suggested, was a 'sensitive barometer of agricultural incomes'.[11] It is, however, impossible to be precise about the relationship between fluctuations in agricultural incomes and fluctuations in bank deposits in this, or indeed any other, period. In the context of the late 1840s it was suggested that several factors influenced deposit levels and a similarly complex picture will emerge from the agricultural depression of the late 1870s. The proportion of Irish bank deposits held by the agricultural sector is unknown. There was, however, an informed and confidential estimate made at the end of 1866 which concluded that the Ulster 'farming population' held at least £4 million of the total bank deposits in the province.[12] This figure was close to the combined total of deposits in the Ulster and the Belfast Banks (£4.55 million in the autumn of 1866) and represented something like twenty per cent of the Irish total.

Even if the 'farming population' did provide a substantial proportion of bank deposits, which is undeniable, it is far from clear that the nineteen per cent decline in deposits between 1850 and 1863 faithfully reflects a downturn in agricultural incomes. If the late 1870s is any guide, the aggregate deposit data conceal differences in the experience of various banks and differences too in the experience of different branches of any bank's branch network. No disaggregated branch data for the 1860s have been discovered but some relevant figures for three banks are given in Table 25.

Between 1860 and 1863 the decline in total Irish bank deposits and credit balances was seventeen per cent while those in the Ulster Bank remained virtually unchanged. Those in the Belfast Bank fell by only 12.6 per cent and those in the National actually increased by 5.5 per cent. It is clear then that the aggregate figures conceal substantial differences in the experience of various banks. The fact that the aggregate figure falls by a far greater percentage than that for the Belfast and Ulster may reflect the relatively slight impact of depression in the north-east. The National Bank's increase in deposits is at first surprising given that it had an extensive network

Table 25 *Deposits and current accounts in credit in three Irish banks 1859–64 (£000)*

Date	Ulster[a]	Belfast[b]	National[c]	Total[d]
1859	1,396	not available	4,034	16,042
1860	1,486	2,177	3,987	15,609
1861	1,527	2,166	4,261	15,005
1862	1,609	2,028	4,245	14,388
1863	1,489	1,903	4,208	12,966
1864	1,655	1,812	4,284	14,422

Sources. (a) Ulster Bank Balance Sheets, 1859–64.
(b) Belfast Bank Miscellaneous Papers.
(c) *Irish Times*, 26 December 1864.
(d) W Neilson Hancock, *Report on Deposits in Joint-Stock Banks*, p. 6.

in the south and west of Ireland. The National's deposits probably held up so well because of the increase in its London deposit business. The National was the only Irish bank with branches in London (the first of which was opened in 1854) and by 1875, these had amassed £1.5 million in current accounts alone.[13] It is likely that the National's Irish deposits fell considerably in the early 1860s. The inclusion of significant and increasing London deposits certainly influences movements in the National's deposits, and hence the total 'Irish' figures.

4.2 The linen boom

For the Belfast banks the depression of the early 1860s had led to a sustained contraction of agricultural credit. Towards the end of this depression the Irish linen industry, heavily concentrated in the north-east, began a short period of hectic expansion which was of great importance for those banks operating in this region. The background to the linen boom may be summarised very briefly. By 1860 Ulster was the world's leading linen producing area crucially dependent on overseas markets and increasingly reliant upon imported flax. Of particular importance as a market was the United States which took an average of forty-one per cent of Irish linen exports in the quinquennium 1856–60.[14] Any serious disturbance to this market was potentially damaging. Accordingly the outbreak of the American Civil War in 1861 was viewed very darkly indeed and pessimism prevailed for several months afterwards.[15] By late spring 1862 a reappraisal of prospects was under way, based on the recognition that a substitution of linen for scarce and increasingly expensive cotton was taking place.[16] Thus in the autumn of 1862 both the Northern and the Ulster Bank alluded to the dull state of trade for the previous twelve months but both noticed that the province's staple trade had just started to feel the benefit of an increased demand.[17]

As far as the banks were concerned, the linen boom had several short-term effects. First there was a huge increase in lending. This may be illustrated with reference to the balance sheets of the Ulster Bank. Between August 1863 and August 1866 advances and discounts rose from £1.68 million to £2.53 million – an increase of some 50.5 per cent. During this period advances and discounts were constantly larger than deposits, credit balances and paid up capital put together. The proportion of total assets held as advances and discounts rose from 79.3 to 82.3 per cent.[18] The figures strongly suggest a dramatic increase in the demand for accommodation and a willingness on the part of the bank to supply it. Indeed all the evidence points to an immense expansion of bank credit in the mid-1860s.

Specific instances of requests for accommodation are few, but the case of William Barbour and Sons of Lisburn is a good one. In November 1863 Barbour, a prominent linen thread manufacturer, requested that his overdraft limit be extended from £5,000 to £10,000. The Ulster Bank agreed, provided that the overdraft return to its normal limit of £5,000 by April 1864.[19] The stipulated reduction did not, however, materialise and in September 1864 Barbour requested an extension of his temporary limit of £10,000. Again the bank agreed, provided that it would be reduced to the ordinary limit of £5,000 by May 1866. The bank, in agreeing to this second request, made it clear that 'the sum of £10,000 is to be the *maximum* and we can assure you that it is quite unusual for us to agree to so large an overdraft in the absence of collateral security'.[20] Apart from showing that the bank did not always insist on collateral security, this comment demonstrates the bank's willingness to assist a major firm at a time when accommodation was required. The reference to a 'normal' limit of £5,000 is significant since it strongly suggests that Barbour could depend on this sum if and when it was required. How long such an arrangement had been in operation is difficult to say. It is, however, certain that Barbour had been overdrawn £5,035 in August 1852, £6,101 in February 1853 and £9,641 in August 1853. In fact Barbour's account was overdrawn at each half-year balance between 1852 and 1860 at levels which varied between £5,000 and £10,000.[21]

Another example of a linen firm which requested accommodation during the linen boom was McCrum, Mercer and Watson of Milford Mill, Armagh. Early in 1865 Robert McCrum wrote to the Bank of Ireland in Armagh asking for assistance to enable him to extend his powerloom factory. McCrum explained:

> I am about making a small addition to my powerloom factory and find I could make a rather larger one to my purposes better and without very much greater expenses but I am afraid of trenching too close on my working capital. If your directors could give me a little extra overdraft say £700 in addition to my present one of £300 it would enable me to carry out my plans and be a good accommodation to me and I would reduce it to £300 before 1st of January next.[22]

It is not clear whether the accommodation was granted, but it might well have been since there is no further reference in McCrum's letter book. At any rate, the request shows that in McCrum's eyes at least bank finance could be crucial in enabling him to extend his factory without having to encroach too much on his working capital.

The most substantial evidence of bank finance for the linen industry in this period is that of the Provincial Bank, and some examples will help to clarify the picture. The York Street Flax Spinning Company was converted into a limited company in September 1864[23] and in that month it had applied to the Provincial Bank for a credit of £57,000 secured by the guarantee of the directors.[24] This large credit had been authorised by the Provincial's Court of Directors in London. The first balance sheet issued by York Street in December 1864 shows an item 'bankers for advance £26,452 16s 11d' or less than half of this firm's credit facility.[25] The credit was renewed the following September for a further twelve months and indeed was still operative in April 1868 when York Street's directors requested a limit of £60,000 but without a guarantee. The bank agreed to this limit on condition that the guarantee would remain; if not the limit would be fixed at £20,000. In May the York Street directors resolved to continue to bank with the Provincial on the understanding that a cash advance of £50,000 without security would be provided if required, but the bank adhered to its former decision.[26] It would appear that as a result York Street changed its bankers, as there is no further correspondence, but there is evidence that this important account was transferred to the

Belfast Bank.[27]

If the Provincial lost this account over its refusal to compromise on the question of security, it gained other accounts presumably because other banks had been unable to provide accommodation in sufficient quantities or on acceptable conditions. An instance of this occurred in 1866 when the Blackstaff Spinning Company Ltd moved their account from the Ulster Bank to the Provincial 'with an occasional overdraft of £15,000 during the flax buying season, on the security of the seven directors as individuals'.[28] Sometimes accounts were transferred without any apparent increase in the demand for accommodation, although not all accounts offered were accepted by the bank concerned.[29]

The personal guarantee of the directors of a firm was a common form of security, particularly for limited companies.[30] The overdraft facility of £60,000 to York Street appears to have been the largest made by the Provincial Bank to a linen firm in the 1860s, but other substantial advances secured in this way included £10,000 to the Smithfield Flax Spinning and Weaving Company Ltd in January 1866[31] and £30,000 to the Richardson family, then setting up the Bessbrook Spinning Company. This last advance, authorised in September 1867, was granted on the security of the promissory note of J. Grubb Richardson and his son James.[32] Not all overdrafts were secured although banks preferred some kind of security for the larger advances. Thus in February 1864 J. T. and M. Greeves, Belfast flax spinners, operated an unsecured overdraft totalling £8,298. The Provincial thought this sum too large and requested deposit of the promissory note of the four directors.[33]

The above examples of lending, together with evidence cited earlier, give some indication of the extent to which linen firms drew on local banks during the boom period. Indeed such was the expansion of credit that by the end of 1867 the Provincial Bank Court of Directors declared that 'advances and occasional overdrafts especially' at the Belfast branch were 'too high'.[34] This state of affairs continued and twelve months later total lending at this branch exceeded deposits and cash on hand by no less than £947,000.[35]

If the linen boom was reflected in a marked increase in lending, it was also reflected in bank profits. Between 1862 and the middle of 1867, the lowest discount rates (on English bills of three months or less) were seldom less than four per cent and for much of the period

Towards limited liability

were more than seven per cent. Overdraft rates did not fall below five per cent and remained over seven per cent for months at a time, while rates on deposits ranged between two and four per cent below overdrafts. Given the strength of demand for accommodation during the boom, the effect on bank profits was remarkable. The gross profits of the Belfast Bank, for example, in 1866 reached £173,000, a figure not attained again until 1897. Net profits (gross profits minus interest paid and working expenses) also reached record levels in 1866 to stand at £67,187. This latter figure was not attained again until 1907.[36]

Increased profits enabled all the Belfast banks to raise dividends and add to reserves. The relevant figures are shown in Table 26 and it may be noted here that at no time in the nineteenth century were dividends higher than they were in the mid-1860s. This picture of high profits and dividends and increased reserves in the mid-1860s contrasted sharply with the experience of banks closely involved with the cotton industry in Lancashire, and the contrast is a good illustration of the way in which banking business mirrored the fortunes of the local economy. The Preston Banking Company, for example, suspended payment in July 1866 with deposits of £1 million and advances in excess of £1·3 million. Losses were thought to be around £180,000. This state of affairs had resulted from a run on the bank in addition to large debts owed by local heavily-mortgaged cotton manufacturers who had drawn accommodation bills 'to an alarming extent'. Only after raising capital (by means of calls on existing shares and the issue of new shares) and reconstructing the board of directors did the bank reopen its doors and begin to rebuild its business.[37]

High interests rates were naturally welcomed by the banks, but in September 1864, as the boom continued unabated, the Northern offered a word of caution to its shareholders. If such rates persisted, argued the Northern's board, 'they must materially interfere with the profits of ordinary business, particularly that portion of it which is usually transacted on credit. . . . Experience teaches that seasons of unusual prosperity are uniformly followed by serious reverses which will require to be guarded against.'[38] This was at once a justification for adding to reserves and a warning that the end of the boom, if not in sight, could not be very far away. When supplies of raw cotton resumed, there was no possibility that Ulster linen firms could sustain the freak profit levels of the mid-1860s. Despite this

Table 26 *Dividends and reserve funds, 1859–71*

Date	Belfast		Northern		Ulster	
	(a)	(b)	(a)	(b)	(a)	(b)
1859	16	?	10	61	9	67
1860	16	?	10	71	9½	72
1861	18	?	13½	84	10	84
1862	18	182	10	88	10	88
1863	18	192	10½	92	12	96
1864	30	200	18	104	16	100
1865	20	250	18½	112	18	103
1866	30	250	18½	132	20	110
1867	28	250	16	155	20	115
1868	22	250	16	173	20	120
1869	26	250	16½	183	20	125
1870	24	250	16½	191	20	130
1871	28	250	16½	191	20	135

Notes. (a) = Dividends + bonus (%).
(b) = Reserve funds (£000).
Sources. Belfast Bank Miscellaneous Papers; NBCM, Ulster Bank *Annual Reports*.

there is no doubt that the linen industry shared in the international boom which lasted at least until 1873 when the UK economy was profoundly affected by financial crises, bankruptcy and slack trade in many parts of Europe and the United States.[39]

The general prosperity of the early 1870s and the downturn of 1874 are reflected in the trend of bank profitability (see Appendix). Consistent with the change in economic climate is the fact that the first major failures of linen firms occurred in 1874–5. Easily the largest failures were Lowry, Valentine and Kirk in 1874 and William Spotten and Co. in the following year. These failures came hard on the heels of revelations about a spectacular fraud carried on by the Cookstown manager and Chief Accountant of the Belfast Bank. These two officers had cashed drafts on the bank's London agents (The Union Bank of London) for the purpose of stock exchange speculation. The fraud was discovered in December 1873 and the net loss to the Belfast was £135,142. This loss, which was much larger than the total bad debts incurred by the bank in the previous few years, resulted in the reserve fund being halved to £125,000. The other £10,142 was charged to the profit and loss account.[40] The fraud was large by contemporary standards, and it was actually the largest single loss suffered by any of the Belfast banks in the nineteenth century.

No sooner had the full extent of the fraud become public

knowledge than it became known in Belfast that one of the leading flax and tow merchants, Lowry, Valentine and Kirk, was in difficulties. Lowry, Valentine and Kirk is a good example of a firm which had grown far too quickly in the mid-1860s only to find itself unable to meet its huge obligations when the inevitable downturn began. The account had been opened, anonymously enough, in October 1863 with the deposit of their capital of £20,000 at the Provincial Bank in Belfast.[41] Very little is known about the course of the account over the boom period but the Provincial's Court began to express concern early in 1868. Between then and 1874 the Court discussed this account at least fourteen times, probably more than any other single Provincial Bank account in the period 1825 to 1914. The fundamental problem was that the firm's obligations had reached £307,153 in February 1868, and despite the best efforts of the Belfast manager acting on instructions from the London Court, this figure remained obstinately in excess of total credit limits. A limit of £250,000 in July 1868 was consistently exceeded, as was the lower limit of £200,000 imposed in 1870. Not until July 1874 did Thomas Hewat, the Provincial's Chief Officer and Superintendent of Branches, recommend to the Court that bankruptcy proceedings should begin.

This case demonstrates the problems faced by a bank when trying to make a customer conform to its demands, and the Provincial's lack of success in this regard was not unique.[42] Foreclosure on a small firm whose creditors were few and relatively unimportant was a quite different matter from forcing the closure of a large firm with wide-ranging business connections. As explained below, the size of this failure clearly conditioned the bank's response. Other firms closely involved with Kirk's were the Whiteabbey Flax Spinning Company and the Killyleagh Flax Spinning Company, both Provincial Bank customers and both with extensive obligations in 1874. In June of that year the secretary of the Killyleagh Spinning Company summed up how Kirk's failure would affect his firm. He wrote to a shareholder:

> You will have heard . . . of the commercial disasters at Belfast; to the surprise of nearly everyone L V and K stopped payment with immense liabilities and of course as they have been from the first our mainstay in providing floating capital, we have felt the loss in this point very much, however, unfortunately, our chief loss will arise from acceptances of other parties which they paid us for our sales as they gave up the practice of cash settlements . . . long since.[43]

In August 1874 the Provincial decided to accept an offer from Killyleagh to pay 'a portion of its creditors including the Bank' by instalments of 1s 8d per £ every three months with interest at five per cent.[44] In the case of Whiteabbey the Provincial nursed the company along and kept its credit open. Indeed in an unusual move the bank accepted an invitation from the Whiteabbey directors to nominate a bank officer to their board. Accordingly the Provincial's Belfast manager was appointed to the Whiteabbey board in December 1876 and his successor as manager also sat on the board and in fact became its chairman. The bank appears to have sold its interest in Whiteabbey in 1891, although a condition of sale was that its nominee remain chairman for twelve months after the sale was completed.[45]

Many firms which failed in the 1870s were products of the linen boom period and they found themselves unable to withstand the pressure of the downturn of 1874. A tone of helplessness informs the correspondence and annual reports of many firms in this period, a result of a combination of high fixed costs, falling prices, lack of reserves, and frequent inability to raise capital from shareholders.[46] The banks were aware of the traumatic effect Kirk's failure would have on the credit system of the region's principal industry. For this reason, all the banks agreed to do what they could to soften the blow. The procedure was clearly spelled out by the Northern: '. . . fearing that any sudden suspension of payment would result in very great disaster to the whole mercantile community the banks had agreed to turn over bills for four months with Lowry, Valentine and Kirk's name on them, if the other parties to the bills were unable to meet them sooner . . .'[47]

The banks proposed to appoint inspectors who would oversee the gradual winding up of the firm and thereby give an opportunity for any assets to be realised, and for 'solvent people' to take up bills with their names on. This type of response was unprecedented, but then there had never been a failure of such dimensions in the Ulster linen industry. In point of fact none of the Belfast based banks was directly involved with Lowry, Valentine and Kirk to any great extent. The main casualty of the failure was the Provincial Bank, which lost around £75,000.[48] Nevertheless, the failure did result in a severe tightening of accommodation to other firms which were, or were thought to be, involved with Lowry, Valentine and Kirk. The Ulster Bank, for example, wrote to its branch managers in major

Towards limited liability

linen areas such as Ballymena, Lurgan and Portadown with a list of firms which it considered to be Kirk's creditors. Managers were told that they could not 'be too careful with all linen bills until the trade emerges from the cloud which at present overshadows it'.[49] Kirk's failure was bound to drag others down, and in September 1874 the Northern Bank rightly believed that the failures of the previous year were 'more numerous and of larger amounts' than had ever occurred in Belfast.[50] The problems were, however, by no means over for the linen industry or the banks because late in 1875 another major firm, William Spotten and Company, linen manufacturers and merchants, was declared bankrupt. The main casualty of Spotten's failure was the Northern Bank whose claim for dividends on the estate was proved in June 1876 at £157,245. This total included Spotten's endorsements of £104,000 of which it was estimated that £35,000 would be paid in full.[51] The Northern also held a guarantee of a Tandragee merchant for £15,000 as well as other securities including life policies.[52] The net loss to the Northern turned out to be around £60,000 which was deducted from the reserve fund.[53] The repercussions of the failures of 1874–5 continued to be felt for several years and in 1879 the Northern had to admit to its shareholders that losses incurred as a result were larger than anticipated. For this reason, a further £27,500 was deducted from the Northern's reserve fund in 1879 to provide for bad debts.[54] It should be stressed that the failures of 1874–5, although large, were rather exceptional. Certainly there were further failures between then and 1914 but, as far as the banks were concerned, none was so significant as those of 1874–5. The evidence suggests that while the major initial failures and their subsequent repercussions did cause some banks to incur abnormally high debts and to exercise extra caution in lending to linen firms, there was no dramatic reversal of lending policy towards firms in this industry. Some examples of the banks' relationships with this industry before 1914 are given in Chapter Five.

At this stage, however, it may be noted that in the last quarter of the nineteenth century total spindleage of the Irish linen industry declined from its nineteenth-century peak of 925,000 in 1875 to 828,000 by 1900 – a decline of 10·5 per cent. In weaving, however, the position was quite different because the number of powerlooms increased from 14,834 in 1871 to 32,245 in 1899, that is by 117 per cent. This very substantial increase in the number of powerlooms resulted in an increase in the total numbers employed in Irish linen mills: 55,000 in 1871; 69,000 in 1897. Ulster's weaving firms certainly benefited from the generally low prices of yarn (both domestically produced and, to an increasing extent, imported). These, together with improvements in marketing methods, credit facilities and the use of foreign agencies, ensured that in the weaving, finishing and making-up branches of the linen industry significant progress was made before 1914.[55] In short, then, while the position of the spinners was by no means reassuring, there were real technical and commercial improvements in other branches of the industry and these, together with the retiral of Scottish and English competition, went a considerable way to protect the overall position of the industry in the last quarter of the century.

4.3 The agricultural depression of the late 1870s

An unusual coincidence of many factors combined to depress Irish agriculture for several years after 1877. Appallingly wet weather for months at a stretch seriously affected yields of the main crops. 1877 was a bad year, 1878 somewhat better, 1879 and 1880 were disastrous. If Ireland had been a closed economy, some compensation for farmers would have come from higher prices. As it was, such compensation was not forthcoming because of the influx of cheap foreign imports, particularly North-American grain.[56] As always, the regional impact of depression varied enormously. Western counties were most affected, but considerable hardship was felt in many other areas, including Ulster. The agricultural depression affected Irish banks in a number of important ways: note circulation and deposits fell sharply, as did the rate of branch expansion. Indeed the average note circulation in the third quarter of 1879 amounted to only £5,498,000 or eighty-seven per cent of the authorised issue. This was the lowest quarterly average figure in the period 1870–1914. Furthermore there was a noticeable restriction of credit to the agricultural sector. This restriction was applied to farmers and shopkeepers in rural areas as well as agriculture-related industry such as milling.

Between 1863 and 1876 deposits and credit balances in the Irish banks had risen each year from £13 million at the start of the period to £33 million in 1876. Between 1876 and 1880 they fell to just under £30 million, that is by about twelve per cent: this was the largest sustained fall in any four-year period in the nineteenth century. In

Towards limited liability

the same period note circulation declined from £7·5 million to £5·7 million, or by twenty-four per cent.[57] The dimensions of the decline in deposits and credit balances of the Belfast banks between 1876 and 1881 are shown in Table 27. From these figures it is clear that the Belfast banks experienced considerable variations in the rate and scale of the decline in deposits and credit balances. Professor Cullen has claimed that the decline in aggregate deposits and credit balances 1876–81 was a sensitive barometer of prosperity in countryside and rural towns.[58] Such a claim is open to a number of objections.

Table 27 *Deposits and current accounts in credit in the Belfast banks, 1876–81 (£000)*

Date	Bank			Total Irish
	Belfast	Northern	Ulster	
1876	2,445	2,547	3,585	32,815
1877	2,399	2,566	3,574	32,746
1878	2,257	2,433	3,514	31,745
1879	2,187	2,258	3,293	30,191
1880	2,061	1,991	3,278	29,350
1881	2,089	1,955	3,180	28,289

Sources. Belfast Bank Miscellaneous Papers; Northern Bank Abstract of Branch Balances; Ulster Bank Balance Sheets.

These may be briefly stated and then examined in some detail. First, the aggregate series comprises deposits and current accounts in credit in all joint-stock banks. Thus the series includes both urban and rural accounts. In an agricultural depression one would, *a priori*, expect the decline in deposits at rural branches to be higher than at urban, yet the series cannot show if, or to what extent, this was in fact the case. A related point here concerns the spatial impact of depression. No depression in nineteenth-century Ireland, whether agricultural or industrial, had the same impact on all areas. Again the aggregate deposit series by its very nature conceals the different spatial impact of depression rather as national unemployment figures conceal important regional variations in the numbers out of work. Second, the aggregate deposit series must be considered against a background of branch expansion. The 1870s saw the highest rate of branch expansion of any single decade in Irish banking history. It is surely reasonable to argue that this expansion gathered in deposits hitherto hoarded. In other words the aggregate series is likely to exhibit an upward bias as hitherto hoarded deposits were brought into the banking system. Third, in the later 1870s as in the later 1840s there is evidence to indicate that deposits in Irish joint-stock banks fell to some extent because they were transferred into other interest-bearing assets.

On the first point, a breakdown of branch deposits and credit balances can help us to estimate the impact of the agricultural depression of the late 1870s. Such a breakdown has been made for the Northern Bank in 1876 and 1881, and the appropriate figures are given in Table 28. During this period the Northern's branch network, although concentrated in Ulster, extended into parts of Connaught and Leinster. Between 1876 and 1881 the decline in the Northern's deposits and credit balances was 23·2 per cent. This was much larger than its two neighbours the Belfast at 14·5 per cent and the Ulster at 11·3 per cent. If we look at the Northern's branch figures over this period as a whole, total deposits declined by thirty-one per cent while total current accounts in credit rose by twenty-four per cent. The extent to which the latter figure includes transfers from the former is impossible to say, but the magnitude of the decline in deposits (£679,000) measured against the increase in current accounts (£87,000) shows that any transfer could not have been very significant. What can be said with certainty is that deposits declined by almost a third while the trend of current accounts was in the opposite direction.

Table 28 *Northern Bank branch deposits and credit balances, 1876 and 1881*

	Deposits			Current Accounts (cr)		
	1876	1881	% change	1876	1881	% change
Ardglass	—	9·1	—	—	0·4	—
Armagh	26·8	16·6	−38	5·0	3·6	−28
Bailieborough	39·2	28·3	−28	3·8	4·2	+11
Balbriggan	17·0	15·9	−6	7·1	6·3	−11
Ballinamore	17·5	14·8	−15	0·1	0·6	+500
Ballybay	31·7	16·1	−49	1·6	1·8	+13
Ballybofey	44·5	34·2	−23	5·8	6·4	+10
Ballycarry	17·5	11·8	−33	0·3	0·1	−66
Ballycastle	52·0	41·3	−21	3·7	3·7	0
Ballyclare	46·2	28·8	−37	0·9	0·9	0
Ballymena	94·8	57·9	−39	3·7	6·2	+68
Ballynahinch	70·0	50·8	−27	3·2	2·7	−16
Banbridge	15·6	16·6	+6	7·0	2·0	−71
Carndonagh	24·8	18·3	−26	0·9	1·6	+78
Carrickfergus	78·3	49·5	−37	2·5	5·1	+104
Carrick-on-Shannon	21·8	14·0	−36	2·0	2·2	+10

Towards limited liability

Table 28 *(contd.)* Northern Bank branch deposits and credit balances, 1876 and 1881

	Deposits			Current Accounts (cr)		
	1876	1881	% change	1876	1881	% change
Castlewellan	78·2	55·2	−29	1·9	2·9	+53
Clady	—	8·7	—	—	1·1	—
Clones	92·0	40·9	−56	5·6	9·9	+77
Coleraine	56·5	32·8	−42	6·5	6·3	−3
Comber	22·5	12·1	−46	1·4	7·1	+407
Cushendall	17·5	13·1	−25	1·7	3·5	+106
Derry	85·2	43·8	−48	19·9	23·2	+17
Downpatrick	177·2	103·4	−42	16·6	13·9	−16
Dromore	47.9	23·4	−51	1·6	2·9	+81
Dungiven	42·1	21·9	−48	1·6	1·5	−6
Fintona	27·1	13·0	−52	1·4	1·8	+29
Fivemiletown	17·0	21·7	+28	1·1	0·7	−36
Hillsborough	13·7	12·1	−12	6·3	1·8	−71
Irvinestown	11·3	9·8	−13	1·7	1·4	−17
Keady	15·6	13·7	−12	2·1	2·2	+5
Kilrea	29·5	20·4	−31	2·9	3·9	+34
Larne	—	9·9	—	—	1·7	—
Limavady	44·5	29·0	−35	5·2	5·3	+2
Lisburn	75·6	54·6	−28	7·3	21·5	+195
Lurgan	50·4	32·9	−35	4·3	3·4	−21
Magherafelt	40·5	25·5	−37	3·6	4·8	+33
Mohill	30·1	18·8	−37	3·3	1·7	−48
Newry	11·8	6·7	−43	2·5	2·9	+16
Newtownstewart	35·7	30·5	−15	1·3	2·0	+54
Oldcastle	25·5	21·6	−15	5·2	13·2	+154
Ramelton	38·5	25·0	−35	6·3	5·7	−9
Randalstown	26·0	21·2	−18	0·9	1·9	+111
Raphoe	36·9	23·4	−36	2·3	3·2	+39
Strokestown	12·3	10·7	−13	1·5	2·1	+40
Virginia	20·9	12·6	−40	1·3	1·2	−8
Holywood Agency	—	0·8	—	—	—	—
Branch Total	1,779·7	1,193·2	−33	164·9	202·5	+23
Head Office	406·8	319·0	−22	196·2	245·6	+25
Total	2,186·5	1,512·2	−31	361·1	448·1	+24

Source. Northern Bank Abstract of Branch Balances. (All figures taken at 31 August.)

Table 28 shows that the decline in deposits was very unevenly spread throughout the Northern's branch system. Of the forty-four branches (including head office) that were open the whole period, only two (Banbridge and Fivemiletown) had larger deposits in 1881 than in 1876, and in both cases the increase was achieved in the last financial year under review ie 1880–1.[59] The remaining forty-two branches registered a decline of between five and fifty-seven per cent. One particularly notable feature emerges from these figures: that there was no clear east-west or north-south division in the extent of the decline in deposits. Thus, of the five branches which registered the lowest percentage decline in deposits, two (Irvinestown in County Fermanagh and Stroketown in County Roscommon) are on the extreme south-west of the branch system, another (Balbriggan in County Dublin) is on the east coast, Keady is in County Armagh, while Hillsborough is in County Down. Of the eleven branches which lost forty per cent or more of their deposits between 1876 and 1881, four (Dromore, Newry, Comber and Downpatrick) are in County Down, three (Coleraine, Dungiven and Derry) are in County Londonderry, two (Clones and Ballybay) in Monaghan, one (Fintona) in County Tyrone and one (Virginia) in Cavan. It is also interesting to note that three of the four branches which lost forty-nine per cent or more of their deposits were in Tyrone and Monaghan. This lends some support to R. W. Kirkpatrick's recent study which shows that parts of mid-Ulster were amongst the most badly affected areas in this agricultural depression.[60] Such disaggregated deposit data afford us a much clearer picture of the impact of agricultural depression than the aggregate series which Cullen has called a sensitive barometer of prosperity in countryside and rural towns. In short, while Cullen's term certainly contains some truth, it cannot be carried very far on the basis of the data which he himself uses, because such data necessarily fail to take account of local experience.

As noted above, a second reason for doubting whether aggregate deposits and credit balances were 'sensitive barometers' is that they include formerly hoarded cash which was deposited with banks only when branches extended further into the Irish interior. Joseph Lee has rightly argued that some of the increase in deposits before 1880 merely reflected a transfer of savings from the mattress to the bank safe, although his figures for the number of branches are a little misleading.[61] It is impossible to calculate the extent of dehoarding but the Secretary to the Bank of Ireland in his evidence to the *Select Committee on Banks of Issue* in 1875 clearly believed that it had been substantial:

Q: I think formerly there was more hoarding in Ireland than is now the case?
A: A great deal more.

Towards limited liability

Q: Do you think it probable that much of the money which used to be hoarded in Bank of Ireland notes, is now paid into banks, and appears as deposits in banks?
A: There is no question about that.[62]

For this reason the extent to which the aggregate deposit series is a 'sensitive barometer' may well be doubted. In the 1870s the total number of bank offices in Ireland increased from about 300 to about 480.[63] Assuming that this increase was accompanied by substantial dehoarding, it becomes clear that an unadjusted aggregate deposit series cannot be used as an accurate reflection of prosperity in countryside and rural towns. In the context of the agricultural depression of the late 1870s it is necessary to remember that about sixty new offices were opened between 1877 and 1880. Figures produced by the *Bankers' Magazine* show that during this four-year period thirty offices were opened in smaller towns and villages which previously had no bank office. Twenty-three of these were opened in 1877.[64] Branch data show that new branches opened by the Northern during the financial year 1876–7 (Ardglass, Clady and Larne) had added about £25,000 to the bank's total deposits and credit balances by the end of that same year.[65] If it were possible to obtain branch balances for all Irish banks during the late 1870s it may be hazarded that, even allowing for accounts which were transferred from one bank to another or from one branch to another, the new branches might have contributed hundreds of thousands of pounds in 'new' deposits. Any figures that were advanced would be highly speculative, but the fact remains that distortion caused to the aggregate deposit series by formerly hoarded deposits is a real one which should not be dismissed, played down or forgotten.

The final problem with attempting to correlate the decline in deposits with agricultural depression is that at least some deposits were withdrawn from joint-stock banks and invested elsewhere. For example, commenting on the decline in deposits since the middle of 1876, the *Irish Banker* in October the following year declared itself 'anxious to dispel the illusory notion that the prosperity or decline of a country is to be reckoned by an unimportant rise or fall in bank deposits'.[66] The article reminded readers that many building societies were accepting deposits on more favourable terms than banks, that new capital issues by a number of important

Irish railways for 'extension and improvement' had led to 'serious' withdrawals and that since savings banks offered a higher rate of interest than joint-stock banks 'people with small savings' simply transferred cash into the former. A more general point was made by the Department of Agriculture and Technical Instruction in 1913, namely that bank deposits could not be used to gauge 'net savings' because the essential requirement for such a calculation was 'a complete account of savings on the one hand, and of indebtedness on the other'.[67] This argument clearly has validity when applied to any period during the nineteenth or twentieth centuries. Above all these comments serve to emphasise the need for eclecticism in any interpretation of movements in deposit levels even for relatively short periods such as a year.

The marked decline in deposits during the agricultural depression was bound to affect bank profits adversely. In May 1880 the board of the Provincial Bank told its shareholders that the harvest of 1879 was the most unsatisfactory for thirty years.[68] The Northern, too, admitted that the year 1879 had not been favourable for bank profits:

> . . . chiefly due to the pressure upon the resources of the farming classes which compelled them to withdraw deposits from the banks to a very considerable extent to meet current expenses. . . . The directors moreover have felt it their duty to act with the greatest caution in the face of depression of trade generally and have preferred diminished returns rather than incur any avoidable risk.[69]

This reference to general depression applied both to industry and agriculture in the late 1870s. We have seen already examples of how the banks were taking steps to restrict the supply of accommodation to the linen industry at this time and it is now necessary to examine how a similar restriction was applied to agriculture. The agricultural depression was, to a considerable extent, responsible for the formation of the Land League in 1879. For the banks, widespread agrarian agitation added to their combined problems of depression and low interest rates. Late in 1879, the Bank of Ireland commented coldly that if Irishmen could be persuaded to spend less time on politics and 'more to keeping a credit balance at their bankers, they would see things looking better all over the country'.[70]

As the agricultural depression deepened there were a number of reports of attacks on bank staff carrying cash from branches to agencies and local markets in the Westport region of County Mayo.

Towards limited liability

On several occasions in the late 1870s the Ulster Bank requested, and received, a police escort for its officers travelling between Westport and Louisburgh and Westport and Newport in view of the 'unsettled state of the country in that neighbourhood'.[71] In this region, conditions were particularly grim and it is perhaps not surprising that the earliest Land League agitation developed here. About the same time, the Ulster's manager at Longford wrote to his board to suggest the conversion of the Edgeworthstown agency into a full branch. The board declined to convert Edgeworthstown and considered that because of a succession of bad harvests, subsequent impoverishment of the region, and decline in agricultural creditworthiness, a new branch would not promise well.[72]

Bearing in mind bad harvests and agrarian agitation at the end of the 1870s, it was only to be expected that the banks felt themselves justified in exercising extreme caution in the provision of agricultural credit. As a recent study by Samuel Clark has shown, there is no doubt that credit was squeezed hard,[73] but it remains true to say that we still know very little about the actual mechanics of the squeeze. The best evidence on this aspect of the depression is two circulars sent by the Northern Bank to branch managers. The first of these was sent to all branches in November 1877 when the downturn in agriculture began.[74] Managers were advised to be 'more than usually cautious' in their transactions with small farmers and shopkeepers, and strict limits were imposed on new accommodation. Occasional overdrafts without security were to be discontinued 'where any risk is apprehended', and managers were asked to consider carefully 'the best way of acting on these instructions without losing any good business or making their management unpopular'.

If the Northern Bank began to restrict agricultural credit in 1877, three years later (when the second circular was sent) the depression was far deeper and the instructions to managers were far more uncompromising. Branch managers to whom this second circular[75] was sent were requested to discount no new bills for farmers apart from exceptional cases where the parties were 'very respectable', had their rents fully paid and who were 'undoubtedly safe independently of any interest in their farms'. Further, managers were asked to discount no new bills for shopkeepers on farmers unless the endorsers could be depended upon for cash payment if the acceptors failed to pay when the bill matured.

The bank was aware, as it could hardly fail to be, that if farmers were hard pressed the whole structure of agricultural credit would be severely shaken. Because this was so, the circular went on to warn that 'struggling shopkeepers are likely to try to get bills discounted, both to obtain ready money and to put the bank between them and their debtors to assist themselves in collecting debts. This you must not permit.' These instructions relate only to new bills, but managers were further instructed to do all they could to 'get rid' of farmers' and shopkeepers' bills then under discount. If any such bills were renewed strenuous efforts were to be made to strengthen them with an additional name if it could be obtained.

Apart from the light it throws on the restrictions of agricultural credit, a further point may be made about this second circular. This circular, unlike the first, was sent to only eight branches, all of which were in the south or west of the bank's network: Ballinamore, Carrick-on-Shannon and Mohill in County Leitrim; Bailieborough and Virginia in County Cavan; Carndonagh in County Donegal; Oldcastle in County Meath and Strokestown in County Roscommon. This would seem to indicate that really severe restriction on bill discounts in 1880 was applied selectively. Why the bank singled out these particular branches is not altogether clear. By no means all of them suffered the heaviest decline in deposits during this period, so a relatively high percentage of deposit loss cannot have been the reason for their special treatment. Again, one can only wonder why the circular was sent, for example, to Carndonagh and not to nearby Ballybofey, Raphoe or Ramelton.

4.4 Inter-bank relations

It was noted in Chapter Two that the three Belfast banks had signed a collusive agreement in 1839 which formally bound them to uniform levels of interest rates and prevented canvassing for each other's accounts. Since 1839 the agreement had continued in force, and there is no evidence to suggest that any of the signatory banks showed a desire to abandon or even to modify it. A further indication of collaboration was that the three banks sent just one witness to represent them all at the parliamentary enquiries into commercial distress in 1848, and into the operation of the Bank Acts ten years later.

After 1860, while the essential spirit of collusion was maintained, the agreement itself was modified more than once. Indeed, the available evidence indicates that in the last forty years or so of the nineteenth century the Belfast banks had to work much harder to preserve their agreement than they had hitherto. During this period the Belfast banks had to face much fiercer competition from several others, notably the National and Hibernian Banks. The aim of this section is to show how they responded to such competition, and in what ways competition led to tensions between the Belfast banks themselves. It will be argued that competition from the National and the Hibernian reinforced the determination of the Belfast banks to act in concert, and that the policy of the latter at every stage was dictated by the need to preserve their collusive agreement at all costs.

The key determinant of inter-bank relations after 1860 was the growth in the branch systems of all Irish banks. As might be expected, the rate of expansion varied greatly between banks and through time. In addition, expansion itself took two different forms. Up to 1870, all banks concentrated their efforts into opening full branches. After 1870, this emphasis changed and the next forty years or so saw an unprecedented proliferation of sub-branches and agencies. Table 29 illustrates these developments in the period 1850 to 1913.

As far as the Belfast banks were concerned, the total number of new offices opened by other banks did not necessarily mean that competition increased by anything like the same extent. Only if others opened offices in or near the places served by the Belfast banks did the latter have cause for concern. Some banks, such as the Royal and the Munster, operated principally in regions away from the main body of branches of the Belfast banks. For the latter, the main thrust of new competition in the later nineteenth century came from the National and, even more so, the Hibernian. The Belfast banks' reaction to this was a mixture of defence and retaliation, but in both cases reaction took place after trilateral discussion of procedure and tactics.

In 1862, the Ulster Bank opened a Dublin branch. It was the first of the Belfast banks to do so. Significantly, the joint agreement on interest rates of 1839 did not apply to Dublin, so here the Ulster Bank was enabled to exercise a degree of discretion over interest rates which it was formally denied at all its other branches. Such discretion could be important either as a defensive weapon in the event of price competition from a rival, or as a means to enable the

Table 29 Bank offices in Ireland, 1850–1913

	1850	1860	1870		1880		1890		1900		1910		1913	
	(a)	(a)	(b)	(c)	(b)	(c)	(b)	(c)	(b)	(c)	(b)	(c)	(b)	(c)
Bank of Ireland	24	27	37	2	58	2	59	1	61	7	70	26	71	34
Belfast	21	24	33	—	37	—	38	22	45	26	47	30	48	30
Hibernian	5	4	17	2	39	12	37	16	42	27	47	32	50	34
Munster and Leinster	—	—	30*	6*	44*	4*	38	12	44	12	54	26	61	27
National	48	50	55	—	83	27	85	9	87	12	90	29	91	34
Northern	12	13	33	9	48	19	49	32	53	40	60	41	63	43
Provincial	38	42	44	—	47	—	51	4	52	12	55	30	58	30
Royal	1	1	5	—	6	—	8	—	8	—	9	3	10	3
Ulster	16	19	31	—	53	1	56	52	64	69	73	87	77	89
Tipperary	9	—	—	—	—	—	—	—	—	—	—	—	—	—
Total	174	180	285	19	415	64	421	148	456	205	505	304	529	324
			304		479		569		661		809		853	

Source. Report of the Departmental Committee on Agricultural in Credit in Ireland, BPP 1914, XIII, p. 18.
Notes. * Refers to Munster Bank which was replaced by the Munster and Leinster Bank.
(a) Offices open.
(b) Head office and branches.
(c) Sub-offices and agencies.

Towards limited liability

Ulster to compete 'legitimately' for the business of the Northern and the Belfast.[76] There is ample evidence to show that the Ulster used its Dublin branch to *protect* business from poaching rivals, but there is none to suggest that it used Dublin to *attract* business away from its two Belfast neighbours.

The first occasion that the Ulster used its discretion over rates in Dublin was early in 1865. The National had written to one of the Ulster's valued clients in Moy, County Tyrone, offering him four per cent on his deposit if he transferred it from the Ulster. This customer, who had £7,000 on deposit at the Armagh branch of the Ulster Bank, showed the National Bank's letter to his branch manager who then contacted head office in something of a dilemma. Under the joint agreement, the rate for deposits at this time was three and a half per cent. The rate offered by the National was that prevailing at its London offices. The Ulster's head office acted promptly to prevent the transfer of this account, and the following extracts from the correspondence with the relevant branch managers illustrate well the tactics employed. First, head office contacted Armagh branch with the following suggestion:

> We feel obliged to Mr S— for allowing us to see his letter from the National Bank about the rate on deposits.
> We are not under any terms as to rate in Dublin, so if Mr S— remits his money to our Dublin branch and takes out a Deposit Rect. we will allow him 4 per cent for the loan for 6 months, same as proposed by the National Bank.
> We don't allow this to become generally known as it would disarrange our plans, but in Mr S—'s case we must meet him as he is so good a friend to the Bank.
> PS
> You may give him an order on Dublin free.[77]

The next week, head office wrote to Dublin branch and informed the manager that

> ... in self defence we propose to meet this action of the National by using the Dublin Branch and retaining the deposits of such friends as may be tampered with in this way ... it would not be advisable to say anything public on the subject.
> Further action of this kind will tend to increase your deposits, but we hope not to have many such exceptional cases to deal with.[78]

These comments show that the Ulster Bank was able, and intended, to use its Dublin branch to protect threatened deposits at other branches. Without a Dublin branch, the Ulster could not have protected accounts in this way unless it was prepared to break the long-standing agreement with the Northern and Belfast Banks. This it was not prepared to do, and on several occasions branch managers were told the agreement must not be broken.[79] If the Ulster was thus at an advantage as regards interest rates, what of the Northern and the Belfast, neither of which had Dublin branches until 1888 and 1891 respectively?

In March 1865, as a protective measure, for the first time in their history the Belfast banks introduced differential rates for various levels of deposit. Initially, deposits less than £5,000 attracted three per cent; those over £5,000, subject to six days notice, received three and a half per cent.[80] The latter rate was the same as that given by joint-stock banks in London. The differential rate on deposits became a permanent feature of the Belfast banks' policy after 1865. While there is no direct evidence on this point, the timing strongly suggests that it was a reaction to the National's actual and potential 'poaching'. Competition from the National was thus met by the Belfast banks without any change in the basic terms of their agreement and relations between the latter remained cordial. Indeed, by late 1865 there were signs that relations between two of the three Belfast banks might become closer still.

In December 1865, the senior director of the Belfast Bank made an informal approach to at least one Northern Bank shareholder suggesting the two might amalgamate. As we saw in Chapter Two, such a suggestion was not new, and had been broached several times since 1834. On each occasion the initiative had been taken by the Belfast Bank and 1865 was no exception. The response of the Northern Bank to this proposal reveals something about its philosophy towards collusion. The Northern's board discussed the proposal with the advisory committee and both agreed that amalgamation was impracticable. Recalling the rejection of a similar proposal of 1845, the board felt bound to state that its main objection remained the same, namely that amalgamation of two banks would simply 'clear the way for the third or some other bank'. In 1845 the Northern refused to entertain amalgamation unless all three Belfast banks were parties to the deal. This was accordingly discussed, but nothing came of it.

The view of the Northern Bank in 1865 was that:

> These objections to the proposals exist as strongly at present indeed more strongly than ever – a time in which new projects are put forth

Towards limited liability

every day is not a favourable one for clearing the way and therefore on this ground alone this course would be objectionable –

Were any junction with the others likely to be satisfactory in its working and to preclude further competition on the ground occupied by the local banks there is no doubt that a considerable saving of expense and diminution of risk might arise from it but there is no reason to hope for such a result and in many other respects the plan would be impracticable.[81]

Whether the Northern actually communicated these opinions to the Belfast's board is not entirely clear. It seems unlikely, since the proposal had been an informal one and there is nothing in the records of either bank even to hint that any reply had been made. In October 1866, however, the Belfast did make a formal proposal to the Northern suggesting amalgamation. The proposed bank would have a capital of £500,000 and a reserve fund of £125,000.[82]

Bearing in mind the attitude of the Northern the previous year, one might suppose that the new, formal, approach would be rejected out of hand, but it was not. Indeed the Northern gave at least a lukewarm reception to the plan. The Northern's board and committee considered that the scheme was not 'sufficiently matured' and told the Belfast quite frankly that its proposal would not be accepted as it stood. For one thing, the Northern was adamant that any amalgamated bank should not start business with a reserve fund of less than £200,000. Nevertheless the Northern's board was authorised to go ahead with amalgamation if it was thought desirable 'on full consideration'.[83] Both Alexander Johns of the Belfast and James Bristow of the Northern took legal advice in London 'as to the possibility of carrying out the amalgamation'. The result of this advice was that amalgamation could not be carried out under existing acts of parliament, and would need a private act. Doubts were expressed whether Lord Redesdale would sanction such an act. It was therefore decided to wait for a suitable opportunity in the next session of parliament to persuade the government to introduce an amendment of the Public Acts 'as would meet this and similar cases'.[84] This is the last we hear of the amalgamation proposal and there do not appear to have been any more such proposals during the period with which this study is concerned.

One can only speculate as to why it was the Belfast Bank which made the amalgamation proposal and why it should have been thought appropriate to approach the Northern Bank in 1865–6. It may be hazarded that, as the oldest banks in the town, the Belfast and the Northern felt a closer affinity between themselves than they did with the Ulster, which was many years younger and had no roots in the more intimate age of private banking before 1824. This is certainly possible, but we shall probably never know for certain why the Belfast always approached the Northern rather than vice versa.

Can we say anthing about the timing of the approach of 1865–6? Both the informal approach of 1865 and the formal one of 1866 took place against a background of boom conditions and exceptionally high bank profits. Shortly before the informal approach was made the Belfast had decided to double its paid up capital to £250,000. The necessary £125,000 was to be raised by the issue of 2,500 shares of £100 each, £25 paid up at a premium of £10, together with 5,000 half shares of £50 each, £12 10*s* paid up at a premium of £5. The amount received from premium payments was to be added to reserves. Assuming this new issue was all sold, the Belfast's capital account and reserve fund would be as follows:

Capital account

	£
5,000 old shares (£25 paid up)	125,000
2,500 new shares (£25 paid up)	62,500
5,000 new half shares (£12 10*s* paid up)	62,500
Total	£250,000

Reserves

	£
Reserve fund at present (24 October 1865)	200,000
Premium on 2,500 new shares	25,000
Premium on 5,000 new half shares	25,000
	£250,000

This was the first increase in the bank's capital since August 1829. New shares were to be offered to existing shareholders in proportion to their holdings, that is, for every old share held, one new full share or two half shares could be purchased at £35 and £17 10*s* respectively.

For the bank, there were obvious advantages in a one for one rights issue of this kind. Without a local stock exchange, an open share issue of these dimensions may have been extremely difficult to manage. In addition, a rights issue avoided the necessity of extensive and costly advertising. Of course, the bank had to make the shares an attractive proposition to existing holders and so the offer price had to be fixed at a level below the expected market price. The Belfast believed that the new (full) shares would immediately attract a premium of £15 on the open market.[85] On this assumption, which was not only reasonable but, if anything, conservative, given that the bank's dividend had been at least sixteen per cent since 1858, the existing shareholders were offered new shares at a substantial discount. Existing shareholders did indeed buy the new issue with alacrity, and by November 1865 all but 400 out of 7,500 had been taken.[86]

Shortly after the Belfast Bank's increase of capital and reserves it made the formal amalgamation proposal to the Northern. The actual timing may have been no accident. The boom in Irish linen in the mid-1860s occurred at about the same time as London was shaken by a major financial crisis. In May 1866, one of Britain's leading bill brokers, Overend, Gurney and Co Ltd, failed with disastrous consequences. This firm had adopted limited liability only a few months before its collapse, and there seems little doubt that this served to preserve the suspicion surrounding the concept of limited liability as a suitable status for financial concerns.[87] This is discussed in rather more detail below (section 4.5). The Belfast Bank made the formal amalgamation proposal only a matter of months after the Overend, Gurney crash, and it may possibly be that the bank directors believed that amalgamation without limited liability was the best way simultaneously to preserve confidence, increase resources and stability. Again this hypothesis is only tenuous, but in the complete absence of evidence, it is at least plausible.

Shortly after the 1866 amalgamation proposals had evidently been abandoned, the Northern Bank decided to increase its capital and reserves. The bank believed that such a step was necessary to match the rapidly growing regional economy. In addition, the board was acutely conscious of the fact that the Belfast Bank had already increased its capital and believed that the Ulster Bank was about to do the same. The Northern's board bluntly told its advisory committee that 'the position before the public of the Northern Bank would not continue to be what it should be as compared with other establishments unless some step of this kind be taken'.[88]

The Northern had not increased its capital since 1839 and now in 1866 it proceeded in a similar, though not identical, way to the Belfast. The board recommended the issue of 5,000 new shares of £100 each, £30 paid up, at a premium of £10. As was the case with the Belfast, the amount received from premiums would be added to reserves and the new shares were to be offered to existing holders on a one-for-one basis. Unlike the Belfast, however, the Northern issued no half-shares. In the event of any new shares not being taken, the board was authorised to sell them on the open market at not less than £45.[89]

If all shares were sold the capital account and reserve fund of the Northern would be as follows:

Capital account

	£
5,000 old shares (£30 paid up)	150,000
5,000 new shares (£30 paid up)	150,000
	300,000

Reserves

	£
Reserves (as at 1866)	131,912
Premiums on new shares	50,000
	181,912

Thus the new issue would give the Northern a larger paid-up capital, but a smaller reserve fund, than the Belfast. The rights issue was a success, all but 600 of the new shares being taken by early March 1867. Applications for these 600 were received, but for some reason the board declined to issue them.[90] Just three years later, however, all the new shares in the Northern Bank had been issued.[91]

The rights issues of the Belfast and Northern Banks left the Ulster Bank with the smallest paid-up capital and reserve fund of the three banks, standing in 1871 at £183,405 and £135,000 respectively. The question of increasing the Ulster's capital had been 'under consideration for several years' when the decision to go ahead was made in 1871.[92] The way in which the Ulster increased its capital

Towards limited liability

contrasted markedly with its two neighbours. The capital of the Ulster had originally been 100,000 shares of £10 each, £2 10s paid up. However, not all these had been issued and by 1871 the bank had some 25,000 unissued shares. These were now to be offered to existing shareholders on a one-for-three basis at a premium of £5 per share.[93] The proceeds from payments were to be added to the reserve fund with the intention of raising this to £250,000. Any balance beyond this figure was to be added to undivided profits. In other words, unlike the Belfast and the Northern, no category of 'new' shares was created. Again, if all these were sold the capital account and reserves would be as follows:

Capital account

	£
100,000 shares (£2 10s paid up)	250,000

Reserves

	£
Reserves (as at August 1871)	135,000
Premium on 25,000 remaining shares (max. £115,000)	115,000
	£250,000

All shares had been taken by September 1872.[94]

Thus by the early 1870s the resources of all three Belfast banks had been increased considerably without any appreciable change in share ownership. The success of each rights issue must be seen as a demonstration of shareholders' confidence: in their minds the increase in personal liability which necessarily accompanied such an issue was outweighed by consistently high levels of distributed profits. It is important to note, however, that the rights issues had altered the relative size of the resources of the Belfast banks. In 1865 the Ulster's combined paid-up capital and reserves had been larger than either the Belfast or the Northern. By 1872 they were smaller. To rectify this, the Ulster decided to increase its capital and reserves again in 1876. One hundred thousand new shares of £10 each were created. Only 20,000 were issued with £2 10s paid up and £2 10s premium. Again these shares were offered to, and were taken by, existing holders so that by September 1877 the bank's paid-up capital stood at £300,000 and reserves also at £300,000.[95]

How did the position of the Belfast banks compare with other joint-stock banks in Ireland in the mid-1870s? Some available figures are given in Table 30. These figures, while self-explanatory, nevertheless deserve some comment. From Table 30 it can be seen that the number of shareholders in the Belfast banks was well below the average. In terms of paid-up capital, the Irish average is strongly distorted by the Bank of Ireland and, to a lesser extent, by the National Bank. Even allowing for this, however, the paid-up capital of the Belfast banks was substantially less than all other banks apart from the Royal Bank. Their dividends, on the other hand, were higher than any other bank. The average yield (that is dividends per share as a percentage of share prices) is again distorted by the Bank of Ireland, and if this bank is omitted the yield on shares of the Belfast banks was slightly below the average. The dividend yield is perhaps the best single index of the esteem of any share in the eyes of investors: the higher the esteem, the lower the yield. We may conclude that in this respect shares in the Belfast banks compared favourably with those of several other Irish banks. Indeed in a wider context it is worth pointing out that average yields on bank shares in Ireland were lower than in any part of the United Kingdom. Lower yields in Ireland and Scotland than in England and Wales in the mid-1870s reflected, according to Dun, 'the greater popularity of bank shares as an investment' in the former. Similarly, average share premiums in Ireland (212 per cent) were higher than in Scotland (176) and in England and Wales (142).[96]

In 1875, only five Irish banks published their balance sheets: the Hibernian, the Munster, the National, the Royal and the Ulster.[97] Any bank which published balance sheets certainly gave rivals some indication of its overall position. On the other hand, no bank needed the balance sheets of others to tell it if the actions of rivals were seriously affecting its own business. If the Belfast banks had been forced to respond to price competition from the National Bank in the 1860s, in the 1870s they were faced with a still more aggressive rival: the Hibernian Bank. As a non-issuer, the profitability of the Hibernian depended crucially on its ability to attract and retain deposits. With the abolition of free issue in 1845, the importance of deposits as a source of profit had increased. For this reason all banks, whether note issuers or not, were keenly aware of the need to maximise deposits. If follows that, as branch systems expanded, the competition for deposits became fiercer. In general,

Table 30 *Irish joint-stock banks in 1875*

	Paid-up capital (£)	*Reserve and balance after last dividend (£)*	*Number of proprietors*	*Number of shares*	*Amount per share (£)*	*Paid-up per share*	*Dividend and bonus %*	*Price per share (£)*	*Premium %*	*Yield % (£sd)*
Bank of Ireland	2,769,320	1,072,000	n.a.	—	—	100	13	306	206	9 5 0
Northern	300,000	170,000	718	5,000	100	30	15	91½	205	4 8 4
				5,000	100	25	7½	46	53½	4 17 8
Hibernian	500,000	239,916	1,380	20,000	100	25	12	57½	130	5 4 4
Provincial	540,000	213,255	2,000	20,000	100	25	18	88¼	253	5 2 0
				4,000	10	10		34¼	242½	5 5 1
Belfast	250,000	196,030	648	5,000	100	25	20	103¼	313	4 16 10
				5,000	100	25	8	41¼	65	4 16 11
National	1,500,000	150,000	4,000	50,000	50	30	11	69½	131⅔	4 15 0
Ulster	250,000	291,568	1,020	100,000	10	2½	20	10½	320	4 15 3
Royal	300,000	200,000	1,350	30,000	50	10	14½	29¾	197½	4 17 6
Munster	350,000	167,251	1,163	100,000	10	3½	12	8¾	150	4 16 0

Source. John Dun, 'On the analysis of joint-stock banking in the United Kingdom', *Journal of the Statistical Society*, XXXIX, 1876, p. 19.

any bank felt most threatened when a rival moved into or near those areas where its own branch deposits were highest. As branch systems expanded, this became an increasingly frequent occurrence. The Belfast banks not only feared competition in this respect from other banks, but from each other. By the end of 1865, for example, the Ulster bank was clearly aware that its move into Lisburn and Newtownards, where there were already branches of the Belfast and the Northern, might lead the latter 'to retaliate on us at other points'.[98] Any signs of retaliation were to be immediately communicated to head office.

There were obvious dangers that competition for deposits, typified in retaliatory branch expansion, could wreck the long-established spirit of collusion between the Belfast banks. No sooner had such a prospect become apparent than the banks discussed the possibility of entering into an arrangement 'for mutual non-interference'. Such an arrangement was in fact made, and came into operation on 18 November 1870.[99] The gist of the agreement was that none of the three banks would open an agency or branch at any place within five statute miles from where either or both of the others had an office *unless* any other bank actually opened, or there were 'reasonable grounds' for believing that it would open, at the place in question. If there were no 'reasonable grounds' for such a belief, the place remained 'forbidden ground';[100] if there were, the place became 'a free town'.[101] Although this agreement was appropriate defensive action against other banks, friction between the Belfast banks could and did arise as a result of it. If one of them thought there were reasonable grounds for believing that an outsider was about to open in a town already occupied by either or both of the others, but the latter thought the evidence insufficient, then friction occurred. Several examples of this could be cited, but two will suffice to make the point. The first occasion concerned proposed expansion into Letterkenny in 1873. Of the three banks, only the Belfast had an office in this town and it was a major source of deposits. The Ulster believed it had 'reasonable grounds' for believing that the Hibernian was about to open in Letterkenny which would then become a 'free' town. The Belfast, obviously mindful of the importance of Letterkenny as a source of deposits, was evidently determined to forestall the Ulster if at all possible, and decided to write to the Hibernian to ask if the latter did have plans to open in the town. When the Ulster learnt of this direct

Towards limited liability

approach, it protested to the Belfast and did not mince words:

> Our Mr McCance has reported to us that you informed him that you had written to the Hibernian Bank asking whether it was their intention to open a branch in Letterkenny. We feel it to be our duty to protest against such a step as being in our view, in contravention of the spirit and intention of the second clause of the Agreement of 18 November 1870 which contemplated 'reasonable grounds' and not absolute certainty. In our opinion we have such grounds and submitted them to you yesterday, but as you did not deem them sufficient we promised to have and lay before you further and stronger proofs, stating at the same time that if we did not satisfy you we would call in the aid (as we were entitled to do) of the Northern Bank.
>
> That our interpretation of the agreement is correct appears quite clear, because the object of the clause in question was to enable one of the three banks to open in a place where one of the others was already established, in case of a stranger 'threatening' to invade such a place, so as to forestall and thereby probably prevent the action of such a strange bank.
>
> Under these circumstances, we think you were not warranted in making a direct application to the Hibernian Bank and thus placing us in a false position with them in the event of our opening in Letterkenny.[102]

This was the first occasion that the agreement of 1870 had been tested and despite the strong language of the above letter the aim of the Ulster was to clarify, rather than opt out of, the terms of the agreement. The Ulster decided to go ahead and open in Letterkenny, but its determination not to antagonise the Belfast can be illustrated by the rejection of an offer from an officer of the latter in Letterkenny for the post of manager. The offer was rejected by the Ulster for three reasons: that it could fill the post with one of its own men, that it never negotiated with any person still working at another bank, and finally that even if the officer had resigned from his position

> we would be restrained by a regard for etiquette and a sense of honour from engaging your services with the view of turning against the Belfast Bank, the knowledge and experience you have gained as their officer and, through you, making a business for ourselves at their expense. In our view such a proceeding would not be fair or neighbourly.[103]

Thus it is clear that the Ulster was prepared to compete with the Belfast only within the parameters set by the joint agreement and had no desire to provoke its neighbours in any way. Friction between the two banks in this instance was a result of the different interpretation of the phrase 'reasonable grounds'. A similar dispute occurred in 1877, this time between the Ulster on the one hand and the Belfast and the Northern on the other. The Ulster believed it had reasonable grounds for believing that the Hibernian intended to open in Coleraine. This town was a major source of deposits for both the Belfast and the Northern and, probably for this reason, the latter refused to accept that the Ulster's evidence amounted to reasonable grounds. With its two neighbours united, the Ulster could do little at this stage and simply replied that it had no wish to press its view in opposition to theirs 'if the Hibernian can be kept out without our making any movement we shall be better pleased'.[104]

Two months later an announcement that the Hibernian intended to open in Coleraine appeared in the *Irish Banker*. The Ulster wrote to its two neighbours and asked them pointedly if they still refused to admit the existence of reasonable grounds.[105] The Belfast and the Northern again rejected the Ulster's evidence and argued that the latter had to prove the Hibernian's 'fixed determination to open at a specific time'. The Ulster protested strongly that such an attitude was in contravention 'not only of the spirit but of the letter' of the agreement, and informed the Northern that 'if such be your view, it is clear that we must come to an understanding with you and the Belfast Bank on this point'.[106]

The cases of Letterkenny and Coleraine are interesting in several respects. First, they show the determination of banks already established in those towns to forestall and possibly prevent the opening of new branches of other banks. The evidence strongly suggests that this determination derived from the importance of both places as sources of deposits. Second, friction between the Belfast banks, although generated as a result of the necessarily ambiguous wording of the 1870 agreement, was strictly temporary and superficial. The agreement remained in force. Finally, in both cases the threat to the Belfast banks came from the Hibernian. The response to this threat was a clear demonstration that the primary goal of their policy was concerted action to thwart the deposit-gathering drive of the Hibernian wherever possible.

In addition to moving into towns where one or more of the Belfast banks already operated offices, the Hibernian offered higher rates for deposits than the three Belfast banks. The true extent of this type of price competition was concealed to some degree since the Hibernian professed to offer the same rates.[107] As the Hibernian's tactics became increasingly obvious, the Belfast banks modified their strategy to enable them to meet the competition at whatever point in their branch system it arose. It was noted earlier that the differential scale of rates for deposits had been introduced as early as 1865 to meet competition from the National. In April 1877 branches of the three Belfast banks were authorised to vary rates 'to such an extent as to place . . . customers on as favourable footing as those of the Hibernian Bank'. The authorisation was given on the understanding that rates would be varied only in exceptional cases where competition from the Hibernian was in evidence, and managers were ordered to keep details of any such special arrangement a secret between themselves and the parties with whom it was made.[108]

Extra rates on deposits could be granted for three reasons: on deposits likely to be transferred to the Hibernian in consequence of its offer of a higher rate; on deposits which, by offering a higher rate, the Belfast banks could attract from the Hibernian; and on new deposits which, but for the offer of a higher rate, would be taken by the Hibernian. The Northern cautioned its managers that these instructions were 'not intended as a precedent for canvassing for deposits belonging to any other bank than the Hibernian, much less are you authorised to make any such offer to divert deposits from the local (that is, Belfast and Ulster) banks who are parties to the arrangement now made'.[109] Managers were further advised to use their discretion 'sparingly' since the banks could not afford to pay extra rates on all their deposits.

This leads us on to another important aspect of banking in the second half of the nineteenth century: the increasing strain on, and responsibility of, branch managers. In order to understand more fully the pressure on managers during this period, it is necessary to recall the terms of the original agreement between the Belfast banks in 1839 and recognise too the determinants of managers' salaries. The 1839 agreement had attempted, *inter alia,* to prevent canvassing for the accounts of the signatory banks. However, because of the need to maximise deposits in the second half of the nineteenth century, the pressure on managers was obvious. Not only did deposits play an important role in bank profitability, they were also (and for the same reason) major determinants of managers' salaries. Salaries were not fixed on any set scale but they were decided by the bank's directors, who had to consider a number of factors. Among these were the age and experience of the person concerned and the size and type of business at the branch in question. If a manager asked for an increase in salary, directors took account of the recent overall performance of his branch: deposit levels, profits, bad debts, and operating costs.[110]

That deposit levels were a key factor in the directors' decision to increase or peg managers' salaries cannot be doubted. In the autumn of 1861, for example, the Ulster Bank agreed to increase the salary of its manager at Strabane, but the latter was told curtly that the board hoped to see deposits at his branch increase by £50,000 within twelve months.[111] Similarly, when the board agreed to raise the salary of its Omagh manager, he was told: 'do not relax in your endeavours to increase your deposits'.[112]

With such stress placed upon deposits, it is understandable that branch managers of any of the Belfast banks might be tempted to flout the 1839 agreement by canvassing for the deposits of one or both of the other signatory banks. There are, however, few references to such canvassing in the second half of the nineteenth century.[113] It would appear that the determination of bank directors not to canvass for each other's customers' accounts succeeded in preventing managers from succumbing to this particular temptation.

So far, our discussion of inter-bank relations has been confined to joint-stock banks, but it would be incomplete without a brief examination of the growth of savings banks and the effect of the latter on joint-stock concerns. Trustee Savings Banks had operated in Ireland since 1816 and Post Office Savings Banks since 1861. The former had been subject to several failures and some spectacular frauds.[114] They had been particularly hard hit by the Famine in the late 1840s, and their deposits which had increased steadily until that time would not surpass their peak of 1845 until after 1914.[115] In 1880 their deposits stood at £2·06 million. The Post Office Savings Banks, on the other hand, were latecomers to the financial scene, but their deposits had increased steadily to reach £1·48 million by 1880.[116]

Individual deposits in savings banks, unlike joint-stock banks, were limited by law. The annual limit of deposit was £30 while the total deposit of any individual was limited to £200. In other words, competition between savings banks and joint-stock banks was limited to the smaller amounts of deposit. In 1880, however, a bill was introduced which, if passed, would raise the ceiling on individual savings-bank deposits to £300 and so increase competition for

Towards limited liability

larger deposits. The response of joint-stock banks to this bill is interesting in several respects.

Joint-stock banks in Ireland and Scotland[117] opposed the bill in the strongest possible terms. In Belfast, the lead was taken by the Ulster Bank which solicited not only the support of the Belfast and Northern Bank, but other Irish banks as well as several MPs. The Ulster Bank opposed the bill for a number of reasons. First, it was of the opinion that the bill would have 'the inevitable tendency to induce parties superior in point of position to the class for which savings banks are properly intended to place their unemployed money in those banks instead of in the commercial banks and even to withdraw the deposits now held by these banks'.[118]

If the Ulster Bank had definite, not to say rigid, ideas about the social class of depositor for whom savings banks were designed, it also considered that should deposits be transferred from commercial banks to savings banks the necessary consequence would be a drain of funds from Ireland into British Government coffers, which in turn could seriously impair the ability of commercial banks to lend to Irish industry and trade. In addition, since interest on savings banks' deposits did not fluctuate with market rates, depositors would have a positive inducement to transfer cash into savings banks. Strongly implicit in this last point was the view that government-backed competition was 'unfair' because it could be carried on without regard to the vagaries of market conditions. Indeed, this particular complaint has a distinctly modern ring to it, and is employed today by banks and building societies against government competition in the market for savings.

The extent to which deposits in commercial banks might be depleted by the proposed bill depended very largely on the proportion of individual deposits of £300 or less. Table 31 illustrates the structure of deposits in the three Belfast banks in June 1880. The most striking feature of these figures is the similarity of deposit structure: in all cases around ninety per cent of depositors held amounts less than £300 although this category of deposit accounted for only about fifty per cent of the total. The net effect of the bill, then, would be to introduce new competition for deposits between £200 and £300 which, for the Belfast banks, accounted for about ten to twelve per cent of the total. Most of their deposits would remain immune to competition from savings banks even if the bill were passed. Nevertheless, bearing in mind the connection between deposits and profitability and remembering also the potential drain of funds from Ireland, the response of the Belfast banks to the bill was both predictable and reasonable. Their response was entirely consistent with a long-established policy of protecting deposits from competition irrespective of where such competition came from.

Finally, it is worth noting that the Belfast banks sought the support of other Irish banks in their opposition to the bill. Approaches were made either directly[119] or indirectly through MPs[120] one of whom, William Shaw, was chairman of the Munster Bank. Not since the threat to small notes in the early nineteenth century had Irish banks shown such unanimity in opposition to a government proposal. All Irish banks, whether note issuers or not, shared the need to protect deposits. Indeed, it is difficult to conceive of anything other than a threat to deposits which would have persuaded them to form a united front. As far as the Belfast banks were concerned, the response to the bill was just one more example of collaboration for the purpose of united action. We have seen that relations between these banks, although subject to periodic strain, remained cordial. In the next chapter we will see how, for the first time, they attempted to persuade other banks to join them in this spirit of collaboration.

We might note that the 1880 bill in its original form did not survive, but further bills were to be introduced in future years. In 1882 and again in the early 1890s arguments used against the bill of 1880 were reiterated by bankers on both sides of the Irish Sea. The complaint against 'unfair' competition became louder. After the City of Glasgow Bank failure when many frightened depositors ran for cover, it was only natural that some would choose a post office savings bank.[121] As George Rae pointed out in 1882, ' "government security" is a word of power in England'.[122] However much the joint-stock banks might complain, competition for deposits from savings banks was already clearly evident in the later nineteenth century and was to become a permanent feature of financial life in the United Kingdom.

4.5 The adoption of limited liability

It remains for this chapter to discuss a decision which effected a major and permanent change in the organisation of the Belfast banks: the adoption of limited liability in the early 1880s. The legal

Table 31 *Deposit structure of the Belfast banks, June 1880*

Category (£)	% of deposits in each category				% of depositors in each category			
	Belfast	*Northern*	*Ulster*		*Belfast*	*Northern*	*Ulster*	
Under 100	16.46	22.00	18.32		62.71	68.75	66.77	
100–199	16.55	18.75	15.78		18.53	17.50	17.53	
200–299	12.21	11.15	10.45		7.79	5.75	6.44	
300+	54.78	48.10	55.45		10.97	8.00	9.26	
Total	100.00	100.00	100.00		100.00	100.00	100.00	

Source. Derived from returns of each bank contained in two letters: UBHO to Sir Thomas McClure, MP, 23 June 1880 and UBHO to John Givan, MP, 2 July 1880.

background to this decision is rather complex, but a brief survey of the relevant legislation is essential.

In common with the English joint-stock banks that were established in the 1820s and 1830s, those in Belfast were co-partnerships. Every subscriber to such partnerships was personally liable to his or her 'last shilling or acre' for all debts incurred by the partnership.[123] While the risk attached to shareholders was real enough, the generally accepted view of bankers was that depositors had much more confidence in unlimited liability banks.[124] Between 1855 and 1856 company law was revolutionised with the introduction of general limited liability, but banks were excluded from registration. However, the commercial crisis of 1857 and the consequent failure of several banks persuaded parliament to permit the formation of new banks with limited liability and old banks to become limited.[125]

Despite the permissive legislation of 1858,[126] there was no rush to register. A number of reasons may be offered for this. Any bank which registered under the 1858 Act had to display in a conspicuous place at all its offices a statement of assets and liabilities on 1 February and 1 August each year. Divulgence of such data could be seen as contrary to the necessarily secretive business of banking. Any bank which considered registration had to bear in mind that an unregistered rival was under no obligation to publicise its financial position. Crick and Wadsworth have noted that the objection to display statements may have deterred the registration of old banks more than new, but for the latter a further obstacle to registration was the requirement of a minimum share denomination of £100.[127] This last obstacle was removed by the consolidating Companies Act of 1862.[128]

What was the reaction in Belfast to these momentous changes in company law? As the voice of local business, the Chamber of Commerce set up a sub-committee to monitor and report on the original limited liability bills before parliament in 1855. Admitting that it was not entirely competent to judge the technicalities, the sub-committee reported that:

> the principle of limited liability should be restricted to companies possessing a sufficient amount of capital to be an adequate guarantee to the public, and engaged in undertakings of considerable magnitude and importance, and further that to make partnerships with small capitals liable to all the enactments proposed and to Chancery proceedings in the event of anything going wrong would defeat the object of the Bill as

Towards limited liability

regards them by absorbing such small capitals by such expensive proceedings . . .
The principle might be properly applied to companies with a capital of £5,000 in shares of not less than £25 each the whole amount of such shares to be paid up.[129]

This less-than-wholehearted support for change in the law was consistent with opinion in several important manufacturing districts in England.[130] The Belfast banks, in common with all Irish banks formed in the 1820s and 1830s, shunned registration under the 1858 Act, and there is no evidence in the records of the former that registration was even discussed.

As co-partnerships, they had successfully survived all previous commercial crises and evidently directors and shareholders alike were happy enough with this form of organisation, although there were certain advantages for the banks to register under the 1862 Companies Act. One of these was the acquisition of company status. A co-partnership did not have a legal entity separate and distinct from its partners, nor did it have a perpetual legal existence. In addition, under the 1862 Act, any shareholder who transferred his or her shares was personally liable for debts incurred by the company for one year after transfer instead of the normal three.

These features could be acquired without the sacrifice of unlimited liability, and would be advantageous to both directors and shareholders. Accordingly, all the Belfast banks registered between 1866 and 1867. The first to abandon its co-partnership status was the Belfast Bank early in 1866, following a unanimous decision by shareholders on 18 December 1865.[131] Late in 1866 the Northern Bank followed suit.[132] The Ulster Bank, however, seems to have entertained some doubts about registration, despite the knowledge that its two neighbours were well satisfied with the move, and despite admitting the advantages. The reason for the Ulster's delay was that it was unaware of any other joint-stock bank in the United Kingdom, apart from the Belfast and the Northern, which had actually registered under the Act. As it admitted to the London and Westminster, one of the banks from whom it sought advice: 'It appears strange to us that the Act referred to has not been taken advantage of by unlimited banks anywhere except in this town, and we are anxious to satisfy ourselves that there is no good reason for this before we move in the matter.'[133]

Presumably, the banks from whom the Ulster sought advice

foresaw no disadvantage in registration and the latter's board and committee in September 1867 asked their shareholders for the necessary authorisation to register. Authorisation was given at a special general meeting, and the Ulster Bank became an unlimited company in October 1867.[134]

The net effect of changes between 1856 and 1862 was to make company law in the UK the most permissive in Europe.[135] However, as the speculative boom and crash of 1866 proved, there was ample scope for unscrupulous company promoters to take advantage of this situation for their own ends. The name most closely identified with 1866 crisis was Overend, Gurney and Company, the largest discount house in London. Overend, Gurney had become a limited company only a few months prior to its failure in May 1866. This fact, together with the failure or weakening of several limited banks, served to preserve the suspicion which had long surrounded the suitability of limited liability for financial institutions.[136]

We have noted that this particular crisis passed Belfast by because of the sustained linen boom and the 'avoidance on the part of both merchants and bankers of such ventures as by promising sudden and extraordinary gains were liable to perils of a similar character'.[137] The fact that Irish banks were virtually unaffected by the 1866 crisis may account for the absence of a condemnation of the principle of limited liability by them. Significantly, the only bank in Ireland to adopt limited liability before the later 1870s was a brand new concern: the Munster Bank, which was set up in 1864 on the initiative of southern merchants and traders to cater for the relatively underbanked south and west.[138] Whether or not older banks in Ireland 'looked down on the limiteds', as Clapham has suggested was the case in England and Scotland,[139] is not entirely clear. If they did, they certainly kept quiet about it, but since none of them adopted limited liability it may be inferred that they maintained a strong preference for unlimited status. This preference changed abruptly in the late 1870s, and the reason for change is not difficult to find. Between 1867 and 1878 the monetary system of the United Kingdom had operated smoothly and there were no major bank failures. A decade of such relative tranquility was an exceedingly rare phenomenon in the banking world, and the new limited banks were given an opportunity to consolidate their position. All joint-stock banks formed in England since 1860 had adopted limited

Towards limited liability

liability by 1876, and even seven banks dating from 1840 or before had become limited.[140] In Scotland, traditionally the most stable part of the banking system, none of the banks converted to limited liability.[141] Indeed, so stable were Scottish banks thought to be that one leading commentator considered that the likelihood of any of them stopping payment was 'very improbable'.[142]

This picture of relative calm was rudely shattered on 1 October 1878 with the failure of the City of Glasgow Bank. The details of this disaster are too well known to require recapitulation here. Suffice it to say that calls of £2,750 were made on each £100 share and, not surprisingly, only 254 of the bank's 1,819 shareholders remained solvent after its affairs had been wound up.[143] In Ireland, this major failure had several repercussions. Two days after the City of Glasgow closed its doors, branch managers of the Northern were instructed to take the notes of the former 'in the ordinary course of business, unless offered in amounts or under circumstances which would lead you to suspect that other banks or parties across the water were relieving themselves at our expense'.[144] Over the next two or three months, as the true dimensions of failure became increasingly apparent, the Belfast banks' anxiety became correspondingly greater. None of them was actually owed anything by the City of Glasgow, and the Ulster in fact owed it between £8,000 and £10,000.[145]

Undoubtedly there was some unusual demand for gold, reflecting a degree of distrust in the banking system, but it does not seem to have been significant. In so far as such demands were made, they appear to have been more frequent in the south and west of Ireland than the north and east.[146] This would be consistent with the former regions' higher propensity to show symptoms of distrust, the reasons for which were explained at the end of Chapter Two.

The banks, however, were clearly in no mood to take any chances. As bank shares fell on the Dublin Stock Exchange (see Table 32) managers were reminded that, in this instance, the interests of all banks were bound up together.[147] The Northern told its managers that demands for gold were to be met 'with great readiness, showing no hesitation and asking no questions'. Any demand was to be immediately telegraphed to head office, but in order to minimise the risk of knowledge of demands becoming public, managers were instructed to codify their messages. The wording of the message would be the same as if a bill was being retired: the amount of the 'bill' corresponding to the sum paid out, and its due date representing the number of people who made the demand. Thus, a telegram reading 'Retire Bill seven hundred due this third instant or proximo' would mean 'seven hundred in gold paid out to three persons'. If the manager felt his stock of gold to be inadequate, a further codified telegram was to be sent to head office. In this case, 'Cheque ten hundred in letter' would mean 'Send me ten hundred in gold immediately'. The name of the branch applying for assistance was to be added as the last word on the telegram.[148] This was the first occasion that code was used for communication between a head office and branches. It was not, however, the last, since code was again used in a similar way during the Home-Rule crisis of the early 1890s.[149] This precautionary measure against demands for gold was further reflected in the instruction from head office that branches were to furnish a daily statement of their gold stock. This extraordinary instruction was kept in force for no less than six months after its introduction in December 1878.[150]

Table 32 *Bank shares on the Dublin Stock Exchange, 1878–9*

	June 1878 £ s d	June 1879 £ s d
Bank of Ireland	310 00 00	305 00 00
Hibernian	64 00 00	45 19 00
Munster	9 05 00	7 02 03
National	75 00 00	65 10 00
Provincial	80 00 00	66 14 00
Royal	33 10 00	30 03 06

Source. *The Irish Banker*, IV, 1879, p. 378.

Another possible effect of the City of Glasgow crash was a tightening of accommodation; this applied to both bills and overdrafts. It was only to be expected that bills on Scotland would be treated with much more care than hitherto, but it is clear that extra care was given to more than this type of bill. The following circular from the Northern's head office illustrates the point well: 'The caution recently given you respecting Scotch bills may now be applied to Wales and the West of England as well as the manufacturing districts of England. You cannot be too cautious about all these at present.'[151] With regard to overdrafts, the precise effect of the City of Glasgow failure is difficult to ascertain. This difficulty arises because the failure occurred at a time when the Belfast banks

Towards limited liability

were already cutting back their accommodation to many linen firms following the major failures of 1874–5 and their unexpectedly serious repercussions. In addition, the banks were restricting the supply of agricultural credit as a result of the agricultural crisis of the late 1870s. Even without the City of Glasgow's failure, then, the banks would undoubtedly have continued to restrict lending to these two key sectors.

Such evidence as exists on this point, and it is admittedly fragmentary, sugggests that the failure served to strengthen the banks' resolve to cut back. In particular, the banks became keener than ever to insist on collateral security for overdrafts. Thus, when W. A. Ross of Clonard asked the Ulster for permission to overdraw his account to the extent of £10,000 to purchase flax, the bank replied that

> ... if we agree to give the required accommodation we would hope that you would see your way to give us security in conformity with the ordinary rule of the bank. You can easily understand that at times like the present the board feels it to be their duty to apply this rule with more than usual stringency.[152]

About a month after this, the Belfast Flax and Jute Company applied for an extra overdraft of £5,000. Supporting their application was a testimony from James Barbour, one of the region's foremost linen manufacturers and an old and valued customer of the Ulster, to the effect that the firm was efficient and in perfect order. The bank, whilst acknowledging the 'importance and value' of Barbour's opinion, declined the application because 'of the circumstances of the time as affecting banks, and the disfavour with which overdrafts are now, more than ever before, regarded in banking circles ... we are impressed that it is our imperative duty to reduce rather than increase our overdrafts'.[153]

If the failure of the City of Glasgow Bank forced the Belfast banks to become generally more cautious in their lending, it also forced them to reconsider their attitude towards limited liability. Prior to this failure the only Irish bank which had adopted limited liability was the Munster. By the end of 1883, however, all joint-stock banks in Ireland had become limited. The move to limited liability was an extremely important one and, as far as the Belfast banks were concerned, taken only after careful consideration and mutual discussion.

One legal change brought about by the City of Glasgow failure was the Companies Act of 1879.[154] This introduced the principle of 'reserve liability' which permitted banks to acquire additional capital which would not be called unless the bank was wound up. There is no doubt that this Companies Act made limited liability a far more attractive proposition than it had ever been before. It is difficult to be precise about when individual banks made their decision to take advantage of the new Companies Act. The directors of the Belfast Bank, in their annual report of 1879, said that they felt unable to recommend that the unlimited status of the bank should be changed unless 'other Irish banks shall determine to change their status in like manner.'[155] At the annual meeting of the next year some shareholders in the same bank expressed a 'general feeling' that the Belfast should register under the 1879 Act, but no action was taken.[156]

The first Irish bank of issue to propose registration under the 1879 Act was the National. As soon as this proposal became known, James Carr, a director of the Ulster Bank, confided to the National's manager in Belfast that it 'would provide a strong impetus to others to adopt it'.[157] The validity of this observation is shown by the fact that directors of the three Belfast banks met together in January 1882 and decided that a proposal to adopt limited liability should be put to shareholders in the spring of that year. If shareholders agreed the three banks would become limited in the autumn of 1883.[158]

Limited liability gave an unprecedented degree of protection to shareholders but, by the same token, meant that any loss incurred by a bank beyond its capital would necessarily fall on the public. For this reason the Belfast banks, prior to registration under the 1879 Companies Act, decided to increase substantially both capital and reserves. This was a common precaution taken by banks in all parts of the United Kingdom before conversion to limited liability,[159] and it was one that was recommended by leading contemporary commentators on banking. John Dun, for example, in his comprehensive review of the United Kingdom banking system in 1875, considered that 'from the creditor's point of view the limited bank exposes itself to unfavourable comparison with the unlimited bank, unless it maintains an adequate margin upon its shares'. In assessing just what 'adequate' meant in this context, Dun analysed the major bank failures in Britain between 1857 and 1867 and concluded that a limited bank with an uncalled margin of three

Towards limited liability

times the amount paid up on its shares was *'ceteris paribus,* as regards security to its creditors, practically as safe as an unlimited bank'.[160]

The increases in capital and reserves of the three Belfast banks may be briefly summarised. The Belfast Bank issued 6,000 shares at £35, £10 of which was a premium to be added to reserves. These shares were offered to existing shareholders on a pro-rata basis on the same terms as those of 1866. In addition, the nominal value of each share was increased from £100 to £125 and this increase of £25 represented the bank's reserve liability. All but 122 new shares were taken and the residue was sold 'for the benefit of the bank'.[161] The Belfast Bank became a limited company on 16 August 1883.[162] The Northern's procedure was rather more complex. The original 5,000 shares of the bank had been £100 Irish, the equivalent of £92 6s 2d sterling. These were now subdivided into 15,000 shares of £30 15s 4d of which £10 was credited as paid up. Henceforth such shares were known as 'A shares'. The new shares issued in 1867, 5,000 in number, were sub-divided into 15,000 of £33 6s 8d with £10 credited as paid up. These were now known as 'B shares'. The nominal capital was increased by £200,000, consisting of 100,000 shares of £20 each. When all instalments on these had been paid, they were amalgamated with the A shares. Five thousand shares were issued in 1883 at £18 each, of which £8 was added to reserves. This operation raised the bank's capital to £2 million, £400,000 of which was paid up, with a reserve fund of £140,000. Approval for registration under the Companies Act was given by shareholders on 18 December 1882, and the Northern Bank became limited on 1 September 1883. In the October of the latter year it was decided that the reserve liability would be £30 per share.[163]

In September 1882 the Ulster Bank announced the issue of 40,000 £10 shares to existing shareholders on a one-for-three basis. Each of these was offered at £5, £2 10s of which was a premium added to reserves. In addition, the nominal value of each share, 160,000 in all, was to be raised to £15 and reserve liability was set at £10 per share. When all shares had been sold, the Ulster's paid up capital would stand at £400,000, with an identical sum callable for carrying on business, and £1·6 million as reserve liability. The Ulster Bank became a limited company on 1 September 1883.[164] Additions to capital and reserves of the Belfast banks between 1882 and 1883 had greatly increased their resources and had more than satisfied Dun's recommendation that the ratio of uncalled to paid up capital should be three to one.

As we have seen, the banks had only become limited liability companies after an interval of more than twenty years following the enabling legislation of 1858. It may be useful here to ask whether or not their suspicion of this form of organisation was reflected in an unwillingness to lend to limited liability companies during this same interval. There is, *a priori*, perhaps some reason for expecting such unwillingness since subscribers to a limited company by definition were not liable to their 'last shilling or acre' for debts incurred by the company. Before we consider some specific instances of bank lending to limited companies it is relevant to consider a published piece of evidence which throws light on this point.

Just after the failure of the City of Glasgow Bank, when shareholders in every unlimited bank must have felt at least uneasy, the president of the Belfast Chamber of Commerce, Alexander Johns, reviewed the history of limited liability and judged that:

> When the introduction of the principle of limited liability gave enormous impetus to joint-stock enterprise we can all remember the suspicion with which it was first regarded in many quarters. For example, bankers at first declined to make advances to limited companies unless some of the directors or other chief shareholders would come under personal arrangements. But this suspicion has given place to an exactly opposite current feeling, and it is now so much insisted on, that shares in limited companies are the most likely to be held by strong people, that there are found many to recommend the extension of the principle to banks themselves.[165]

This cannot be regarded as uninformed comment because Johns was a director of the Belfast Bank, and had been so since the 1850s, when general limited liability had been introduced. Johns' view, in short, was that the banks' attitude to lending to limited companies had altered markedly in the twenty years or so before 1879. Can his view be substantiated from the records?

One example of a firm which changed its bankers was the Blackstaff Flax Spinning and Weaving Company. When floated as a limited company in 1866, the Ulster was appointed as banker, but later the same year the account was given to the Provincial. A shareholder then asked why the account had been transferred; the secretary told him that the company believed it would 'get accommodation (when required) on more liberal terms than a private firm, but as the directors did not accede to our request, the account

Towards limited liability

was given to the Provincial'.[166] There is no reference to the Blackstaff's requests for accommodation in the records of the Ulster Bank, but it may be that the bank's objection lay in the fact that Blackstaff was a limited company. Another point to bear in mind is that limited liability was very much an unknown quantity in the Ulster linen industry at this time. The first firm to adopt it, the York Street Flax Spinning Company, did not do so until 1864. Unfortunately the evidence relating to the Blackstaff Company tantalises rather than satisfies, but it does hint that the Ulster Bank was not willing to become heavily involved with a new limited company in the mid-1860s.

Some examples of lending to limited companies were given in Section 4.2 and it was there suggested that directors' guarantees were common forms of security for limited companies from the mid-1860s. Despite this, there do not appear to have been any definite rules laid down until the early 1880s. As will be shown in the next chapter, rules for directors' guarantees as security for advances seem to have become more formalised in the 1880s although a guarantee was not always a necessary condition for an advance even to a limited company. Lending by banks to limited companies certainly became commonplace from the 1860s; the Belfast Bank alone had more than fifty such accounts in 1885.[167]

CHAPTER FIVE

INTO THE NEW CENTURY

5.1 The cartel widened

Substantial changes in the Irish banking structure in the period 1880 to 1914 were very few. Only one bank, the Munster, failed and out of this failure the Munster and Leinster was established as a non-issuing limited liability concern in 1885.[1] No new joint-stock banks were formed and only one private bank, Ball's of Dublin, was taken over. Ball's was taken over by the Northern Bank in 1888 and became the latter's first branch in Dublin. The Northern decided to take over Ball's Bank for two reasons: to give the Belfast-based bank a Dublin branch and also to relieve it from paying heavy commission charges to its Dublin agent, the Bank of Ireland. Such charges were 'of yearly increasing importance'.[2] Following this takeover, which cost the Northern £22,850, only two private banks remained in Ireland: Boyle, Low, Murray and Co., and Guinness, Mahon and Co., both non-issuers and both based in Dublin. The Northern's move into Dublin left the Belfast Bank as the only one without a branch in Ireland's largest city. At least one Belfast Bank director was not at all certain that such a branch would be profitable, and even in 1890 considered that it 'would be attended with great expense to start there in a credible way, and considering the long start the other two local banks have had and the efforts they have made to acquire any business worth having, would leave but a poor chance for another coming in now'.[3] Despite this pessimistic assessment, the Belfast Bank opened in Dublin in 1891.

In the late nineteenth century the Irish banking structure differed markedly from that in England and Wales where in the late 1870s there were still almost 200 private banks with some 450 offices chiefly in agricultural districts and over ninety joint-stock banks with about 840 offices mainly in manufacturing areas.[4] Thus in England and Wales there was enormous scope for bank amalgamations which did not exist in Ireland. One of the motives behind the amalgamation movement of banks in England and Wales which gathered force after about 1870 was the acquisition of supra-regional or even national branch systems and deposits.[5]

In Ireland the emergence of such systems occurred much earlier than in England and Wales and the formation of large branch systems was undertaken mainly by a small number of long-established banks rather than through amalgamation. Whether or not there were any discussions between Irish joint-stock banks on amalgamation is not at all clear, although there was a rumour that the Bank of Ireland was negotiating to take over the precarious Hibernian Bank in 1886.[6] Moreover in 1892 there was a suggestion put forward in the *Bankers' Magazine* that amalgamation of a few Irish banks would make substantial economies, one of which was the elimination of duplicate offices.[7] Whatever rumours circulated or suggestions were put forward, no amalgamations took place, although there were a number of attempts to reduce the level of price and non-price competition between banks. The three Belfast banks had signed a consolidating agreement in January 1886 with a view to clarifying, and to some extent altering, the scope of existing agreements. As before, none of the signatory banks could open a new branch or agency within five statute miles of one of the others. Exceptions to this were towns whose population at the preceding census exceeded 10,000, towns in which 'some other bank' had either just opened or had taken premises to do so, and towns where there were reasonable grounds for believing another bank would open. Moreover expansion within Belfast itself was strictly controlled. Each of the banks had one suburban branch early in 1886: in the Markets area (Belfast Bank), Falls Road (Ulster) and Shankill (Northern). No further suburban expansion was permitted unless any bank (other than those with head offices in Belfast)

> which now has an office in Belfast shall actually open, or announce an intention of opening, an additional branch in Belfast then that district in which such additional branch bank shall have been opened, or be about to be opened, shall be an 'Open' district and any or all of the signatory banks may establish a branch or branches therein.[8]

Given the rate of Belfast's growth such a restrictive policy was likely to break down sooner than later and, as we shall see, this policy did lead to problems. The rest of the agreement detailed common rates and charges, but there were some exceptions, one of the most important of which was that rates on 'special loans' – those made for fixed periods against stock exchange or other convertible securities – were not regulated and each bank was free to strike the rate it saw fit.

Within two years of the consolidating agreement coming into effect, the Provincial Bank became party to it. The first move in this direction was made late in 1887 when the Provincial Bank approached the three Belfast banks and suggested a uniform scale of interest rates on certain categories of special deposits.[9] This initial suggestion was eventually modified and extended and by April 1888 the four banks signed a joint agreement to prohibit any of their officers from canvassing for each other's deposit and current accounts. In addition, the Provincial agreed not to allow extra interest on deposits under £2,000 at any of its offices located in places where there was also an office of any of the three Belfast banks,

> reserving however the right to give at any Country Branch or Agency where there is an office of the said three banks an extra rate for deposits of £500 and upwards if they should find it necessary to do so for the purpose of meeting the undue competition of the Hibernian Bank, but for no other purpose.[10]

The joint agreement of 1888 was thus an extension of the long-established spirit of collusion which had been adopted by the three Belfast banks almost fifty years before. The motive behind the Provincial Bank's approach was apparently to protect itself from fierce competition from the Hibernian Bank which was, of course, nothing new to the Belfast banks. Although this was the first time that the latter had made a formal agreement with any other bank, there were to be a number of attempts before 1914 to widen the scope of collusive agreements to include most, or even all, Irish banks.[11]

The origins of such attempts are rather obscure, although it is certain that in March 1885 the Ulster Bank asked the Provincial whether it was 'not possible for all the Irish banks or a preponderating majority of them, following the example of the Scotch banks to come to some agreement as to charges and rates that would put a stop to this competition'.[12] This reference to Scotland applied to the General Managers' Committee which effectively controlled interest rates and commission charges of Scottish banks and had done so since the 1840s.[13] The Scottish cartel was generally successful in eliminating price competition and by the 1870s the banking system in Scotland was undoubtedly more cartelised than in any other part of the United Kingdom.

If the Ulster Bank hoped that a similar cartel would be introduced into Ireland, it would be disappointed. Ironically perhaps, when the question of a wider agreement between most of the Irish banks began to be discussed in the early twentieth century, the Ulster Bank showed itself more unwilling to enter into it than either of its two neighbours. In November 1905 the Bank of Ireland wrote to the Belfast Bank and suggested that all Irish banks of issue should agree on a uniform tariff for all interest rates and charges. The Belfast Bank expressed itself wholeheartedly in favour of the suggestion, drew up a draft schedule and submitted it to its two neighbours. The Northern Bank followed the Belfast in welcoming the proposal, but the Ulster Bank did not. The latter wanted any agreement to apply to all Irish banks, not merely to the issuers, and for some reason judged that an agreement between issuers only would lead to a reduction in profits. Both the Belfast and the Northern were keen for an agreement between banks of issue, but recognised that 'the withdrawal of the Ulster Bank is fatal to the successful carrying out of such an arrangement'.[14]

Over the next few years, the Ulster Bank became more co-operative. Although no agreement, between issuers only or all banks, was arrived at before the First World War, a conference of all Irish banks did take place some time between late 1913 and early 1914. The participants were unable to agree amongst themselves and the two banks most unwilling to join a general agreement were the Munster and Leinster and the Provincial. The Bank of Ireland asked the three Belfast banks to persuade the Munster and Leinster and the Provincial to change their minds as it had already tried to do. The Belfast banks were not optimistic about their powers of persuasion, and told the Bank of Ireland that 'it would be too much for us to expect to succeed in an attempt to bring in the two banks referred to where the Bank of Ireland has failed'.[15] Thus, on the eve of the First World War, the Irish banking system was only partially cartelised. Despite the failure of most Irish banks to enter into a joint agreement, the agreement signed by the Belfast banks and the Provincial continued in force, but there were many disagreements and the correspondence generated as a result was very substantial. However, a mutually satisfactory solution was reached in virtually all cases, and all bank staff were told 'to act in all things in letter and spirit strictly in accordance' with the terms of the agreement.[16] The two most important sources of friction were branch expansion and canvassing for accounts.

In 1897, for example, the Belfast Bank asked its two neighbours, as it was formally bound to do, for permission to open in Donegall Square in Belfast because its own head office was no longer large enough to handle the volume of business.[17] In less than a week, however, both the Northern Bank and the Ulster Bank had refused to grant the request, whereupon the Belfast Bank suggested that the city of Belfast should be placed on the same footing as Dublin so as to enable any of the signatory banks to open offices anywhere within the municipal boundaries without requiring the consent of the others. The view of the Belfast Bank's directors, which was made plain to their neighbours, was

> that any agreement between ourselves which prevents our moving forward so as to keep pace with the progress and development of the City must, if we would desire to retain the position we have all hitherto held in the past, be so modified as to enable us to keep ourselves abreast of modern requirements.[18]

Despite this reasoned plea, the Northern and the Ulster continued to refuse to accede to the Belfast Bank's request, so the latter took the unprecedented step of serving formal notice of partial withdrawal from the agreement. Three months after 1 September 1897, the Belfast Bank said it would no longer be bound by that clause in the agreement relating to the opening of offices within Belfast, and 'shall hold ourselves at liberty to open such branches or agencies within the City of Belfast or the suburbs thereof as we think fit'.[19]

It would seem that the agreement was changed and Belfast was placed in the same category as Dublin for the purposes of branch expansion. At any rate, by the end of 1901 all the Belfast banks had opened offices in districts which would certainly not have been permitted before 1897.[20] It would appear then that the agreement, although generally effective, was not strong enough to prevent the partial withdrawal of the Belfast Bank which had decided that one clause in the agreement militated against a 'progressive policy'.[21] There can be no doubt that the change of strategy *vis-à-vis* suburban offices led to an immediate proliferation of such offices and provided all districts of Belfast with much easier access to banking services than had ever been the case before.

Into the new century

The multiplication of suburban offices, beneficial though it was to customers, did lead to friction between the banks themselves. Whenever and wherever a new office was opened, the pressure upon the manager to acquire business was substantial, and the evidence suggests that the incidence of canvassing for accounts was markedly higher at new offices, in Belfast and elsewhere, than at older ones. In their search for business, managers at new offices sometimes offered important clients of other banks cheaper accommodation than they were already receiving. This was the case in 1898 when the Bank of Ireland's manager at its new York Street branch in Belfast offered the Belfast and Northern Counties Railway 'any sum they might require' at three and a half per cent which was less than the prevailing rate charged by the railway company's bankers, the Belfast Bank.[22] The Northern Counties Railway had held their account with the Belfast Bank for more than fifty years and were clearly regarded as an important client. For the Belfast Bank, however, it was the actual canvass of their client, rather than the offer of lower interest rates, which caused it to complain to the Governor of the Bank of Ireland. Despite a reassurance from the Governor that the York Street manager had acted without the Bank of Ireland's approval, the Belfast Bank stressed that what it

> wished to bring clearly before you was that by direct solicitation and open canvass your manager had endeavoured to take away from us one of our oldest and most valuable account holders. That is the gist of my complaint and that is my raison d'etre for writing to you – the whole matter is one of canvass and the rate offered has no bearing on the case.[23]

In addition to this example, there were a number of others where managers at new offices were 'caught' canvassing and whenever this happened the bankers of canvassed clients complained directly to the board of the canvassing manager's bank.[24] From the limited evidence available on this point it seems that Belfast city branches could be important centres of business, especially as far as lending is concerned. Table 33 details business at two such branches and the figures explain why banks felt them to be significant enough to be well worth protecting in the period under review.

5.2 Banks and politics

On several occasions before 1914 Irish banks were reminded of the

Table 33 *Business at two Belfast city branches, 1896 and 1906 (£)*

Belfast Bank Markets branch, 6 June 1896			
Bills	28,500	Deposits	35,800
Overdrafts	84,900	Current accounts	42,500
Total	113,400	Total	78,300

Bank of Ireland York Street branch, (?) June 1906			
Local bills	21,500	Deposits	12,928
Outstanding bills	1,306	Current accounts	8,559
Other bills	49,689		
Collateral loans	96,440		
Overdrafts	156,918		
Total	325,853	Total	21,487

Source. Belfast Bank Secretary's Letter Book, 6 June 1896; Bank of Ireland Branch Inspector's Report Book, 1909.

extent to which domestic political issues impinged upon their business. This was particularly the case from the 1880s during the debate on Home Rule. For the banks, the agitation which accompanied, and the uncertainty created by, the Home Rule question was a source of some anxiety. Between the 1820s and 1880 politics had impinged on the business of Irish banking, but only to a limited extent. Politically motivated runs on some Irish banks which had occasionally been a feature of the repeal agitation of the 1830s were not serious, and during the next forty years or so only the abortive Fenian insurrection of 1867 had caused any comment at all in banking circles.[25] In the mid-nineteenth century, however, the Provincial Bank warned its staff in the run-up to each general election not to engage in open discussion of political questions and they were further reminded that the directors' 'steady aim' had been to preserve the bank 'from bias in favour of any political party'.[26] During the Home Rule debate a similar policy was also followed by the Belfast banks.

The origins and early history of the Home Rule movement need not concern us, but the question assumed far greater and more permanent significance with the introduction of the first Home Rule bill in 1886. Although this bill did not pass the House of Commons, a second bill, introduced in February 1893, fared rather better but was still rejected in the Lords. In the interval between these two bills, the militant anti-Home Rule movement, centering on northeast Ulster generally and Belfast in particular, gathered force, and 'one simple, powerful conception of the political conjuncture was developed: Ireland was not one nation but two'.[27]

One obvious effect of the Home Rule debate was a decline in bank shares. Between October 1885 and May 1886 the average premium on Irish bank shares fell from 171 to 116 per cent. Expressed in market values the aggregate paid up capital of £6·72 million declined from £18·21 to £14·83 million, a fall of some nineteen per cent. For this 'Irish bank shareholders have to thank the Nationalist agitation and the political unsettlement produced by Mr Gladstone's Irish schemes'.[28] According to *The Economist*, by 1893 Ulster was drifting into a position which would certainly lead to civil war should the Home Rule bill pass into law. It further noted that the anti-Home Rule movement now included 'men who in an English provincial town would be leaders of the non-conformists and Liberals – men of the middle class as a rule devoted to business and municipal affairs, but compelled by a great urgency to take up a strong political position'.[29] Parallels were drawn between the Ulster Defence Union and the Anti-Corn Law League. As far as the banks were concerned the decline in share prices which accompanied the second HomeRule bill was noticeably less than the first. Between May 1892 and May 1893 the market value of Irish bank shares fell from £18·47 to £16·94 million, or by eight per cent.[30] This compared with a slight rise in Scottish, and virtually unchanged English, bank shares during the same period.

The anti-Home Rule movement in Ulster embraced a number of mutually reinforcing cultural, religious and economic arguments. The view of the Unionist business community was that Home Rule would seriously impair the outstanding progress made by the Belfast region since the Act of Union. This view found its clearest expression in the heavyweight delegation organised by the Belfast Chamber of Commerce in 1893 to protest to an aged but resolutely unimpressed Gladstone about the possible implications of the latter's second Home Rule bill.[31] Chief spokesman for the delegation was John Greenhill, who summed up the 'deep-rooted conviction' of the commercial community that the prosperity of the Belfast region was 'owing to the sense of security and protection which has been afforded them by the Imperial Parliament and its laws combined with the frugality and the enterprise of the people'.[32] One of the many complaints of the delegation was the sharp decline in the value of Irish railway and bank stock which followed the introduction of the second Home Rule bill on 13 February 1893. Between that date and 18 March, some £983,000 had been wiped off the value of the stock of seven Irish banks, and about £1 million off Irish railways.[33] It was no wonder then that a writer in the *Bankers' Magazine* of 1893 considered that 'Ireland cannot afford the luxury of experimental legislation'.[34]

The Home-Rule crisis of 1893 was unlikely to pass without comment from the Belfast banks, but they were studiously careful not to make such comment in public. Indeed, the policy of deliberate public silence was sustained throughout the entire period of debate on Home Rule between the 1870s and the First World War. When it became known that the second Home Rule bill would be introduced, there were runs on the deposits of Post Office and Trustee Savings Banks as well as joint-stock banks. The Belfast Bank admitted to their London agent that while

> this marked distrust is a powerful argument against Home Rule to be used by a politician it might not be so judicious for a Banker to make use of an argument which by the very fact of its publication would probably extend the trouble to his own domain. We have a phrase here in occasional use which though more expressive than elegant conveys exactly the bearing of my argument. 'If you are in the field with *crows* you are liable to be shot at.'
> ... although the general knowledge of the shrinkage in Stock Exchange values of Irish securities is public property and may be freely commented on with advantage to the Unionist cause.[35]

This was explicit recognition of the point expressed by *The Economist* that a company 'that deals in credit can afford less than any other to see a thriving industrial city turned into an armed camp'.[36] The logical extension of this view was that the banks came down hard on any of their staff who trespassed openly into the political arena. Few staff did so, but one who did engage in 'unseemly religious wrangling' was ordered to stay out of all 'future public controversy in politics or religion'.[37]

The silent public facade maintained by the Belfast banks during the Home Rule crisis in 1893 concealed frantic activity to meet the run on deposits. The banks anticipated the run before it began, and were making appropriate plans from late February 1893. Managers of the Northern were instructed to telegraph head office in code and inform directors of any abnormal demands for notes and deposits, making a careful distinction between these two types of demand.

The code was constructed so as to enable directors to see at a glance both the dimensions and type of pressure experienced at any branch in the network. Thus, if gold was paid for notes to three people amounting to £100, or paid for deposits to two people amounting to £150, or paid for notes to three people amounting to £100 *and* to two people for deposits for £150 the appropriate ciphers would be respectively:

> Please retire bill on London No 3 £100.
> Please retire bill on Liverpool No 2 £150.
> Please retire bill on London No 3 £100 and also bill on Liverpool No 2 £150.[38]

Gold was to be paid without hesitation to 'any nervous person' and in exchange for the notes of any Irish bank.[39] Any requests for extra gold were also to be codified. If £500 extra were needed, the cipher would read 'Send First Volume', if £1,000 were needed, 'Send Second Volume' and so on.[40]

One factor in the crisis of 1893 which the banks had evidently not expected, and which appeared only three months or so after the Home Rule bill was introduced, was the threat issued by *The Irish Catholic and Nation* to urge Roman Catholics to withdraw their deposits. This threat led the Northern's directors to make an unprecedented request for a return from all its branches of deposits held by Catholics, and managers were ordered 'to say nothing about it to either your cashier or to anyone else'.[41]

While the threat to bank deposits was real enough, it is important to recognise that the source of this threat changed somewhat during the 1893 crisis. Shortly after the Home Rule bill was introduced there was 'some uneasiness amongst the Protestants' at certain points in the Belfast Bank's branch network and additional gold was sent to these points as a precautionary measure.[42] Initially, then, the threat to deposits seems to have come from Protestants who were alarmed at the possible implications of the Home Rule bill passing into law.

At this stage the banks recognised that it was in their own interest to assist each other whenever possible. Thus the Ulster Bank's manager in Monaghan was told that, if called upon to do so, he would be 'right to give the Belfast Bank and the Provincial Bank a few thousand – in the case of the Hibernian a few hundred would probably be as much as they would ask for'.[43] This instruction is interesting since it implies that the Ulster Bank's directors believed that any run on the Hibernian Bank would not be as great as on the Belfast Bank or the Provincial. This is certainly plausible because the Hibernian was one of the only two Irish banks with a Catholic and Nationalist tradition,[44] and so may have been expected to lose fewer deposits than other banks. If deposits were likely to be withdrawn by anxious Protestants in the first weeks of the Home Rule crisis, they were probably even more likely to be withdrawn by Catholics in the later stages of the crisis because of the threat issued by *The Irish Catholic and Nation*. There is no way of calculating the extent of deposit withdrawal, but it does not seem to have been very great and it is certain that the crisis did not extend to noteholders.

After the second Home Rule bill was rejected, the issue did not become prominent again until just before the First World War when a third Home Rule bill was introduced and passed but suspended because of the outbreak of hostilities. During the third Home Rule crisis, when militant Ulster Unionism reached a new peak, the Belfast banks continued their established policy of keeping a low profile. This can best be illustrated in their collective rejection of an invitation from Colonel R. G. Sharman-Crawford to attend a meeting of businessmen to 'discuss affairs in the event of a Provisional Government being formed'. The invitation was 'carefully and fully' considered by directors of all three banks, but turned down because banks had 'at all times consistently abstained from taking any part whatever in politics, or from interfering in any way with political questions, and they cannot but feel that no good purpose would be served by their now departing from this long established practice . . .'[45]

Even if the Belfast banks told staff to stay out of politics, the strength and sincerity of their unionism cannot be doubted. As Table 34 demonstrates, bank staff during this period were predominantly Protestant, especially in Ulster, and therefore presumably opposed to Home Rule on religious as well as economic grounds.[46] In the upper reaches of the banking structure the link with Unionism was most obvious in the membership of the bank's advisory committees, some of whom were leading Unionists. Shortly after Gladstone's conversion to Home Rule in the mid-1880s, the Liberal-Unionist cause in Belfast was led by Thomas Sinclair,[47] who was a member of the Northern Bank's advisory committee from 1878 to 1900, and chaired that committee from 1901 to 1913.[48] Robert Sharman-Crawford himself was a long standing member of the Belfast Bank's Board of Superintendence.[49] This may well explain the fact that it was the Belfast Bank which held the account of the Ulster Unionist Council and assumed the management of the Sir Edward Carson Unionist Defence Fund which financed, *inter alia,* anti-Home Rule propaganda in Britain after 1912.[50] At the height of the third Home Rule crisis and the famous Larne gun-running episode more than £50,000 was spent on two ships and weapons. As one prominent UUC member was later to recall, payments for these 'were made through the Belfast Bank and there never was any query about the account being overdrawn'.[51]

We may conclude then that the Belfast banks, while staying 'out of politics', gave moral and financial support to the Unionist cause, and so played an important role in the anti-Home Rule movement, particularly in the critical period just before the First World War.

5.3 Aspects of lending before 1914

Historians of the British economy before 1914 are generally agreed that there were peaks of economic activity in 1882, 1890, 1899–1900 and 1907 with troughs in 1879, 1886, 1893, 1904 and 1908–9.[52] In the Belfast region, it would appear that the general trend of economic activity was broadly similar. Evidence from the letter books shows, perhaps predictably, that in known bad years the Belfast banks became far more reluctant to extend accommodation to many clients, whereas relatively good years appear to have been more favourable for firms to seek advances. Before we look at some specific instances of bank lending in this period two further points should be made here. First, while the performance of the linen industry was by no means as impressive as it had been in the mid-1860s, spinning firms were more often in difficulties than those engaged in weaving and finishing. Furthermore, after the 1870s other industries including shipbuilding, engineering, distilling, food-processing and tobacco played a far more strategic role in the economy of the north-east than they had done previously.[53]

Virtually all the output of the Ulster shipbuilding industry was produced by two Belfast yards: Harland and Wolff, and Workman Clark, which in terms of employment were amongst the largest manufacturing employers in the UK in the early twentieth century.[54] Shipbuilding, engineering and ropemaking all experienced rapid growth at the end of the nineteenth century and through their demand for male labour usefully complemented the

Table 34 *Religious affiliation of bank directors and clerks, 1881 and 1911 (all males)*

	Roman Catholic	Church of Ireland	Presbyterian	Methodist	All other persuasions	Information refused	Total
Banker							
1881	30 (3)	73 (17)	14 (6)	0 (0)	5 (2)	0 (0)	122 (28)
1911	23 (0)	31 (5)	7 (7)	1 (0)	7 (3)	0 (0)	69 (15)
Bank clerk							
1881	701 (71)	1,086 (337)	394 (232)	45 (19)	56 (15)	3 (3)	2,285[a] (667)
1911	1,057 (95)	1,236 (405)	498 (379)	85 (43)	88 (42)	0 (0)	2,964[b] (964)

Notes. Figures in brackets are totals for province of Ulster.
(a) Census shows 2,185.
(b) This omits six women clerks, four Roman Catholics working outside Ulster and two, one Methodist and one Church of Ireland, in Ulster.

Source. Census of Ireland 1881 and 1911.

traditionally female-dominated production of linen goods. In general then, the period from the 1870s to 1914 was one of far-reaching structural change in the economy of the Belfast region and as a result the economic base became far more diversified than hitherto. Such diversification was to a large extent responsible for sustaining the economic health of this region down to the First World War. The second relevant point is that despite year-to-year fluctuations the trend of the Belfast banks' advances was firmly upward, although the rate of increase between the early 1880s and 1914 was by no means as rapid as the increase in deposits. This development is explored in more detail below.

As noted earlier, during the last quarter of the nineteenth century there were certain periods during which the banks became far more reluctant to extend accommodation and these periods conform well to marked downturns in economic activity such as the late 1870s and later 1880s. One industry whose prospects deteriorated rapidly during and after the late 1870s was flour milling. The effect of North-American competition on Irish milling from the later 1870s can best be described as devastating. Contemporary evidence from those engaged in this industry is replete with complaints about the results of competition, but one graphic comment will give a good idea of the problem. In 1883 William Mitchell, a beleaguered grain trader in Derry, wrote to Messrs Gill and Fisher of Baltimore thus:

> Flour at your figures would not pay our first cost here as it is being laid down here by New York and St Louis firms very cheap; besides demand is quite dull and we would need a war or something of that nature to give us a boom. If we remain much longer as we are we will get mildewed all over. As it is I am getting rusty already from inaction.[55]

The abrupt decline in milling affected many parts of Ireland and was bound to have an impact on the banks. Thus in March 1878 the Provincial Bank accepted the offer of 15s in the £ from a miller at Dunmurry near Belfast, and another of 10s in the £ from a Belfast grain merchant, both of whom had recently failed.[56] In 1880, a rumour reached the Ulster Bank in Belfast that an important Dublin miller, R. N. Haines, had failed and that the Munster Bank would lose at least £10,000. The Ulster wrote immediately to its Dublin manager asking if he had heard anything about the failure.[57] Clearly the Ulster was concerned about the effect that the state of milling might have on the banks. Three years later, the decline of milling had become so serious as to merit comment in the annual report of the Provincial Bank. In its report of 1883, the Provincial noted that milling had recently 'suffered materially' and went on to specify how this had caused the banks to modify their lending policy to the industry: 'It was the custom very often for banks to advance money on the security of mills, good going concerns, which were very legitimate security. Now they were obliged to refuse advances on such security.'[58]

This comment reveals one way in which banks curtailed accommodation to the ailing milling industry. Another way in which banks could squeeze those engaged in this industry was, of course, by the reduction of discount and/or overdraft limits. A good example of this occurred in 1884 when the Belfast Bank wrote to James Gallagher, a grain merchant of Waring Street, Belfast, and bluntly informed him that 'in these times of anxiety and depression in the corn trade and milling trade we think you are extending your operations too far'.[59] When this letter was written, Gallagher had under discount bills totalling £49,000 and the bank informed their client that this figure was 'about as much as we would wish to see'. Gallagher was told that the bank wished to see his discount line reduced to £25,000–£30,000, although he was given no specific instructions as to when the lower figure should be reached. Despite the letter, Gallagher was either unwilling or, more probably, unable to comply. Indeed, by June 1885 Gallagher's bills under discount with the bank had increased to no less than £68,000.[60] It is very difficult to avoid the conclusion that Gallagher was leaning heavily on the Belfast Bank in an attempt to see him through this particularly adverse period in his trade. It is also worth mentioning that the Belfast Bank was hardly adopting a tough line with Gallagher. Fourteen months between the first reminder and the second cannot be described as excessive pressure. The second reminder was only very marginally stronger than the first, and concluded by merely asking Gallagher 'to carefully consider this matter and arrange to keep your banking accommodation in reasonable bounds'.

As far as the linen industry in the late nineteenth and early twentieth century is concerned, the available evidence indicates that lending policy was determined above all by the state of trade. In periods of generally depressed trade such as the late 1870s and later 1880s the banks endeavoured to curtail lending to many clients in various branches of the industry. At other times, however, no such policy seems to have been followed. Some idea of the adversity experienced by the spinning section can be gathered from William Crawford's 1910 survey of the linen industry. According to Crawford, in the thirty years or so before 1900 some thirty-six spinning mills became actually insolvent or were in such financial trouble that half of them (with 200,000 spindles) disappeared. The other half continued under new ownership and of these six changed ownership twice. In spinning during this period there were 'about seven lean years to one fat one'.[61] Even in the spinning section, however, there is evidence to show that the banks were more willing to extend accommodation to some firms than others.

In his review of the linen trade for 1878, the president of the Linen Merchants' Association remarked:

> It is almost needless to say that the state of the linen trade during 1878 was most unsatisfactory. The decline in prices which extended over 1876 and 1877 has continued during 1878, while the small increase in exports which was established in 1877 and encouraged hopes that the last stage of depression had been passed having again been lost, the amount of the foreign linen trade of 1878 has sunk to the low level of 1876.[62]

In a climate such as this, it was only to be expected that the banks felt themselves justified in exercising some caution with regard to accommodation. Thus in the summer of 1877 the Ulster Bank refused to extend the overdraft limit of the Whiteabbey Bleaching Company from £2,000 to £5,000.[63] The bank did not give a reason for its refusal, but presumably the unfavourable economic environment was a major factor in the decision. In March the following year the same bank informed the County Down Flax Spinning and Weaving Company, whose overdrawn account then stood at £12,466, that it would not allow 'the account to be further overdrawn until we get the additional security for which we have asked.[64] The banks' determination to restrict accommodation in the late 1870s, and the effects of such restriction, can be illustrated by the following comment of Thomas Gaffikin, a Belfast linen yarn merchant, in 1879:

> Regarding our yarn account due last month which you wished us to draw for at 4 months we have delayed doing so as our bankers have informed us that they do not wish our discounts increased. We have tried to convince them to the contrary but they still object.[65]

Gaffikin's bankers were in fact the Belfast Bank which, like the Ulster Bank, responded to the downturn of the late 1870s by attempting to restrict lending. Despite the difficulties of the late

1870s, one general feature of the linen industry which contemporaries pointed out was the fact that there were very few failures, and these were 'the consequence of exhaustion rather than imprudence'.[66]

If most sections of the linen industry experienced difficulties in the late 1870s, the early 1880s saw a qualified revival. In 1882 the industry, 'while somewhat sluggish in some branches was lively in others and was . . . on the whole healthy', and two years later the manufacturing sections were aided by 'cheap flax and cheap money'.[67] We can illustrate this turnaround in fortunes by a glance at the following profit figures for McCrum, Mercer and Watson, a firm of linen manufacturers and merchants in Belfast and Armagh. Profits were £4,476 for the year ending 31 October 1875, falling to £2,925 in 1875, £835 (1877), £897 (1878), £3,738 (1879), £6,700 (1880), £5,136 (1881), and £6,792 (1882).[68] Similarly, the profit and loss account of the Blackstaff Flax Spinning and Weaving Company showed a loss in 1879 for the first time in eleven years, but returned to surplus in the early 1880s. In 1879 Blackstaff passed its dividend for the first and last time before 1893.[69]

While the linen industry recovered in the early 1880s, there was another downturn later in the same decade and in the mid-1880s the industry 'participated in the general depression so universally felt, not only in this country, but in other seats of manufacturing industry'. To judge from the banks' correspondence, the later 1880s resembled the late 1870s in that attempts were made to restrict lending to specific customers. In 1887 the Linen Merchants' Association noted the 'generally unsatisfactory' return on capital, particularly in the spinning sector, 'the year closing with some descriptions of yarns at the lowest price recorded in the history of our trade'.[70]

One major casualty of the mid-1880s was John Hind and Co. of Durham Street Mill in Belfast, 'one of the oldest, largest and most respectable firms in the spinning trade'.[71] When Hind failed in 1884 the Belfast Bank was left with the mill, the title deeds to which had been pledged as collateral. However, the economic environment proved highly unfavourable for the bank to sell. The problem which this property posed for the bank is shown by a number of discussions of the Board of Superintendence on how best to sell it. As late as October 1887 there was still a 'want of success' in the bank's many attempts to dispose of the mill which included advertising the

Into the new century

property in England and Scotland hoping to find a buyer who would use it as a woollen mill.[72]

In addition to the Durham Street Mill, there is further evidence of problems facing the banks in the mid-1880s. In 1887 the Belfast Bank informed a director of the Ulster Spinning Company that 'in the present state of the spinning trade we cannot continue an advance of £30,000 to your company'. He was told that at his firm's next meeting he would have to declare an intention to call up not less than £10 per share. The case of the Ulster Spinning Company is interesting not only because it shows the kind of pressure which the bank was putting on a spinning company in a depression, but also because this spinning company had received substantial accommodation from a merchant bank. The name of the merchant bank is not known but the Belfast Bank was clearly aware of its lending to the Ulster Spinning Company.

The Belfast Bank's suggestion as to calls on shares was due to a desire to reduce simultaneously the Ulster Spinning Company's indebtedness to it and to the merchant bank. It was put to the spinning company that they should make £5 payable directly and a further £5 instalment payable by January 1888. If the merchant bank agreed to an advance of £20,000, the Belfast Bank said it would to do the same until the second instalment was paid. After that, the spinning company would pay each bank £10,000 and still have the proceeds from instalments for its own use 'to wipe off expensive borrowing'.

The success of the Belfast Bank's proposal depended crucially on the willingness of shareholders to meet their calls promptly and in full, but this was precisely what most of them failed to do. The refusal of so many shareholders to pay calls made the Belfast Bank 'very anxious'; so anxious in fact that the bank advised the shutdown of whichever of the Ulster Spinning Company's two mills was suffering the heavier loss. In a candid and revealing letter, the bank explained the rationale of its advice:

> There are occasions when to stop machinery hurts credit but we cannot possibly think that this would be the result in the present case, because it is a matter of public notoriety and public comment that a weekly loss is being sustained at the Company's spinning mills, so that the stoppage of part of your spinning machinery would tell to the Company's advantage.[73]

If the Belfast Bank was putting considerable pressure on the

Ulster Spinning Company, it put even more on the Ards Weaving Company in the same year. In April 1887 this weaving company exceeded its overdraft limit. The Belfast Bank informed the company's directors that 'after considerable hesitation' a cheque for £444 4s 1d had been cleared, thereby making the account almost £500 over the 'very liberal temporary advance' which had recently been granted. Despite a telephone call and a letter to the weaving company's managing director asking him to visit the bank to discuss his company's affairs, the director had not appeared. If this or any other director failed to visit the bank on the following Saturday the bank warned that it would 'have no option but to refuse your cheques and we need not point out to you how disastrous this would be to your credit'.[74]

Both the above examples point to a strict control of accommodation to linen firms in the depression of 1887. Just as the downturn of the late 1870s was followed by a revival in the early 1880s, so the subsequent downturn was followed by a revival in the very early 1890s. According to the President of the Linen Merchants' Association, speaking in January 1893, 'there are few towns in the United Kingdom where at present employment is more constant and trade depression less felt' than Belfast.[75] In the mid-nineties, however, this picture changed again and, according to the Belfast Chamber of Commerce, 1894 was the most disastrous year ever experienced by Belfast industry and trade.[76]

The banks' correspondence which, as noted above, suggests a restriction on lending to several linen firms in the depression of 1885–7, also suggests that the early 1890s was a more favourable time for such firms to receive advances. In Feburary 1892, Gunning and Campbell Ltd, flax and tow spinners in Belfast, were told by the Ulster Bank that their unsecured overdraft facility of £10,000 which had been granted 'for some years past' could remain, this despite the fact that Campbell's uncalled capital, which the bank naturally regarded as an important asset, had recently been reduced from £70,000 to £10,000. The bank concluded, however, that 'while this is our view of the case at the moment, it might well happen that our ideas would undergo a change if the company should have a turn of bad trade and were losing money instead of making it'.[77]

The York Street Flax Spinning Company had been reorganised at the end of the 1880s and as a result its uncalled capital (£140,000) had by 1890 been paid. The Belfast Bank pointed out to the firm

Into the new century

that under these circumstances their traditional credit facility of £30,000 at any time and another £30,000 with six months' notice would have to be reviewed. The bank eventually agreed 'to enter into an agreement that the arrangement should be for a period of 3 years from say 1st March next provided that during the currency of that period we shall have the power to terminate it at any time on 12 months' notice'.[78] York Street were also requested to provide twice-yearly balance sheets, although the bank did stress that it 'did not in the least anticipate' that early repayment would be demanded.

The mid to late nineties was a difficult period for many firms in the linen industry and particularly for the spinners. In 1901 there were over twenty limited companies spinning flax in Belfast, but only six were mentioned in the local stock exchange list and in only two, Brookfield and York Street, were there any regular dealings in shares. These last two appear to have been more integrated than the others, and had an extensive warehousing business in addition to their spinning interest.[79] The difficulties which were faced by many firms after 1894 can be illustrated by several pieces of evidence.

Between 1894 and 1900 the Blackstaff Flax Spinning and Weaving Company, which had succeeded in paying a dividend throughout the 1880s and early 1890s, passed all its dividends both interim and final. Not surprisingly, by 1900 this company's shares had no market value.[80] According to one historian of the linen industry, by the end of the nineteenth century it was still regarded as 'a sort of heresy' to reduce yarn production and put mills on short time. The usual strategy of spinners was to continue yarn production and, when they needed money, to deposit such stocks with yarn merchants as security for advances on bills. By 1897, however, yarn stocks all over the trade 'had risen to huge proportions and prices rapidly fell. The banks wanted more in yarns to cover the bills.'[81]

One firm which went into liquidation in 1898 was the Belfast Flax Spinning Company. The figures from its balance sheets (see Table 35) show how the depression of the later 1880s and mid-1890s had affected its financial position. Between 1886 and 1897, then, the uncalled capital had been paid up, the reserves had disappeared, and the debenture indebtedness had almost trebled, while the firm's liquid assets had dwindled by over forty per cent. When the company went into liquidation it owed the Ulster Bank more than £20,000.[82]

Table 35 The Belfast Flax Spinning Company, 1886–97 (£)

	Paid up capital	Reserves	Debentures	Stock and debtors
1886	75,000	12,000	20,000	117,028
1893	80,000	16,000	57,000	87,408
1897	80,000	0	56,000	67,494

Source. Ollerenshaw 'Industry 1820–1914' p. 81.

Again in 1898 the Belfast Bank informed the chairman of Durham Street Weaving Company that his loan and overdrawn accounts, then totalling £24,000, were too large. The bank thought that £10,000 was a reasonable limit, with a further £20,000 discount line. The chairman of Durham Street agreed to reduce his accommodation within two months, and the bank, which believed itself 'quite too considerate', insisted that the loan account 'must be reduced at the rate of £2,000 a year which is the deferred annual reduction as arranged three years ago, but never endeavoured to be carried out'.[83]

The undoubted dificulties of the later 1890s can be further illustrated by the following extract from a letter sent by the Belfast Bank to the Island Spinning Company in 1897. After drawing attention to the amount of bills under discount, which was some £27,000, and asking for a reduction of £7,000, the bank concluded:

> ... we wish to state that we have no fault to find with the quality of the paper, but having regard to the existing state of the linen trade when nearly all our customers in your line are in a similar position as regards banking accommodation, it becomes necessary for us, having a desire to treat all our friends in a spirit of fairness to limit the individual advances sought for.[84]

As noted earlier, the evidence available on bank lending to the linen industry suggests that the banks were guided above all by the state of trade. Moreover it would appear that, even in bad years, the banks' response was often to ask for collateral for unsecured loans or for more collateral in the cases of those advances which were only very partially secured. In other words, even bad years did not necessarily lead to a reduction in the absolute level of lending.

Turning to bank lending to other industries there are several references in the records which will be noted here, if only to show something of the range of industries with which the banks were involved. It was pointed out in Chapter Three that James Combe of the Falls Foundry operated an overdrawn account with the Ulster Bank throughout the period 1846–60. This firm, renamed Combe, Barbour, Combe, went on in the second half of the nineteenth century to become one of Belfast's leading engineering concerns. In 1883 Combe's total accommodation in bills and on overdrawn account was around £20,000. It would appear that this account had never been secured. In March 1883 the Ulster Bank, while expressing 'great confidence' in the firm and its management, requested that the directors provide a guarantee for their advance, and concluded by saying that it was 'our earnest wish to be enabled to afford you all the reasonable accommodation you require and at the same time to maintain intact the cordial relations which have always subsisted between your firm and this bank'.

A week after this was written, the firm had apparently informed the bank that it was inconvenient for them to provide the requested guarantee. The bank replied:

> While it is our desire to see your account secured and so brought within the scope of our rule, which governs our dealings with other large accounts, we have no wish to press the question of security in a way that does not fall in with your own views, and as it appears that the idea of a guarantee is not altogether acceptable to you we will let it drop.[85]

There is no further reference to Combe's account in the Ulster Bank's correspondence. If the Ulster Bank adopted a flexible policy towards Combe, the Belfast Bank did the same with another leading engineering company, Victor Coates Ltd. Coates's account with the Belfast Bank had been opened in 1882 with an overdraft facility of £5,000–£10,000. No guarantee for this had been requested in 1882, but in 1887 the bank asked Coates to provide one to cover his overdraft which had 'stood pretty much about £8,000 of late'. Coates considered that the request should have been made at the time his account had been opened, but the bank informed him that this had not been thought necessary since trade had then been comparatively good. In the intervening period there had been a 'marked declension in local trade generally', so the bank felt justified in its request.

The bank's view was that it was in Coates's own interest to provide the guarantee and so 'give the bank confidence to continue the advance until better times. . . . Altered times compel an altered policy.'[86] It was argued above that bank lending to the linen industry was determined above all by the state of trade. Coates's case is just another example of this. In other words, just as Coates had not been asked for a guarantee when trade was good, so he was asked to provide one when trade took a turn for the worse. This was the way in which 'altered times' compelled an 'altered policy'. As we have seen, the generally depressed period 1885–7 (as well as the late 1870s) provoked a similar response from the banks in their lending to the linen industry.

Another example of a banker's response to the difficulties of the mid-1880s was the Belfast Bank's advance to the Belfast and Northern Counties Railway. The depression of 1886–7 hit this railway hard and in 1886 it paid the lowest dividend in its history (two per cent), accompanied by a decline in the value of its shares. In the spring of 1885 the Belfast Bank advanced £40,000 to this railway company. The following May, however, when trade was much worse than it had been when the loan was made the bank informed its client that:

> The advance of £40,000 made about 12 months ago will fall due on 8th prox. Perhaps you have it in mind to repay same, but if on the other hand you propose to renew the loan we shall require to have it reduced to such an extent as to leave us a fair margin on the security held. In view of the decline of Irish Railway Prices all round we would require to see the loan brought down to £35,000 and we think it well to give you this early intimation on the subject.[87]

If we turn now to consider the finance of Belfast shipbuilding it should be remembered that shipowners often financed builders by extending credit as construction proceeded.[88] This does not, of course, preclude the possibility that bank finance might be required and indeed there is considerable evidence for this before 1914. As far as Irish banks were concerned it was the Bank of Ireland which played by far the most important role in shipbuilding finance. In the later 1860s Harland and Wolff operated an 'occasional' unsecured overdraft facility of £10,000.[89] Ten years later, possibly because the firm was then constructing an expensive engine works, the unsecured overdraft limit was raised to £35,000.[90] The growth of this shipyard continued to be matched by increasingly extensive bank credit. Thus in 1888 an overdraft facility of £120,000, secured by debentures of the City of Liverpool Steam Navigation Company, was provided and later in the same year a further £50,000 unsecured credit for 'occasional' use was granted.[91] In addition in 1891 the Belfast Bank lent £50,000 to Harland and Wolff on the security of fully paid-up shares in the African Steam Ship Company, though this was probably repaid the following year.[92] By 1903 Harland and Wolff's 'occasional' unsecured overdraft limit with the Bank of Ireland was raised to £150,000.[93]

The other major Belfast shipbuilders, Workman Clark and Co., also received extensive bank credit. This firm, set up in 1879, approached the Provincial Bank in Belfast in 1884 for an overdraft of £12,000 secured by the guarantee of Francis Workman and George Clark but the Provincial's directors rejected the request, deeming the security inadequate.[94] It would seem that after this unsuccessful request Workman Clark received some credit from the Ulster Bank,[95] but their main source of bank finance was the Bank of Ireland. By the late 1890s their overdraft limit was £50,000, secured by the directors' guarantee, with a further discount facility of £10,000. Again in 1904 the Bank of Ireland provided Workman Clark with a loan of £100,000 for seven years secured by £100,000 of the firm's debentures guaranteed by the United Trust Company of America.[96] Four years later this shipyard requested, and was granted, a loan of £230,000 secured by the guarantee of the three directors (Workman, Clark and Charles Allan) to help finance construction of a ship for the Oriental Steam Navigation Company. However, after about a year, much to the disappointment of the bank, 'unfortunately the Co. have been so flush of funds they have not yet availed of any of the accommodation'.[97] Such a comment speaks volumes for the financial position of this shipyard before 1914, and no-one could then have foreseen the problems of the 1920s which finally led to closure in 1935.[98]

In addition to loans and overdrafts, both Belfast shipbuilders discounted the acceptances of their customers with the Bank of Ireland and the scale of this business was extensive. As an example, Table 36 details the level of acceptances discounted at the beginning of 1909 and the shipping companies on which they were drawn. Even if shipowners did finance builders, then, such finance often took the form of acceptances which involved banks in their discount.

There are further examples of lending to new and growing industries in this period. In July 1895 the Ulster Bank lent £20,000 to Robinson and Cleaver, a large retail store in Belfast.[99] Three years later the account of one of the city's distillers, wine and spirit merchants Peter Keegan and Co., was overdrawn to the extent of

Table 36 *Acceptances discounted by Bank of Ireland for Belfast shipbuilders at 6 January 1909*

Harland and Wolff	Amount (£)	Workman Clark	Amount (£)
African Steamship Co.	50,000	Elder Dempster & Co.	20,000
Elder Dempster & Co.	61,800	Oriental Steam Navigation Co.	30,000
International Navigation Co.	75,000	Tyser Line	51,000
Royal Mail Steam Packet Co.	120,000	Ulster Steam Ship Co.	11,000
Thompson and Co.	25,000		
Ulster Steam Ship Co.	1,377		
Wilson and Furness, Leyland Line	25,000		
Total	358,177	Total	112,000

Source. Bank of Ireland Acceptance Book, 1908–10.

£14,450. The Ulster Bank informed the firm that not only was the account unsecured, but the firm had not even asked the bank for permission to overdraw in the first place. The bank simply asked for Keegan's balance sheets, 'expressed satisfaction' having examined them, merely asked Keegan what limit of finance he required and added that 'you will understand even with our best customers it is inconvenient that overdrafts should be taken without pre-arrangment with us'.[100] Again, in 1883 the Provincial Bank provided a credit of £5,000 to William Higgin's Avoniel Distillery, built the previous year, upon the guarantee of the Revd William Edwards and Thomas C. Higgin.[101] Just over twenty years later the same bank granted a request from Dunville's Distillery for an overdraft of £25,000 for four months secured by deposits of a £500,000 Consol certificate.[102]

In this section we have said something about the nature of diversification within the economy of the Belfast region, and emphasised how fluctuations in economic activity affected bank lending to several customers. It should be pointed out that in periods of relatively depressed trade, when the banks tried either to reduce accommodation to particular customers or to request some or more security for advances, it was not always easy to persuade customers to meet the bank's request.

The length of the period over which a bank was prepared to negotiate with a client for a restriction of accommodation depended on several factors. These included the size of the account in question, the length of time it had been operated to the bank's satisfaction, the prestige and 'morality' of the account holder, whether or not he was a shareholder in the bank, and, of course, the bank's estimate of the creditworthiness of the firm or individual. Evidence illustrative of these factors is fragmentary, and scattered over several decades of correspondence, and there is no possibility of ranking their relative importance. What we can do is to demonstrate, by example, how the different factors played a part in determining bank lending policy.

As was shown in the last chapter the banks, by mutual arrangement, attempted to soften the impact of the collapse of Lowry, Valentine and Kirk by turning over that company's bills. The explicit intention of this move had been to defer the consequences of the sudden failure of this major firm. The banks were mindful, as they could not fail to be, of the potential repercussions of the bankruptcy of a large firm with extensive and long-established connections. For this reason it is understandable why the decision to take drastic action such as stopping a company's cheques was taken only as a last resort. Clearly, then, in the case of Lowry, Valentine and Kirk, the banks were heavily influenced by the size of that firm.

The importance which the banks attached to old and valued clients can be illustrated well with reference to the Ulster Bank's relationship with Jaffe Brothers Ltd, linen merchants and bleachers in the 1870s. When Jaffe's account had been opened, the bank agreed to advance £30,000 on open account and discount Thomas Sinton's drafts on Jaffe Brothers to the extent of £10,000. In return for this accommodation of £40,000 Jaffe agreed to provide title deeds of his properties in Tandragee and Banbridge as collateral security. In 1878, the Ulster's board thought this level of accommodation 'large', but nevertheless agreed to continue it. Jaffe was informed that in case of advances to limited companies, the rule of the bank was to require the personal guarantee of the directors,

> but as this point was not mentioned at first, and as we now find it would not be agreeable to you, we will not insist on it in the present instance. In your case we naturally take into account our long and satisfactory relations with your firm and our high estimate of your business character and capabilities.[103]

The importance of a long-established relationship in influencing bank lending policy is shown again in the case of the Belfast Bank and J. S. Boyd in the 1890s. Boyd had two principal business interests, the Old Bushmills Distillery Ltd and the Belfast Warehouse Co. Ltd. In April 1892 Boyd's total accommodation amounted to some £70,000. While the bank hoped that this amount would be adequate, Boyd evidently needed and availed himself of a substantially higher amount without prior permission from the bank. By January 1893, when Boyd's accommodation had reached almost £106,000, the bank requested a reduction, indicated how this should be achieved and concluded: 'We hope a ready compliance with our views will facilitate the continuance of the pleasant business relationship which has existed between your good self and this Bank for so many years . . .'[104] Although the bank could have taken steps to curtail Boyd's accommodation well before it reached £106,000, it did not do so, presumably because Boyd was an old and valued client. What security had been provided is not known, but the fact that the bank informed Boyd that it looked to his 'personal management largely for our security and the success of your companies' strongly implies that his account was only partially covered by collateral.

The flexibility with which the bank treated Boyd did, however, create problems over the next two years or so. During this period the bank struggled hard, but with very limited success, to reduce Boyd's accommodation to acceptable levels. Numerous detailed reminders about the state of his various accounts in the summer of 1893 were eventually followed by more extreme pressure in October of that year. The bank was in a dilemma not only because of its long and generally satisfactory relationship with Boyd, but also because his two major business interests experienced very different fortunes. Of the two, the Old Bushmills Distillery was very successful, while the reverse was true of the Belfast Warehouse Company. In October 1893, the Belfast Bank informed Boyd that it wished to have the distillery's account transferred elsewhere. The question arises: why did the bank want to rid itself of the account of a successful distillery? There appear to have have been two reasons. First, the bank was clearly influenced by the length of the period over which it had tried to make Boyd meet its views as to the level of accommodation. Second, the bank felt, or at least told Boyd, that the future success of the distillery 'will require a very considerable increase in accommodation, and we think it would be well to have this arranged elsewhere before the necessity for its use actually

Into the new century

arises'.

A month after the bank was attempting to dispose of the Old Bushmills Distillery account, it also put a great deal of pressure on Boyd to bring the account of the Belfast Warehouse Company under control. By November 1893, the latter, which had previously been very active, had suddenly become 'practically dormant' except for the payment of cheques which the bank had paid to preserve Boyd's honour. At this date, the account was £6,615 overdrawn and, in the bank's view, 'in such a state as to warrant our declining to pay many of the cheques presented'. Despite this apparently final demand, the account was overdrawn by a further £130 two days later, and both accounts were still operative in May 1894. By this time, the bank demanded deposit of collateral security if Boyd's accounts were to be continued, so as 'to avert a trouble that we would all sincerely regret'. In the same month, however, the Belfast Warehouse Company failed, and Boyd finally had to acknowledge the bank's lien on whiskey warrants, certificates, other securities and property in order to settle his debt. This particular example of a bank's attempt to reduce the accommodation of an old and respected client over several years was similar to several others which could be cited from the records of the Belfast banks.

If the banks sometimes had difficulty with customers such as Boyd, what was their policy on the accounts of shareholders? The power of all three Belfast banks to lend on the security of their shares was unquestionable since it was written into their deeds of co-partnership, and the evidence suggests that such lending was common.[105] Occasionally, however, the accommodation afforded to shareholders did become a matter of some concern to the bank's directors. Two examples of this, both from the last quarter of the nineteenth century, will suffice to show the bank's policy.

The first case is that of Charles Duffin, a flaxspinner, shareholder in the Ulster Bank and a member of that bank's advisory committee. Between 1874 and 1878 the bank had aimed to limit Duffin's overdraft to £7,500 on the security of shares, and in view of Duffin's promise to comply had agreed to take his drafts on his son, Edmund Grimshaw Duffin, to the extent of £2,500. Evidently, however, the promised reduction was not made and in March 1878 his overdraft was £10,028. The sum was £2,648 more than the market value of his shares which then stood at £12 each.

The bank made it clear that, although the account was considered 'unsatisfactory', the directors agreed to continue to advance up to the full value of Duffin's shares but 'appealed' to their client to try to reduce his overdraft to the stipulated limit. Early in the next month, Duffin was told 'While we are anxious – the more especially because of your position as a member of the Committee – that you should use every effort to reduce your balance to the limit we have named, or to fully secure it – we have no intention of pressing you at present.'[106]

Implicit in this comment is the directors' view that a member of the bank's advisory committee should set an example to others by keeping to his agreed limit. In Duffin's case membership of the committee may also have played a part in the directors' decision not to press their client. Nevertheless, the bank directors went so far as to satisfy themselves that Duffin had £5,000–£6,000 worth of yarn stocks on hand and that his total liabilities outside the bank were less than £2,000. He was further advised not to do anything 'to make the bank's position worse than it is in relation to your creditors'.

Duffin's case is interesting because it shows that the Ulster Bank's directors did not make members of their advisory committee exceptional cases in their attempts to restrict accommodation. This policy is shown even more clearly in our second example, which concerns the Belfast Bank and John Browne, a prominent timber merchant, owner of large sawmills and former mayor of Belfast, in the mid-1880s. In this case the correspondence became rather acrimonious.

Browne was a member of the Belfast Bank's Board of Superintendence. In April 1884 the directors of the bank, with the approval of the Board of Superintendence, had decided to make it a rule that advances to limited companies should be secured by guarantees of the directors of those companies, except in cases of advances of 'small amount'.[107] Accordingly they had written to Browne to request the provision of such a guarantee, but eighteen months later he had not complied. Browne in fact accused the bank directors of 'peremptory' treatment.

If Browne was expecting special status as a result of his membership of the bank's Board of Superintendence, he must have been surprised by the tone of the directors' response:

> If we had avoided to make it (i.e. the request for a guarantee) and you had died or any other disaster had befallen the Limited Co. the directors of this bank would have been blamed *and justly blamed* for their

Into the new century

conduct, and it would have been, naturally, supposed that this dereliction of duty was due to a cowardly unwillingness to deal with a member of the Board of Superintendence in the way any other customer would have been dealt with . . .

. . . we would have been undeserving of the confidence of our shareholders if we had acted otherwise . . .[108]

The problems which banks faced when they were forced to reduce or secure accommodation show that the banks were sometimes placed in a difficult, occasionally almost powerless, position. If the banks had felt confident enough to make advances on the security of a client's good name, or waive their rules on personal guarantees for advances to a limited company because such a company was believed to be sound and its prospects good, but were subsequently obliged to revise their judgements in the light of deterioration in the economic climate, it was by no means always easy to translate the revised policy into practical results.

It is all too easy for the historian to assume that a bank exercised absolute control over the level of accommodation provided to clients. Often, particularly in the short term, this was not the case. It must be said, however, that the directors of the Belfast banks, each of which was supported by an advisory committee whose members were almost all engaged in local business, were as well placed as any bankers could be to gain a reasonable idea of any particular client's creditworthiness. The quality of their judgement on this score was especially important in their decision to lend only on the security of a particular client's good name or business acumen.

If a bank did decide to satisfy itself that a client's credit was good, it could do so by asking him to provide recent balance sheets. This was where the question of the client's morality became important. Occasionally balance sheets were provided which later proved to be highly misleading. The best surviving example of this occurred in 1878. In February of that year the Ulster Bank asked one customer to provide balance sheets to satisfy the bank that his position was sound. As a result, the bank was convinced that his credit was good. Two months later, he had failed. The bank made it absolutely plain that, in their view, he had taken advantage of their good nature in the intervening period:

> We cannot forget that for two months you left us to believe that your statement showing a surplus of about £12,000 over and above your liabilities was a fair and true statement, and that upon the faith of its

being so we were induced to let you go on with your trading with the result as it appears, that every item in your estate has been very seriously deteriorated.

We feel very strongly that we have not been fairly treated and . . . it will be best to wind up your estate in bankruptcy.[109]

What had actually happened during the two months between submission of balance sheets and failure was that the customer had accepted accommodation bills drawn by his brother-in-law (who was also in dire financial straits) to such an extent that when he, the customer, 'had almost stopped payment he protected his brother-in-law at the expense of the Bank'. Such business ethics appalled the Ulster Bank, which continued to complain, with good reason, that it had 'not been fairly dealt with'.[110] This customer had deceived the Ulster Bank, and had been able to do so because the bank believed his own statements of his financial position. There do not appear to have been many other cases like this, but even this example shows how a desperate client could exploit the bank for his own financial gain.

Evidence from the period between 1880 and 1914 points to a pragmatic approach to bank lending. Each case was assessed on its merits and, as noted earlier, took into account a range of considerations. It is sometimes argued that, as far as British banking was concerned, the City of Glasgow Bank failure marks a watershed in the development of the system by convincing bankers that the risks involved in long term industrial finance were too great. W. P. Kennedy, the most forceful exponent of this view, has suggested that in the mid-nineteenth century long-term bank lending was common and that British banks played a role comparable to that of the German Great Banks at the end of that century. However, his conclusion is that after 1878 'no longer would banks become willingly involved in the long term financing of industry'.[111] As far as the Belfast banks and indeed the Provincial were concerned, there is no evidence that 1878 marks a turning point in the history of bank lending. Certainly the later 1870s saw a contraction of bank credit, but this was primarily the result of both industrial and agricultural depression and the policy pursued in this downturn was the same as in previous and subsequent downturns. The City of Glasgow Bank failure did not result in any abrupt reversal or fundamental reappraisal of bank lending, either in the short or long run.

Lending was, of course, an important but not the only aspect of

Into the new century

banking business. It remains for us briefly to consider the broader changes in Irish banking down to 1914.

5.4 Irish banking before 1914

So far in this chapter we have commented on the nature of inter-bank relations, on the bank's reactions to political developments and on some aspects of lending. An indication of the general structure of Irish banking is provided in Table 37. Throughout this period the Bank of Ireland retained its position as Ireland's premier bank with the National in second place, although both experienced some decline (4·1 per cent and 6·6 per cent respectively) in their share of deposits between 1886 and 1912. The data also throw some light on the growth of the Munster and Leinster Bank which had developed into a considerable force in Irish banking on the eve of the First World War. Further, the rather precarious state of the Hibernian in the mid-1880s is apparent, particularly its virtually non-existent reserves. The rapid expansion of the Hibernian's branch network, which caused the Belfast banks some problems was also clearly a great strain on the Hibernian itself, and indeed the bank passed its dividend in 1881.[112] Recovery was slow and erratic and even by 1912 it paid a mere six per cent dividend – well below that of other Irish banks.

To contemporaries one of the most obvious features of Irish banking in the later nineteenth and early twentieth centuries was the disappointing performance of the Provincial. Third in terms of both deposits and total assets in the mid-1880s, the Provincial had fallen to fourth place by 1912. This decline contrasted strongly with the bank's innovative image in its early years. It has been suggested that the slow growth for the thirty years or so after 1860 meant that when branch expansion (mainly in the form of sub-branches and agencies) did eventually take place it was too late to make a significant contribution to regaining the bank's former position. Moreover it suffered more than most from competition from the Hibernian and the Munster and Leinster.[113] As for the Belfast banks, it was undoubtedly the Ulster which made most ground. Measured in terms of number of branches, deposits, total assets or profitability, the Ulster was clearly ahead of its two neighbours.

All Irish banks in this period experienced a decline in the ratio of advances to deposits. Indeed in all parts of the UK both advances and deposits increased in the last thirty years of the nineteenth

Table 37 Irish joint-stock banks, 1886 and 1912 (£ million)

Bank		Paid-up capital	Reserves	Notes in circulation	Deposits and credit balances	Advances	Investments	Cash	Total assets/ liabilities
Bank of	1886	2·769 (17·5)	1·191 (7·5)	2·423 (15·3)	9·446 (60·0)	5·921 (37·4)	8·413 (53·1)	1·402 (8·9)	15·830
Ireland	1912	2·769 (11·9)	0·932 (4·0)	3·005 (12·9)	16·377 (70·5)	10·064 (43·3)	9·732 (41·9)	3·305 (14·2)	23·235
Belfast	1886	0·4 (11·6)	0·346 (10·1)	0·412 (12·0)	2·270 (66·1)	2·273 (66·2)	0·667 (19·4)	0·446 (13·0)	3·435
	1912	0·5 (6·5)	0·450 (5·9)	0·566 (7·4)	6·046 (78·7)	4·714 (61·4)	1·470 (19·1)	1·421 (18·5)	7·678
Hibernian	1886	0·5 (23·5)	0·016 (0·7)	—	1·234 (58·2)	1·630 (76·8)	0·164 (7·7)	0·212 (10·0)	2·122
	1912	0·5 (10·7)	0·196 (4·2)	—	3·942 (84·5)	3·159 (67·7)	1·194 (25·6)	0·171 (3·6)	4·666
Munster and	1886	0·137 (23·5)	0·001 (1·7)	—	0·444 (76·3)	0·228 (39·2)	0·058 (10·0)	0·263 (45·2)	0·582
Leinster	1912	0·2 (3·0)	0·340 (5·1)	—	5·787 (87·2)	3·511 (52·9)	1·623 (24·5)	1·173 (17·7)	6·637
National	1886	1·5 (12·6)	0·304 (2·6)	1·201 (10·1)	8·764 (73·9)	7·561 (63·8)	1·608 (13·6)	2·313 (19·5)	11·852
	1912	1·5 (8·9)	0·440 (2·6)	1·254 (7·4)	13·321 (79·0)	10·033 (59·5)	2·211 (13·1)	4·101 (24·3)	16·862
Northern	1886	0·342 (11·0)	0·164 (5·3)	0·367 (11·8)	2·230 (71·8)	2·302 (74·1)	0·369 (11·9)	0·437 (14·1)	3·108
	1912	0·5 (7·3)	0·320 (4·7)	0·635 (9·3)	5·320 (77·6)	3·630 (53·0)	2·053 (29·9)	1·062 (15·5)	6·855
Provincial	1886	0·540 (10·5)	0·207 (4·0)	0·687 (13·4)	3·710 (72·1)	3·282 (63·8)	0·911 (17·7)	0·801 (15·6)	5·144
	1912	0·54 (7·2)	0·375 (5·0)	0·715 (9·5)	5·838 (77·7)	4·202 (55·9)	2·500 (33·3)	0·711 (9·5)	7·514
Royal	1886	0·3 (13·7)	0·234 (10·7)	—	1·621 (74·3)	1·312 (60·1)	0·558 (25·5)	0·282 (12·9)	2·182
	1912	0·3 (12·1)	0·205 (8·2)	—	1·902 (76·5)	1·383 (55·6)	0·893 (35·9)	0·180 (7·2)	2·485
Ulster	1886	0·4 (7·9)	0·465 (9·2)	0·551 (10·9)	3·583 (71·0)	3·517 (69·7)	0·907 (18·0)	0·565 (11·2)	5·043
	1912	0·5 (4·4)	0·7 (6·1)	1·055 (9·3)	8·972 (78·7)	6·968 (61·1)	2·878 (25·2)	1·556 (13·6)	11·402

Note Figures in parentheses represent the percentage of total assets/liabilities of each bank.
Source *The Economist Banking Supplements* (October 1886 and 1912).

Into the new century

century but neither in Ireland, Scotland nor in England and Wales did advances rise as fast as deposits.[114] Most banks did not distinguish between various types of advance in their published balance sheets. Those that did distinguish loans and overdrafts from discounts invariably show that discount business was being rapidly overshadowed by other types of lending. For example, in the cases of the Royal, the National and the Munster and Leinster, loans and overdrafts began to exceed discounts in the early 1890s and the gap widened steadily before 1914,[115] reflecting the increasing popularity of the overdraft as a method of advance.

For the Belfast banks, which did not distinguish discounts from other types of lending, total advances consistently exceeded deposits before the early 1880s; thereafter the reverse was true. It is clear, however, that both advances and deposits rose on trend before 1914 but the rate of increase of the latter exceeded the former. Rapid expansion of branch systems, in addition to gathering deposits, also increased lending opportunities, but the evidence suggests that the banks found it impossible to match lending with soaring deposit liabilities. This is brought out most clearly in the Ulster Bank correspondence. This bank began to speak of 'surplus funds' in the late 1870s. In the 1880s the notion of surplus funds reappears on several occasions. In 1885, for example, the Ulster Bank wrote to its London agents, the London and Westminster Bank, that 'it is of importance to us to find employment for our surplus funds . . . we have £300,000 in London just now and there is no outlet in the way of loans or more legitimate business'.[116] The inability of the Ulster Bank to employ locally all its deposits after 1880 led to the bank to seek the advice of the London and Westminster Bank as to how these funds might be invested in securities outside Ireland. Irish banks made most of their investments through London, and most were in non-Irish stocks. The Dublin Stock Exchange had always been considered so small that sudden purchases or sales of large quantities of securities could not be made without causing unacceptably great increases or decreases in price.[117] This was obviously a crucial consideration for a bank wishing to convert its reserve fund into cash during a liquidity crisis. From the 1880s Irish banks looked to investments not simply as reserves but increasingly as an earning asset to help fill the gap between lending and deposits.

It has been established that the advances of most Irish banks were greater than their deposits until about 1880, and this generalisation holds even for banks such as the Munster which operated in the overwhelmingly agricultural south of Ireland.[118] This view runs counter to mainstream historiography which has generally given the banks very low marks for their contribution to the Irish economy. Representative of the conventional wisdom is Joseph Lee who claims that there was 'probably too much saving' in Ireland between 1850 and 1900, 'money being directed from consumption into deposits which the banks then transferred to England thus reducing consumption without increasing investment'.[119] This view will be evaluated more fully in the conclusion to the present study, but an examination of bank balance sheets and other records will show that Lee's view is both simplistic and wide of the mark. It might also be pointed out that in the later nineteenth century advances to deposits ratios in Irish banks were considerably higher than for banks in most regions of England and Wales.[120]

Finally it may be noted that the extension of branch networks before 1914 brought banking facilities to within reach of most people who wished to use them, although it was still not unknown to have to walk more than ten miles to the nearest branch in 1913. The total number of offices operating in each part of the United Kingdom in 1913 is shown in Table 38, while Table 39 offers a rough approximation of total offices in relation to population and square mileage in several countries. Counting accurately the number of bank offices is very difficult and drawing inferences from the total is equally problematic. However, assuming the approximate reliability of the figures, it would appear that the achievement of Irish banks in facilitating access to deposit and credit services was considerable, particularly when it is recalled that between 1876 and 1913 up to 250 bank offices were opened in Ireland in locations where there had previously been none.[121]

Into the new century

Table 38 *Bank offices in the United Kingdom in October 1913*

	Number of bank offices				
	Open daily	% of total	Not open daily	% of total	Total
England and Wales	5,342	77	1,631	23	6,973
Isle of Man	24	100	—	—	24
Scotland	1,222	98	34	2	1,256
Ireland	539	62	324	38	863
Total	7,127	—	1,989	—	9,116

Source. *Report on Agricultural Credit 1914*, p. 19.

Table 39 *Bank offices in 1912*

Country	Banking offices	Inhabitants per office	Square miles per office
England and Wales (including Isle of Man)	6,733	5,379	8·7
Scotland	1,235	3,854	24·6
Ireland	841	5,220	38·5
Total for UK	8,809	5,150	13·8
Canada	2,933	2,456	1,271·6
Australia	2,043	2,179	1,455·9
New Zealand	392	2,572	266·2
Union of South Africa	460	12,985	1,028·5
Argentine[a]	385	17,334	2,950·3
Belgium	260	28,809	43·7
Denmark	700	3,964	22·2
Finland	550	5,664	228·6
France	4,400	9,000	47·0
Germany	13,000	4,994	16·0
Holland	500	12,045	25·2
Italy	1,700	20,395	65·0
Norway	640	3,737	193·9
Sweden	650	8,496	265·9
Switzerland	900	4,158	17·7
USA	29,000	3,711	123·1

Note (a) In the case of these twelve non-empire countries savings banks are included where they were 'of a public character and authorised to invest their funds, in whole or in part, at their discretion'.

Source. *Report on Agricultural Credit 1914*, p. 20.

CONCLUSION

The aim of this study has been to throw new light on the growth and role of banks in nineteenth-century Ireland. This conclusion reviews the evidence presented in the light of the criteria used by contemporaries and employed by historians to judge the performance of the Irish banking system. Any historian of banking is faced with the task of selecting appropriate criteria by which the banks studied may be judged. No banking system can be taken out of its wider economic and social environment since, as S. G. Checkland has reminded us, 'banking structure and function evolve as part of a larger whole and performance can only be judged in terms of it'.[1] It seems most appropriate to review the history of the Belfast banks in terms of their stability, their contribution to the economy in which they operated and the extent to which they fulfilled the needs of their customers. There is, of course, an overlap between all of these.

Stability

Irish joint-stock banks were, with few exceptions, stable institutions. After the numerous failures of private banks in the five years or so after 1815, the legislative framework was altered and the vast majority of joint-stock banks founded as a result of these alterations was to survive. There were only three important failures: the Agricultural and Commercial Bank in 1840, the Tipperary Joint-Stock Bank in 1856 and the Munster Bank in 1885. The chronology and location of these failures was such that parts of the south of Ireland experienced periodic bank failure until very late in the nineteenth century. By contrast, the province of Ulster, with the partial exception of some branches of the Agricultural and Commercial Bank, was free from bank failure after 1820.

One problem here for the historian is that it is easier to analyse the causes of failure than to discover the reasons for stability. As far

Conclusion

as the banks based in Belfast in the nineteenth century were concerned, we can suggest a number of sources of stability. One of the most important was the spatial distribution of their branch networks. As a generalisation, it is possible to say that a bank with only one office which is heavily dependent for its well-being on the economic health of a single town is more vulnerable than a bank with branches scattered over a relatively wide area. Unitary banks were more vulnerable whether they were private or joint-stock concerns. Another valid generalisation is that banks with large regional or even national branch networks appeared much earlier in Ireland than they did in England and Wales. Both generalisations are relevant when the stability of Irish joint-stock banks is compared to that of joint-stock banks in England and Wales. In respect of the position in England and Wales in the 1840s, P. L. Cottrell has recently written that 'The new joint-stock banks were generally hardly distinguishable from the private country banks in terms of resources, management and branch networks. They were essentially local institutions and their frail fabric was a major contributive factor to the financial instability which continued to plague the economy until the 1870s.'[2] In England and Wales the average number of offices per joint-stock bank in 1861 was about six, whilst in Ireland it was about twenty; thirty years later the averages were, respectively, twenty-three and sixty-three.[3] These are summary figures, but they do give a helpful indication of the relatively large network of offices operated by each bank in Ireland. Branch systems were no guarantee against bank failure, as is witnessed by the cases of the Agricultural and Commercial, the Tipperary and the Munster Banks, nor did a strictly localised business such as that carried on by the Royal Bank in Dublin necessarily lead to failure. Yet it is difficult to avoid the conclusion that a province-wide or nation-wide network helped to prevent the effects of a localised 'run' from becoming serious, and hence it promoted stability.

The province of Ulster, in which most of the Belfast banks' branches were located, enabled these banks to establish well balanced branch systems from the 1830s, comprising branches in both predominantly agricultural and industrially developed areas. While it would not be wise to push the distinction between these too far, it is the case that the Belfast banks operated primarily in a region with a heterogeneous economic base of agriculture, industry and trade. Here again a comparison with England and Wales is relevant.

Nishimura has pointed out that very few banks in England and Wales had balanced systems in both agricultural and industrial areas until the 1890s[4] and so, as has been noted already, the local nature of banks was a factor in exposing them to local crises whether agricultural, industrial or commercial. It was argued earlier in this study that the diversified character of the Belfast banks' business helped to protect them on a number of occasions. For example, the prosperity of the linen industry helped to carry them through the difficult 'Famine years' of the later 1840s, and also through the agricultural depression of 1859–64. The Belfast banks never had a monopoly of banking in Ulster, but from the 1830s no other Irish bank could boast a branch system which was from the start so balanced as those based in Belfast.

If a balanced branch system tended to stabilise the Belfast banks, it also enabled them to gather deposits in rural areas and utilise them for lending in urban centres. Some data on the regional distribution of deposits and advances in Ulster in the mid-nineteenth century were given in Chapter Three. L. S. Pressnell, in his study of English country banks to the mid-1840s, remarked that there were 'but rare cases of firms having offices in 'saving' and 'investing' areas – a not unexpected result of the localisation of banking'.[5] This comment continues to be applicable to banking in England and Wales until well into the second half of the nineteenth century. The consequence was that the transfer of funds had to take place via the London discount market. The distribution of the Belfast banks' offices was such that the transfer of funds could take place within a unified framework. As J. T. Bristow told the *Select Committee on Banks of Issue* in 1875, the deposits of the Belfast banks were gathered 'chiefly' in agricultural districts, and 'our loans are made in the towns'.[6]

A balanced branch network, while tending to increase stability and facilitate the transfer of funds, was never a sufficient condition for stability. In the last analysis, the stability of a nineteenth-century bank of issue depended on the confidence of its noteholders and depositors, the trends in the economy it served and the skill with which it was managed. Confidence in the notes of the Belfast banks was seriously though only momentarily lacking on just one occasion, during the crisis of 1857. Similarly, although depositors sometimes made abnormal demands, these were infrequent and tended to be concentrated in the southern and western branches,

Conclusion

that is to say in areas where confidence in all banks was generally less than it was in the north-east. Moreover, although there were commercial crises in nineteenth century Belfast (at least until 1857–8), just as there were periods of agricultural depression in nineteenth-century Ulster, rarely did the two coincide.

On the question of managerial skill, it should be recalled that an important stabilising influence on the Belfast banks was their declared policy of raising dividends slowly so as to permit the accumulation of reserves. The banks had to call on these reserves only rarely. The largest call was that made by the Belfast Bank in 1873, after the fraud committed by two of its own staff. This call, of £125,000, was entirely unexpected, but the bank's ability to make it vindicated the wisdom of holding a large reserve fund. The point that is being made here is that the gradual accumulation of a reserve fund could prove to be a powerful stabilising factor in the event of a major unforeseen loss. On the question of management structure, the highly unusual structure of the Belfast banks was noted in Chapters One and Two. There is no doubt that a permanent board of directors and an elected committee of management comprising substantial shareholders (predominantly local businessmen) not only allowed directors to devote themselves full-time to all aspects of banking policy but also ensured that directors were kept fully and regularly informed by a well-placed group of businessmen about trends in the local economy, credit needs and creditworthiness. A flow of accurate information on such matters permitted the full-time directorate to make informed judgements, and the very existence of committees of management meant that links between banks and the wider business community would remain strong.

Given that the Belfast banks lent on a large scale, particularly in the north-east, the potential consequences of a failure of one or more of them would have been very grave indeed, but the fact that the banks were stable meant that there were no financial crises induced by bank failure. Indeed, a generally stable financial structure with the Belfast banks as the keystone was a substantial benefit to nineteenth-century Ulster.

Contribution to economic growth

Those acquainted with the economic historiography of Ireland in nineteenth century will not need reminding that banks have always been viewed in a generally poor light. The markedly revisionist character of recent research into many areas of Irish economic history has not yet reached the banks; and it would be fair to say that the standard conception of the role of Irish banks has not changed much for over half a century. The criticisms of Irish banks made by historians are similar to those made by many contemporaries during the nineteenth century. The charges that have been levelled against Irish banks may be briefly summarised and then examined in the light of the evidence available from those based in Belfast. The banks have been criticised for being 'conservative' and unwilling to finance industrial and commercial enterprise and for channelling their resources out of the country. In addition, it is sometimes suggested that the 'English-style' joint-stock banks were inappropriate institutions for Ireland and that the country really needed some kind of investment bank comparable to those which appeared in some states of continental Europe.

The gravity of these charges and the rather uncompromising language in which they have been framed might lead one to believe that they are based on a mass of unconflicting evidence. This is not the case because no published history of an Irish bank contains significant analysis of lending policies, and no history of an Irish business concern contains systematic discussion of its sources of capital and credit. More generally, the evidence that has been used by contemporaries and by historians has often been scanty. Better evidence would be needed for the charges to be declared proven.

Let us take the first criticism that the banks were 'conservative' and unwilling to finance industrial and commercial enterprise. This view was firmly held by George O'Brien,[7] and it has been reiterated by many subsequent writers.[8] But what is conservatism in banking terms? Presumably it relates to a bank which is willing to lend only on first-class collateral security and to one which would not allow unauthorised increases of credit beyond the limits agreed between itself and a customer. From the evidence available on the Belfast banks it is possible to show that while the banks preferred some kind of collateral, there were occasions when they were prepared to accept an entrepreneur's business acumen as sufficient security. Some examples of this were noted earlier in this study, and we can further illustrate the point by quoting a letter from the Ulster Bank head office to its branch manager in Dublin in 1885:

> It very often happens that an unsecured advance to a steady upright practical man with a moderate capital, is quite as safe as a secured

Conclusion

advance. It is for a manager in your position to discriminate such cases and not be bound in his dealings with the public by a hard and fast line that makes no allowance for special circumstances. It is no doubt a sound rule that security should be got for overdrafts, but no bank could prosper which allowed any such rule to dominate every application for an advance.

We fear that it may have been your too inflexible adhesion to such a rule that has kept up the absurd idea in Dublin that the Ulster Bank is not a lending bank. The fact of the matter is that common sense is better than any rule, and every rule must therefore in its application be made subservient to the dictates of common sense.[9]

This comment may be taken as fairly representative of the Belfast banks' lending policy. These banks were, collectively, averse to hard and fast rules on lending in the same way that they had little faith in the hard and fast rules embodied in the Bank Charter Act of 1844. Bank directors used their own discretion in determining lending policy and they encouraged managers to do the same.

The view of the directors was that each branch should pull its weight by contributing a fair share to the overall level of business. This might involve, as in the case of the Ulster Bank Dublin branch just quoted, encouraging a more liberal lending policy, but it might also involve the need to restrain managers from lending too much in relation to deposits. There was in fact no predetermined maximum ratio of advances to deposits permissible at any branch, rather this ratio was left to the discretion of managers. There were occasions, however, when directors felt justified in pointing out to a manager that the advances to deposits ratio at his branch had exceeded their wishes. For example, in 1896 the Belfast Bank wrote to its branches at Enniskillen and Belfast Markets commending managers for their 'zeal and general care exercised both as to bills and to advances'.[10] The directors went on to point out, however, that while they regarded no single advance as unsafe, the gross total of accommodation bore a 'very undue relation' to the resources of the branch in question. In the directors' opinion, managers at these two branches should, 'without any serious or sudden change of policy . . . arrange to place your branch on a proper relative footing'.

The impression given by the surviving bank records is that the Belfast banks, so far from operating a rigidly conservative lending regime, did all that they reasonably could to accommodate their customers. A willingness to lend only on entrepreneurial ability is not a hallmark of a conservative bank; nor for that matter is a willingness to let a client's accommodation exceed limits. Some instances of the latter were cited in Chapters Four and Five. Theoretically a bank could take steps to restrict accommodation if or when accommodation, whether bills or overdrafts, exceeded an agreed limit. In practice, limits were exceeded in many instances, and in such cases bankers had to trust their own judgement. The advice of the Northern Bank directors to their managers in 1888 was that

> . . . when a limit is arranged it should not be exceeded unless for what may appear to be an urgent reason of a temporary character and that reason should at once be fully explained by letter. If a limit is found insufficient the obvious course is to apply for extended accommodation. It is sometimes difficult to restrain a customer but to know how to do it properly is exactly one of those things that test a manager's competency.[11]

The Ulster Bank advised its managers to the same effect in 1863.[12]

A number of possible reasons may be suggested as to why a bank permitted clients to exceed agreed limits of credit. One reason, as mentioned in the Northern Bank circular quoted above, was recognition of a client's temporary difficulties; another was fear of losing custom, because any client was at liberty to go to another bank. In the highly competitive environment of Irish banking, especially towards the end of the nineteenth century when branch managers of the Hibernian, the National and the Bank of Ireland were openly canvassing for custom, it was in the Belfast banks' own interest to operate with flexibility in order to maintain customer loyalty. With regard to discount lines, overdrafts limits and the question of security for advances, rules could be bent and conventions broken with a view to accommodating customers and preventing the transfer of accounts. It is this discretionary element in the policies of the Belfast banks which should warn us against an uncritical acceptance of the charge that they were rigid, inflexible, 'conservative' institutions.

The charge that Irish banks were conservative is usually made in general terms with an implication that they did not lend to industry and commerce. Of all the criticisms made of Irish banks this is the most serious and it is also the one with the longest pedigree. This criticism dates from the early 1820s when the Bank of Ireland came under fire for failing to grant cash credits, for refusing to move outside Dublin, and for the fact that most of its resources were lent

Conclusion

to the government. In the words of one pamphleteer of 1838, the Bank of Ireland was 'the vampire of national prosperity'.[13] Contemporaries continued to be critical of the Bank of Ireland throughout the nineteenth century, but the criticism was particularly acute between 1820 and 1845. During that period most of its privileges were abolished and this, together with the emergence of numerous joint-stock banks, tended to make critics less vociferous.

In fairness to the Bank of Ireland, its special position meant that it was necessarily obliged to lend a disproportionate share of its resources to the government; moreover until 1860 it was specifically prevented from lending on mortgage – a restriction which applied to no other Irish bank.[14] Furthermore critics of the Bank of Ireland usually forgot that this bank had stepped in more than once to assist other banks in times of severe pressure. It is also fair to point out that we still do not know very much about the lending policy of the Bank of Ireland for most of the nineteenth century. The Bank of Ireland was the last Irish bank to publish its balance sheet, which it did not do until 1885. At that date its advances and discounts were £6·43 million, while deposits and credit balances stood at £9·68 million.[15] The advances to deposits ratio (0·66) was well below that of the three Belfast banks in 1885, yet in absolute terms the Bank of Ireland was lending more than the Northern Bank and the Ulster Bank put together. When the full, as opposed to the official, history of the Bank of Ireland has been written, it may well be shown that its lending policy in the second half of the nineteenth century was far more positive than has hitherto been thought. Indeed, our discussion of the finance of Belfast shipbuilding showed that the Bank of Ireland was heavily involved in increasingly extensive lending to both Belfast shipbuilders before 1914, and that much of that credit was either unsecured or secured by directors' guarantee.

The Bank of Ireland may well have been forced to become more venturesome in its lending because of competition from other Irish joint-stock banks. There are glimpses of this in the records of the Belfast banks which, towards the end of the nineteenth century, found some of their customers being canvassed by Bank of Ireland managers who offered accommodation on highly competitive terms. It is impossible to say how typical such cases were, but the Belfast banks took competition from the Bank of Ireland very seriously.[16] Professor Lee has recently written that Irish banks were not 'hungry fighters',[17] but it remains true to say that they did have to fight not only for new custom, but also to hold on to their established customers, failure to do which could only result in loss of business. It is reasonable to suggest that the liberal lending policies of the Belfast banks forced the hand of the Bank of Ireland particularly in those towns where they coexisted. If this was so, it would be analogous to the position in Scotland where the relatively aggressive and liberal lending Glasgow-based joint-stock banks compelled their rather reserved Edinburgh-based chartered rivals to adopt a more sympathetic and positive approach to the requirements of industry.[18]

This study has sought to show some of the ways in which the Belfast banks actively pursued a flexible and extensive lending policy throughout the nineteenth century. They were, as their names suggest, primarily banks of Ulster and for Ulster. It would be strange indeed if these banks, which were locally owned, locally staffed and locally directed from the start, used their resources in a way which ignored the demands of the economy in which they operated. Historians have sometimes alleged that Irish bank deposits were 'idle' or 'sterile',[19] but evidence from the Belfast banks points to exactly the opposite conclusion. Not until the fourth quarter of the nineteenth century did the level of advances and discounts fall below that of deposits and credit balances, and, as has been explained in Chapter Five, total advances and discounts continued on a generally upward trend until the end of the century, although the *rate* of increase was slower than that of deposits and credit balances between 1880 and 1914. Thus to regard deposits as idle, sterile or channelled out of the country is substantially wide of the mark.

Some observers in the second half of the nineteenth century criticised all Irish banks for an unwillingness to lend, but amongst them some drew a distinction between the lending policies of the Belfast banks and other Irish banks. Those who drew this distinction compared the flexible lending policies of, and contribution to the economy made by, the Belfast banks favourably with banks which operated primarily in the south of Ireland. It became fashionable to eulogise the Belfast banks in the same way that Scottish banks were consistently praised for their major contribution to the economic development of Scotland. It is not clear when the distinction between the Belfast banks and other Irish banks began to be made, but it may have been in the early 1860s when Cornelius

Conclusion

Dennehy, in one of a series of letters to the *Irish Times,* paid explicit tribute to the Belfast, the Northern and the Ulster Bank, and went on '. . . the banking system of the North is totally different from that of other parts of Ireland, and . . . until we get the same system of banking that prevails in the North and in Scotland introduced into the other parts of the country, we can have no manufactures. . .'[20] Dennehy was especially critical not only of the Bank of Ireland, but of the Provincial Bank and the National Bank as well. The last two, he argued, tended to be out of touch with Irish requirements because their boards of directors sat in London. His proposal was for a large new national bank, possibly with the Hibernian and the Royal Banks forming the nucleus, which would adopt 'the Scottish system of banking'. By this he meant payment of interest on deposits, cash credits, branches in every Irish town 'no matter how small the population'. Above all such a bank had to be managed and directed by Irishmen.

The distinction between the Belfast banks and other Irish banks was voiced again in evidence before the *Select Committee on Irish Industries* in 1885.[21] By this date, however, criticisms of the Provincial and the National Bank had become more vocal. The main criticism was that because their directors were London-based, all applications for accommodation over a certain limit had to be sent to London for approval, but these were often refused because of the board's ignorance of the requirements and circumstances of potential Irish borrowers.[22] By 1885 in fact, some were actively suggesting the creation of a European-style investment bank.[23]

At this point the distinction between the Belfast banks and other Irish banks becomes somewhat problematic because, as has recently been shown, banks which operated primarily in the south of Ireland were lending on a far more extensive scale than has hitherto been thought,[24] and it is still too early to make valid distinctions between banks. While it is certainly true that there were fairly tight restrictions on the ability of the Provincial's branch managers to grant accommodation without the consent of head office it is inaccurate to suggest that the Provincial's directors took decisions without any background information on the potential borrower's proposal. In fact each such proposal was sent, with the manager's recommendation, to Dublin where it was scrutinised by the Dublin-based Superintendent of Branches and then forwarded to London with a further recommendation. The Provincial's directors' minutes strongly suggest that recommendations by managers and the superintendent were rarely rejected by the directors and for this reason it is valid to argue that *effective* lending decisions were in fact made in Ireland.

It is conceivable that the rather jaundiced view of Irish banks which was put forward by some witnesses before the *Select Committee on Irish Industries* in 1885 reflected the fact that this committee sat during a period when Irish agriculture and industry were generally depressed. The agricultural depression of the late 1870s and early 1880s caused Irish banks to restrict credit and, as we have seen, the contemporaneous difficulties of industry, even in the north-east, led to a sustained attempt to cut back lending to many customers. The criticism that Irish banks pursued a generally restrictive lending policy may have been true in 1885, but if the *Select Committee on Irish Industries* had sat and taken evidence ten or fifteen years before this particular criticism would in all probability have been far more muted. Without evidence from the southern banks it would be rash to take this hypothesis further, but one informed commentator from County Kildare argued in 1887 that the onset of agricultural depression in 1877 led the Munster Bank to order its managers to restrict agricultural credit, but to do so gradually. He went on:

> This step marked the virtual collapse of the long period of inflated credit all over the country; for I have reason to believe that most if not all the Irish banks adopted the same policy about the same time, and that their efforts to prevent new advances being made, and to call in advances except where the security was undoubted, became more stringent from time to time; and by the middle of 1879 the banks were practically in line with individual creditors in endeavouring to call in a large proportion of their advances in all doubtful cases.[25]

This comment, which accords well with the policy pursued by the Northern Bank in the late 1870s and early 1880s, lends some support to our view that this was not the most favourable time for witnesses before a parliamentary enquiry to give a generous picture of Irish bank lending.

It is also worth pointing out that very few parliamentary enquiries in nineteenth century Ireland took evidence from both bankers and 'the general public'; it was usually from one or the other. This, together with the fact that parliamentary enquiries very often took place after major crises or during depressions (for example the

Conclusion

enquiries on promissory notes (1826–7), on joint-stock banks (1837–8 and 1841), on commercial distress (1847–8), on the Bank Acts (1857–8) and on Irish industries (1884–5)) seriously limits our ability to build up a balanced picture of long-term banking practice on the basis of published evidence.

The view that a European-style investment bank would have been more appropriate to the Irish economy is a counterfactual proposition which is in the end unanswerable. Professor Lee has recently suggested that investment banks 'provided a frequent continental solution to the problem of economic retardation' and that 'English-style' joint-stock banks were unsuited to Irish requirements.[26] It would, however, be true to say that recent research has tended to play down the significance of investment banks in European industrialisation,[27] and has shown convincingly that English joint-stock banks did not lend purely on a short-term basis.[28]

Crédit Mobilier banks made their most important contributions where capital goods industries needed large doses of investment, where opportunities for industrial investment were abundant, the supply of capital limited or difficult to mobilise, and where the economy was of high potential in terms of natural resources.[29] In Germany and Belgium such banks did play major roles, but when they were established in several other countries they could not, by themselves, produce economic miracles.[30] One cannot seriously compare the economic (especially the industrial) potential of Ireland with that of Belgium and Germany: Limerick is not Liège, nor Shannon Darmstadt. In Ireland, as in other parts of the United Kingdom, the largest capital projects proceeded without investment banks. Irish railways were constructed with private and public funds, and the ability of an Irish investment bank to create viable integrated steel mills, or chemical works or coal mines, was never tested.

In an implicit comparison between Irish banks and investment banks, G. Ó. Tuathaigh has remarked that the economic role of the former was 'essentially a passive one; that is they did not seek out investment opportunities, they waited for customers to come to them'.[31] But on this criterion all banks in the UK were passive, and a passive role need not be a negative role. Moreover, it has yet to be proved that a credit system which is demand-led is necessarily inferior to one which is supply-led. In Germany, for example, there were complaints that investment banks sometimes foisted 'credit upon firms in too large a volume and at inopportune times'.[32]

The use of bank funds depends upon the nature of liabilities. Almost all of the Belfast banks' deposits were payable on demand or at very short notice and for this reason overdrafts were recallable at short notice. It has been shown, however, that overdrafts often ran on from year to year and sometimes from decade to decade. It would appear that the Belfast banks rarely made explicitly long-term loans, but the overdraft was a more flexible instrument of credit than the fixed-period loan. Similarly, bills could be renewed to extend the period of credit.

It is also important to remember that many investment banks were 'mixed' in the sense that their direct investment business was combined with other functions[33] which Irish joint-stock banks had long performed: deposit-taking, discounting and short-term lending. Furthermore the illiquidity of investment banks produced some major failures in nineteenth-century Europe. The most recent writer on industrial finance in this period concluded by saying that English banks may have contributed just as much to economic growth by operating lending policies which 'did not lead to financial crisis as the German banks did by facilitating industrial capital formation and the export of manufactures'.[34] The same comment may well be appropriate for the Belfast banks.

Within the United Kingdom before 1914 it has always been the Scottish banks which have received most praise for their contribution to economic growth. The Belfast banks were in fact closely and explicitly modelled on those in Scotland. The ease with which financial technology can be imitated and adapted has often been stressed[35] and there was undoubtedly such a transfer of techniques (and trained personnel) from Scotland to Ireland during the 1820s and after. The economic links between the north-east of Ireland and Scotland were always close and as far as Ireland was concerned the ability to import financial technology and successfully to adapt it to a new environment meant that savers and investors were offered a wide range of flexible banking services from the earliest days of joint-stock banking.

Customer satisfaction

The extent to which the Belfast banks fulfilled the needs of their customers has already been partially evaluated in terms of their

Conclusion

stability and lending, but we can go further and point to other, related, contributions. The power of note issue was especially important in the first half of the nineteenth century in three ways: it promoted the use of an economical and portable currency in a region which was short of coin, it lowered discount rates and boosted bank profits. Moreover the power of issue enabled the banks to operate country agencies which (for the Northern and the Belfast Bank) laid the basis of a branch network. One of the conclusions of Cameron's collection of detailed case studies of *Banking in the Early Stages of Industrialisation* is that where a banking system is at a rudimentary stage of development the power of note issue is a most effective way 'both of eliciting a rapid growth in the number of banks and of habituating the public to the utilisation of financial intermediaries'.[36] Our evidence firmly supports this argument. For the customer, branches were superior to agencies because they provided deposit and overdraft facilities. It was suggested in Chapter Two that branches were opened initially in response to competition from the Provincial Bank, but once the nucleus of the branch networks had been formed all the Belfast banks went on to expand from their north-eastern base and open branches well beyond the six counties of the north-east.

It remains for us to ask whether the joint agreement signed by the Belfast banks in 1839 militated against customer satisfaction by reducing competition. Certainly the Belfast banks did not deviate from their agreement, and at no time after 1839 was there significant price competition between them. However, the agreement was modified on several occasions before 1914 in response to competition from other banks (notably the National and the Hibernian) and it was varied explicitly to afford the customers of the Belfast banks the same terms as those offered by others. If the agreement had not been adapted in this way, it would certainly have led to a collective decline in the Belfast banks' competitiveness, but because adjustments took place, there is no reason to suppose that the agreement had a detrimental effect on customer satisfaction.

This study has not asked some questions and it has not fully answered many more. There is still a very long way to go before the role of banks in nineteenth century Ireland is understood, but it has here been shown that many of the criticisms made of Irish banks were never self-evidently true and need to be reappraised. More particularly, this study claims some relevance for the economic historiography of the north-east of Ireland. This is not the place to reiterate the conventional explanations for the industrialisation of Belfast; suffice it to say that very little if any mention is made of the banks. Most writers assert that the quality of entrepreneurship in Belfast was in some way oustanding.[37] Such a view would have greater persuasiveness if we knew anything quantifiable about the 'quality of businessmen', but we do not. The study of Belfast entrepreneurship has not yet gone beyond listing the atypical successful 'giants', which is clearly not enough.[38] More importantly, the economic historian cannot separate banking from entrepreneurship in general; all entrepreneurs, however brilliant, need finance.

If and when business history becomes fashionable in Ireland, historians will be better placed to answer those basic questions on which a fair amount has been written but of which little is known. Hopefully this book has taken a modest step in that direction.

NOTES

Introduction

1 R. Floud and D. McCloskey eds., *The Economic History of Britain Since 1700*, 2 vols., Cambridge, 1981; Peter Mathias and M. M. Postan eds., *The Cambridge Economic History of Europe*, VII Part 1, Cambridge, 1978.

2 G. L. Barrow, *The Emergence of the Irish Banking System 1820–45*, Dublin, 1974; F. G. Hall, *History of the Bank of Ireland*, Dublin and Oxford, 1946; Noel Simpson, *The Belfast Bank 1827–1970*, Belfast 1975.

3 Rondo Cameron ed., *Banking in the Early Stages of Industrialisation*, Oxford, 1967; *Banking and Economic Development*, Oxford 1972.

4 C. P. Kindleberger, *A Financial History of Western Europe*, London, 1984.

5 H. D. Inglis, *A Journey Throughout Ireland During the Spring, Summer and Autumn of 1834*, London, 1838, p. 251.

6 *Belfast and its environs*, 1842, p. 2, cited in R. B. McDowell, 'Ireland on the eve of the Famine', in R. D. Edwards and T. D. Williams eds., *The Great Famine*, Dublin, 1956, p. 15.

7 *Hall's Ireland. Mr and Mrs Hall's Tour of 1840*, reprinted London, 1984, p. 342.

8 L. A. Clarkson, 'Population change and urbanisation' in Liam Kennedy and Philip Ollerenshaw eds., *An Economic History of Ulster 1820–1939*, Manchester, 1985, pp. 138–9.

9 E. R. R. Green, 'The beginnings of industrial revolution' in T. W. Moody and J. C. Beckett eds., *Ulster Since 1800*, London, 1954, p. 28.

10 David Dickson, 'The place of Dublin in the eighteenth-century Irish economy', in T. M. Devine and David Dickson eds., *Ireland and Scotland 1600–1850: Parallels and Contrasts in Economic and Social Development*, Edinburgh, 1983, p. 183.

11 N. E. Gamble, 'The business community and trade of Belfast 1767–1800', *Irish Economic and Social History*, VII, 1980, pp. 93–4.

12 Philip Ollerenshaw, 'Industry 1820–1914' in Kennedy and Ollerenshaw eds., *Economic History of Ulster*, pp. 62–5.

13 L. M. Cullen, 'Landlords, bankers and merchants: the early Irish banking world, 1700–1820', *Hermathena*, 135, 1982–3, esp. pp. 31, 33.

Notes to pp. 4–7

14   S. C. *of the House of Lords on Promissory Notes 1826,* BPP 1826-7, VI, p. 28, evidence of J. H. Houston; J. J. Monaghan, *The Social and Economic History of Belfast 1801–25,* unpublished PhD thesis, The Queen's University of Belfast, 1940, p. 221.

15   W. A. Maguire, *The Downshire Estates in Ireland 1801–1845,* Oxford, 1972, pp. 101–2.

Chapter One

1   The most important contributions focus on Lancashire and West Yorkshire. See in particular, B. L. Anderson, 'The attorney and the early capital market in Lancashire', in F. Crouzet ed., *Capital Formation in the Industrial Revolution,* London, 1972, and M. Miles, 'The money market in the early Industrial Revolution: the evidence from West Riding attorneys *c.* 1750–1800', *Business History,* XXIII, 1981.

2   *Pigot's Directory,* 1824, p. 349, lists two Belfast attorneys with offices in Belfast and Dublin, and the Belfast newspapers of the 1820s show several more.

3   *Belfast Newsletter,* 10 December 1822. This and the following six references cite only a few examples, which could be multiplied dozens of times.

4   *Ibid.,* 1 April 1825.

5   *Ibid.,* 5 October 1821.

6   *Ibid.,* 15 June, 17 July 1824, 11 February, 18 May 1825.

7   *Ibid.,* 29 March, 2 September, 18 May 1827.

8   *Ibid.,* 21 January, 8 November, 9 May 1826.

9   *Ibid.,* 23 April 1822, 1 June 1824.

10   J. J. Monaghan, *The Social and Economic History of Belfast 1801–25,* Unpublished PhD thesis, The Queen's University of Belfast, 1940, p. 221.

11   29 Geo. II, c. 16 (Ire.).

12   33 Geo. II, c. 14 (Ire.).

13   21 and 22 Geo. III, c. 16 (Ire.); F. G. Hall, *History of the Bank of Ireland,* Dublin and Oxford, 1949, pp. 30 ff.; G. L. Barrow, *The Emergence of the Irish Banking System 1820–45,* Dublin, 1974, pp. 2–3.

14   Monaghan, *Belfast,* p. 221.

15   For a lucid discussion of many aspects of Irish monetary history during the restriction period see F. W. Fetter ed., *The Irish Pound 1797–1826,* London, 1955, esp. pp. 9–58; George O'Brien, 'The last years of the Irish currency', *Economic History,* II, 1927, pp. 249 ff.

16   Hall, *Bank of Ireland,* pp. 119–20; Barrow, *Emergence,* p. 208.

17   Neither of these are noted by Barrow or Hall. There are notices of creditors meetings for the Newry bank in *Belfast Newsletter* 7 June, 13 August 1822. Both of these banks seem to have failed around 1816. See Charles MacCarthy Tenison, 'The old provincial private bankers', *Journal*

of the Institute of Bankers of Ireland, XI, 1909, p. 10; *ibid.,* XII, 1910, p. 8.

18   Edward Wakefield, *An Account of Ireland Statistical and Political,* II, London, 1812, pp. 177–8.

19   F. W. Fetter, 'Legal tender during the English and Irish bank restrictions', *Journal of Political Economy,* 58, 1950, pp. 248–9.

20   Wakefield, *Account of Ireland,* p. 168.

21   *Lords' S.C. on promissory notes 1826,* p. 25.

22   Barrow, *Emergence,* p. 32.

23   *L'Estrange and Brett Papers,* PRONI D. 1905/2/207B. I am grateful to Ken Greer of Queen's University Belfast for this reference.

24   C. W. Munn, *The Scottish Provincial Banking Companies 1747–1864,* Edinburgh, 1981, pp. 152–63.

25   Hall, *Bank of Ireland,* p. 119; *Private and Joint Stock Banks Registered in Ireland 1820–44,* BPP 1844, XXXII, p. 445.

26   L. S. Pressnell, *Country Banking in the Industrial Revolution,* Oxford, 1956, p. 6.

27   Sir John Clapham, *The Bank of England 1797–1914,* Cambridge, 1944, pp. 1–2.

28   Hall, *Bank of Ireland,* pp. 127–32; Barrow, *Emergence,* pp. 17–23.

29   Marquis of Lansdowne in Hansard's Parliamentary Debates, 2nd series, 1, 2 June 1820, cols. 799–800.

30   Hall, *Bank of Ireland,* pp. 131–2.

31   See C. W. Munn, 'The emergence of central banking in Ireland: The Bank of Ireland 1814–1850', *Irish Economic and Social History,* X, 1983, pp. 19–32.

32   *Belfast Newsletter,* 16, 20, 23 June 1820. The issue of 23 June contains manifestos from merchants and traders in Dundalk, Newry and Coleraine as well as Belfast.

33   *Hansard's Parliamentary Debates,* 2nd series, XII, 15 March 1825. cols. 1040–1.

34   1 and 2 Geo. IV, c. 72.

35   The petition was reprinted in *Belfast Newsletter,* 6 April 1824. See also *Northern Whig,* 1, 8 April 1824.

36   *Hansard's Parliamentary Debates,* 2nd series, X, 12 March 1824.

37   5 Geo. IV, c. 73.

38   Northern Banking Company Deed of Co-partnership, PRONI T. 1503, no. 2.

39   Conrad Gill, *The Rise of the Irish Linen Industry,* Oxford, 1925, pp. 315–16. Gill mistakenly says that the legal changes of the early 1820s permitted the formation of banks with limited liability, but this was not permitted until 1858, and not adopted by the Belfast banks until the early 1880s.

40   *List of Proprietors of the Northern Banking Company,* Belfast, 24 September 1824. Three calls, totalling £25 British, were made in 1825.

Apart from £5 per share taken from profits in 1839, there were no more additions to capital account until the 1860s.

41 B. L. Anderson and P. L. Cottrell, 'Another Victorian capital market: a study of banking and bank investors on Merseyside', *Economic History* Review, XXVIII, 1975, p. 599.

42 *Northern Bank Deed of Co-partnership,* clause IX. These four directors were joined by James Bristow of the Belfast Bank who became the first elected director in 1828 at a salary of £500: NBCM 25 August 1828.

43 *Ibid.,* clause VIII.

44 See, for example, C. W. Munn, *The Scottish Provincial Banking Companies 1747–1864,* ch. 7: M. Collins and P. Hudson, 'Provincial bank lending; Yorkshire and Merseyside 1825–60', *University of Leeds School of Economic Studies Discussion Paper No. 51,* 1977, Table 2.

45 J. W. Gilbart, *Treatise on Banking,* 1, 1849, p. 189.

46 S. D. Chapman, 'Financial restraints on the growth of firms in the cotton industry 1790–1850', *Economic History Review,* XXXII, 1979, p. 59.

47 *S.C. on the Bank Acts 1858,* QQ. 5214–15.

48 *Northern Bank Deed of Co-partnership,* clause XIII; NBCM 24 September 1835. After 1835, the chairmanship of the committee was held by the person with the largest number of proprietors' votes; i.e. the chairmanship election was part of the annual committee election. The directors decided on this procedure for two reasons. First, a separate election for a chairman distinct from the committee 'would subject them to the solicitations of members of the Proprietary Body for their influential votes, and as all could not be successful the disappointed might relax in their active exertions in favour of the Bank which would be attended with injury to its profits'. The second reason was that the ten years of the existence of the bank had persuaded the directors that the chairmanship of the committee was not a more onerous office than ordinary membership, and so no distinction 'ought to exist save the honour attached to the office'.

49 *Northern Bank Deed of Co-partnership,* clause XIV.

50 *Ibid.,* clause XXXIII.

51 S. G. Checkland, *Scottish Banking; A History 1695–1973,* London, 1975, p. 63.

52 *Commons S.C. on promissory notes 1826,* p. 247.

53 NBCM, 8 October 1827.

54 According to Wakefield some of the private banks in Ireland paid interest on deposits during the restriction period, although he did not name them: Wakefield, *Account of Ireland,* p. 175. In 1826, it was not regarded as 'respectable' for any Dublin banker to pay such interest: *Commons S.C. on promissory notes 1826,* p. 82, evidence of James Robinson Pim. However, this position soon changed and by the mid-1830s both the Dublin-based joint stock banks (the Hibernian and the Royal) paid

Notes to pp. 15–18

interest: *S.C. on Joint Stock Banks 1837*, BPP 1837, XIV, Appendix I, nos. 57 and 97.

55 *Commons S.C. on promissory notes 1826*, p. 248.
56 NBCM, 1 November 1824.
57 NBCM, 3 December 1827, 7 November 1831.
58 *Lords S.C. on promissory notes 1826*, p. 14.
59 NBCM 7 March 1825, 22 September 1834, 21 May 1855. A bank agency in Ulster was a much sought after position attracting applications from a 'great number' of candidates: *Commons S.C. on promissory notes 1826*, p. 107.
60 Northern Bank *Annual Report* 1825. According to J. N. Simpson, James Orr, the Senior Director of the Northern, had made a 'lengthy and detailed study' of Scottish banking before the bank became a joint-stock concern: J. N. Simpson, *The Belfast Bank 1827–1970*, Belfast, 1975, p. 20.
61 6 Geo. IV, C. 42.
62 Thomas Joplin, *An Essay on the General Principles and Present Practice of Banking in England and Scotland, with supplementary observations on the steps proper to form a public bank and the system on which its accounts ought to be kept*, 5th edition, London, 1826, *passim*. Joplin's use of the term 'joint-stock' is a loose one which really meant that banks in Scotland generally had more than six partners.
63 James Marshall, *Report to the Directors of the Provincial Bank of Ireland Suggesting a Plan for Commencing and Conducting the Business of Said Bank*, London, 1825, esp. pp. 16–28.
64 *Prospectus of the Provincial Bank of Ireland*, reprinted in Joplin, *Essay*, p. 116.
65 *S.C. on Joint Stock Banks 1837*, Q. 4320, evidence of James Marshall.
66 *Commons S.C. on promissory notes 1826*, p. 90, evidence of James Marshall, who told the same committee (p. 95) that Provincial Bank managers had no power to discount bills with more than three months to run.
67 Checkland, *Scottish Banking*, pp. 393 ff.; E. T. Nevin and E. W. Davis, *The London Clearing Banks*, London, 1970, pp. 63–4; R. S. Sayers, *Lloyds Bank in the History of English Banking*, Oxford, 1957, pp. 62–4.
68 Joplin, *Essay*, p. 82; C. W. Munn 'The coming of joint-stock banking in Scotland and Ireland c. 1820–1845', in T. M. Devine and David Dickson, eds., *Scotland and Ireland*, Edinburgh, 1983, p. 211.
69 *Report of the Committee of the Loyal National Repeal Association . . . (on) Joint Stock Banking in Ireland*, 1845, pp. 27–8; George O'Brien, *The Economic History of Ireland from the Union to the Famine*, London, 1921; reprinted Clifton, New Jersey, 1972, p. 539.
70 *Northern Whig*, 20 January 1825: 'The present state of banking in Ireland', *Bankers' Magazine*, I, 1844, p. 127.

Notes to pp. 19–22

71 Hall, *Bank of Ireland*, p. 173.

72 *Dublin Evening Post* quoted in *Northern Whig*, 20 January 1825. Articles in the *Dublin Evening Post* critical of the Bank of Ireland were given full coverage in the Belfast press. See especially *Belfast Newsletter*, 25 January 1825.

73 Hall, *Bank of Ireland*, p. 174. Throughout the nineteenth century, the Bank of Ireland designated its managers 'agents'. We will refer to them as 'managers' so as to avoid a confusion with the part-time agencies of the Belfast banks.

74 Hall, *Bank of Ireland*, pp. 174–5, 185.

75 *Ibid.*, p. 181; The Belfast branch opened on 1 August 1825 in temporary offices in Callendar Street: *Northern Whig*, 11 August 1825. The office was moved to Donegall Place in January 1826: *Belfast Newsletter*, 3 January 1826.

76 Hall, *Bank of Ireland*, pp. 189, 241–3. Overdrafts 'for a few days' were granted from the mid-1830s, but it was not until 1855 that the directors gave official sanction to this type of lending.

77 *S.C. on Joint Stock Banks 1837*, Q. 4333.

78 *Ibid.*, Appendix I, no. 85. See Chapter Two for details of the Provincial Bank's branch expansion in Ulster.

79 *Belfast Newsletter*, 15 April 1825. The other towns were Cork, Clonmel, Derry, Galway, Limerick, Newry, Sligo and Waterford.

80 Both the managers and local directors were appointed at the end of 1825, but the branch did not open until March 1826; *Belfast Newsletter*, 20 December 1825; *Belfast Commercial Chronicle*, 20 February 1826; *Northern Whig*, 23 February 1826. Sloane was 'solicited' to become a local director because of his 'very great experience and knowledge of banking and high respectability': *S.C. on Joint Stock Banks 1837*, Q. 4340, evidence of James Marshall.

81 *Commons S.C. on promissory notes 1826*, p. 253, evidence of Pierce Mahony, solicitor to the Provincial Bank of Ireland.

82 NBCM, 21 November 1825.

83 *Ibid.*, 19 December 1825.

84 *Ibid.*, 10, 24 October 1825.

85 *Ibid.*, 30 January 1826.

86 Imitation of the notes of a successful bank by another occurred in 1837 when the Provident Bank of Ireland issued notes which closely resembled those of the Provincial. *S.C. on Joint Stock Banks 1837*, Q. 629, evidence of George Mathews, Secretary of the Loan Fund Board. It may well be that the promoters of the Provident Bank chose this title in imitation of the Provincial Bank.

87 NBCM, 10 October 1826.

88 *Ibid.*, 23 October 1826.

89 There is a concise but comprehensive survey of the background to,

Notes to pp. 22–25

and course of the crisis of 1825–6 in E. V. Morgan, *The Theory and Practice of Central Banking 1797–1913*, Cambridge, 1943, ch.4.

90   Sir John Clapham, *The Bank of England 1797–1914*, p. 98.

91   Morgan, *Central Banking*, p. 83; Checkland, *Scottish Banking*, p. 407. According to Checkland there were only three bank failures in Scotland, 'all minor'. As Kindleberger has pointed out, the ratio of bank failures to total banks was not very different, but it was the large absolute number of bank failures in England and Wales compared with Scotland that made 'a lasting impression'. C. P. Kindleberger, *A Financial History of Western Europe*, London, 1984, p. 83.

92   Clapham, *Bank of England*, pp. 99 ff.

93   As late as 23 December 1825 the *Belfast Newsletter* was 'truly happy' that the crisis was confined to England, and noted that Ireland had been quite free 'from the evil of inordinate speculation'. By the following May, however, the depression was widely noted: *ibid.*, 12 May, 23 June 1826.

94   *Northern Whig*, 11, 18 May 1826.

95   Northern Bank *Annual Report*, 1826.

96   7 Geo. IV, c. 46.

97   E. V. Morgan, *Central Banking*, ch. 4; Checkland, *Scottish Banking*, p. 318.

98   7 Geo. IV, c. 6.

99   *Commons S.C. on promissory notes 1826* and *Lords S.C. on promissory notes 1826*, passim.

100   J. H. Clapham, *An Economic History of Modern Britain*, I, 2nd edition, Cambridge, 1930, pp. 266–9; W. Smart, *Economic Annals of the Nineteenth Century 1821–30*, London, 1917, ch. XXXI, esp. pp. 339, 352.

101   See, for example, Andrew Crockett, *Money: Theory, Policy and Institutions*, London, 1973, pp. 10–13.

102   *Commons S.C. on promissory notes 1826*, p. 76.

103   *Ibid., Lords*, p. 26.

104   *Belfast Commercial Chronicle*, 6 March 1826.

105   *Commons S.C. on promissory notes 1826*, p. 243, evidence of Leonard Dobbin. Dobbin told the Lords Committee that country people could trace a forgery better since they put the name of the merchant from whom they received it on the back of the note: *Lords S.C.*, p. 12.

106   Letter from 'A Bleacher', *Belfast Commercial Chronicle*, 6 March 1826.

107   *Commons S.C. on promissory notes 1826*, pp. 103–4, evidence of J. H. Houston; *Lords S.C.*, p. 22.

108   *Commons S.C. on promissory notes 1826*, p. 77.

109   *Ibid.*, p. 245.

110   *Ibid.*, p. 77; On the currency in Lancashire at this time see S. G. Checkland, 'The Lancashire bill system and its Liverpool protagonists 1810–27', *Economica*, XXI, 1954, pp. 129–42 and T. S. Ashton, 'The bill of

exchange and private banks in Lancashire 1790–1830', in T. S. Ashton and R. S. Sayers eds., *Papers in English Monetary History*, Oxford, 1953, pp. 37–49.

111 The evidence of Scottish witnesses is conveniently summarised in Checkland, *Scottish Banking*, pp. 318–19, 435–9, and Munn, *Scottish Provincial Banking Companies*, pp. 80–5.

112 *Commons S.C. on promissory notes 1826*, p. 106–7. Thomas Joplin believed there were no more than four or five towns in Ireland capable of supporting a bank without circulation: *ibid.*, p. 110.

113 *Lords S.C. on promissory notes 1826*, p. 61. Another point about the power of note issue generally, though it was not made to either of the Select Committees of 1826, was that it was a cheap form of advertising for a bank: *S.C. on Banks of Issue 1875*, BPP, 1875, IX, Q. 3532, evidence of J. T. Bristow, director of the Northern Bank.

114 *Commons S.C. on promissory notes 1826*, especially evidence of John Commelin of the British Linen Company, pp. 178 ff., and James Craig, an Edinburgh solicitor, pp. 265 ff.

115 *Ibid.*, p. 254, evidence of Pierce Mahony.

116 *Ibid.*, p. 224, evidence of Leonard Dobbin who pointed out that the Usury Laws were sometimes evaded because 'there was no person to put them in force'.

117 BCC Minute Book 1802–35, 4 March 1826, PRONI D. 1857/1/2.

118 Report of town meeting in *Belfast Commercial Chronicle*, 15 March 1826.

119 *Report from the Commons S.C. on promissory notes in Scotland and Ireland*, p. 17.

120 *Lords S.C. on promissory notes 1826*, p. 13, evidence of Leonard Dobbin; p. 23 of J. Acheson Smyth; p. 27, of J. H. Houston.

121 See Section 2.6.

122 *Belfast Banking Company Deed of Co-partnership.* I am very grateful to Mr J. N. Simpson of the Northern Bank for sending me a copy of this deed.

123 *Belfast Newsletter*, 3 July 1827.

124 Noel Simpson, *The Belfast Bank 1827–1970*, Belfast, 1975, p. 28.

125 As Barrow *Emergence*, p. 82, has pointed out, the only significant difference between the deeds of the Northern and the Belfast was the absence in the latter of any clause prohibiting a partner in any other Irish bank from holding office or voting at a general meeting.

126 *S.C. on Joint Stock Banks 1837*, Appendix I, no. 82.

127 *Belfast Bank Deed of Co-partnership*, clause II. The initial annual salaries were Thomas Batt (£800), James Luke (£700), John Thomson and Thomas Greg Batt (£600 each).

128 *Ibid.*, clause VII. Robert Callwell was auditor of accounts and acted as chairman of the Board of Superintendence. The deed provided,

Notes to pp. 29–33

however, that after the death or resignation of Callwell the Board would consist of seven partners elected annually. Callwell's salary was £300 p.a.

129   *Ibid.*, clause XV.

130   S. E. Thomas, 'The first English joint stock banks', *Economic History*, II, 1934, p. 128; R. S. Sayers, *Lloyds Bank in the History of English Banking* p. 117; T. Balogh, *Studies in Financial Organisation*, Cambridge, 1950, p. 3.

131   For an indication of the numbers of both types of bank to 1844, see *Private and Joint Stock Banks registered in Ireland 1820–44*, BPP 1844, XXXII, p. 445.

132   Shizuya Nishimura, *The Decline of Inland Bills of Exchange in the London Money Market 1855–1913*, Cambridge, 1971, p. 80.

133   Barrow, *Emergence,* pp. 70, 78.

134   The co-partnership deeds of both the Northern (clause XXII) and the Belfast (clause XXV) gave these banks first lien on the shares of any proprietor in debt to them. The sale of August 1826 referred to here in the text was to settle the debt of John Mullan, a bankrupt general and provision merchant: NBCM, 31 July 1826.

135   *Belfast Newsletter,* 18 August 1826. The premium on Mullan's shares was fifty-eight per cent.

136   NBCM, 1827–8, *passim.*

137   Share price quotations taken from *Northern Whig,* 7 June, 16 August, 20 September 1827, 10, 18 October, 1, 29 November, 4 December 1827, 3, 17 January, 12, 28 February, 13, 20 March, 3 April, 22 May, 10 July 1828. See also *Circular to Bankers,* no. 17, 14 November 1828. The *Circular to Bankers* gives a false impression of the trend of the Provincial Bank's share prices. It was a self-confessed opponent of joint-stock banks, but disliked such 'monopolies' as the Bank of Ireland even more. This antipathy towards joint-stock banks led the *Circular* to assert that between 1826 and 1831, Provincial Bank shares had sold 'only once or twice at an advance of two or three per cent above their original cost': *ibid.,* no. 179, 23 December 1831. This was an understatement.

138   *S.C. on Joint Stock Banks 1837,* Q. 4436, evidence of James Marshall.

Chapter Two

1   BBSM, 23 February 1829.

2   Northern Bank *Annual Report,* 1828, 1831, 1833.

3   BBSM, 25 August 1828.

4   *Ibid.,* NBCM, 21 May, 8 October 1827, 20 October 1828, 24 August, 21 September 1829.

5   BBSM, 22 February 1830.

6   NBCM, 19 April 1825.

7   Northern Bank *Annual Report,* 1835.

Notes to pp. 33–38

8   *Ibid., S.C. on the Bank Acts 1858,* BPP, 1857–8, V, Q. 5200.
9   Northern Bank *Annual Report* 1828. The practice of quoting substantial premiums on Scottish bank shares was used in England in the 1830s to attract shareholders to new banks; F. Stuart Jones, 'The cotton industry and joint stock banking in Manchester 1825–50', *Business History,* XX, 1978, pp. 178–9. See also Bishop C. Hunt, 'The joint stock company in England 1830–44', *Journal of Political Economy,* 43, 1935, p. 339.
10 BBSM, 23 August 1841.
11 *S.C. on Joint Stock Banks 1837,* BPP, 1837, XIV, Appendix I, no. 57. 'The Provincial Bank of Ireland', *Bankers' Magazine,* V, 1846, p. 205. The Provincial paid three bonuses in its first twenty years, in 1836, 1839 and 1842.
12 The eleven Ulster branches opened between January 1831 and August 1835 were Enniskillen, Monaghan, Banbridge, Ballymena, Downpatrick, Cavan Lurgan, Omagh, Dungannon, Strabane and Moneymore: *S.C. on Joint Stock Banks 1837,* Appendix I, no. 85.
13 Hall, *Bank of Ireland,* Appendix I.
14 *Return of the number of applications made to the Bank of Ireland for the establishment of a branch,* BPP, 1844, XXXII, p. 265. The seven Ulster towns whose request for a branch was turned down were Ballybay, Ballymena, Cavan, Donegal, Dungannon, Letterkenny and Omagh.
15 The first 'outside' appointment to a Bank of Ireland branch managership was not made until 1838 when William Fraser of the Royal Bank of Scotland was appointed manager at Limerick: Barrow, *Emergence,* p. 88.
16 NBCM, 11 January, 23 March 1830.
17 *Ibid.,* 8 September 1834; Belfast Bank *Annual Report,* 1835.
18 Northern Bank *Annual Report,* 1834.
19 *Belfast Newsletter,* 16 September 1834.
20 Belfast Bank *Annual Report,* 1835, Northern Bank *Annual Report,* 1835.
21 The chronology of opening dates for the Belfast Bank branches differs from that presented by Barrow, *Emergence,* pp. 82, 215–9. Aware of the pitfalls of using Stamp Office returns which made no distinction between branches and agencies, Barrow claims to have based his chronology on the records of the Belfast Bank. This appears to be a somewhat dubious claim since such records very rarely give precise opening dates. A more reliable source is newspaper notices and Table 10 is based on these. Barrow suggests the first Belfast Bank branch opened in Coleraine in 1828 and the second in Derry in 1833. These dates are, respectively, six years and two years too early.
22 See, for example, NBCM, 6 October 1834.
23 The Northern's managers in Lurgan and Derry were examples of this: NBCM, 22 September, 20 October 1834.

Notes to pp. 38–41

24   *Ibid.*, 22 September 1834, 29 June 1835.
25   Northern Bank *Annual Report*, 1836.
26   Belfast Bank *Annual Report*, 1836.
27   'The Agricultural Bank of Ireland', *Bankers' Magazine*, III, 1845, p. 65. For a similar view see *The Irish Banker*, III, 1879, p. 353.
28   *Belfast Newsletter*, 13 June 1834.
29   *The Origin and Progress of the Agricultural and Commercial Bank of Ireland*, London, 1835, p. 13. This would have made the bank's branch network easily the largest in the world.
30   For more discussion of the Northern and Central Bank see S. E. Thomas, *The Rise and Growth of Joint-Stock Banking*, London, 1934, pp. 281–94.
31   *The Origin and Progress of the Agricultural and Commercial Bank of Ireland*, pp. 13, 21.
32   *Ibid.*, p. 68.
33   By 1 August 1835, 18 branches of the Agricultural and Commercial Bank were operating in Ballina, Bandon, Castlebar, Cork, Ennis, Enniscorthy, Galway, Killarney, Kilkenny, Limerick, Longford, Mallow, Nenagh, New Ross, Roscrea, Skibereen, Strabane and Tuam; *ibid.*, p. 45.
34   Barrow, *Emergence*, p. 109.
35   *Belfast Commercial Chronicle*, 8 February 1836.
36   *Ibid.*, 27 February 1836.
37   *Ibid.*, 19 March 1836.
38   *S.C. on Joint Stock Banks 1837*, QQ. 3156–9, evidence of James Dwyer, a director of the Agricultural and Commercial Bank.
39   *Belfast Commercial Chronicle*, 9 April 1836, expected the branch to open on 1 May 1836.
40   *S.C. on Joint Stock Banks 1837*, QQ. 4015–9, evidence of Pierce Mahony; *The Courier*, quoted in the *Belfast Commercial Chronicle*, 18 April 1836. Opinion on England was divided on the possibility of a crisis. *The Observer*, quoted in the *Belfast Commercial Chronicle*, 18 April 1836, rejected the view of *The Courier* on the grounds that the buoyant demand for products of almost all the staple industries was 'the result of *bona fide* purchases by the manufacturing and other interests, for immediate consumption' rather than for speculation.
41   Arthur D. Gayer, Anna Jacobson and Isaiah Finkelstein, 'British share prices 1811–50', *Review of Economic Statistics*, XXII, 1940, pp. 88–9.
42   See, for example, *Belfast Commercial Chronicle*, 23 April 1836.
43   Prior to the 1830s shares were offered for public sale in Belfast by attorneys, public notaries and general 'brokers'. From the mid-1830s notices from persons styling themselves 'stockbrokers' or 'sharebrokers' began to appear regularly in Belfast newspapers. For an early example see *Belfast Commercial Chronicle*, 30 April 1836. This increase in specialisation has also been identified in Scotland where 'stockbrokers' began to

appear in the mid-1820s, about a decade before their appearance in Belfast. On Scotland see R. C. Michie, 'The transfer of shares in Scotland 1700–1820', *Business History,* XX, 1978, pp. 153–63, esp. p. 160.

44   Clapham, *Bank of England 1797–1914,* pp. 154–5, 429.

45   *S.C. on Joint Stock Banks 1837,* Q. 4036.

46   J. H. Clapham, *An Economic History of Modern Britain,* Vol. I, 2nd edition, Cambridge, 1930, p. 515.

47   The Bank of England's decision had been taken in the light of a deterioration in the state of Anglo-American trade and financial relations. The Bank of Ireland later confessed itself 'entirely ignorant' of this deterioration, and that 'had we known as much then as we do now, in all human probability we should have raised our rates more quickly than we did', *S.C. on Joint Stock Banks 1838,* Q. 875, evidence of Thomas Wilson, Governor of the Bank of Ireland.

48   The Provincial Bank's rate on English bills, for example, followed the Bank of England rate of five per cent except where there was 'fierce competition' for such bills, in which cases it was forced to charge four per cent, 'or else lose our customers': *S.C. on Joint Stock Banks 1837,* QQ. 4027–8.

49   *Hansard's Parliamentary Debates,* 3rd series, XXXVI, (House of Commons), 6 June 1837, pp. 188–9.

50   *S.C. on Joint Stock Banks 1838,* Q. 846.

51   Stuart Jones, 'The collapse of instant banking', *Bankers' Magazine,* March, 1971.

52   The earliest major published survey appeared in three instalments in *Bankers' Magazine,* III, 1845, pp. 65–70, 200–6; *ibid.,* IV, 1845, pp. 280–5. The most recent analysis is Barrow, *Emergence,* pp. 108–19, 146–55.

53   *S.C. on Joint Stock Banks 1837,* QQ. 4143–7.

54   *Ibid.,* Q. 3975.

55   *Ibid.,* QQ. 4190–6. Dundas sent £1,400 to Dungannon branch, £500 to Enniskillen and £1,100 to Clones and Cavan.

56   *S.C. on Joint Stock Banks 1838,* QQ. 1317–33. It should be noted that this evidence from the Hibernian does not accord with that given to the same Select Committee by the Governor of the Bank of Ireland, Thomas Wilson. When asked if he had 'any recollection of any refusal to discount paper which had more than 21 days to run', Wilson answered 'never, that I recollect'. *Ibid.,* Q. 870.

57   *Ibid.,* Q. 1430.

58   *Ibid.,* Q. 1325–6, 1334.

59   *Ibid.,* Q. 891. The Agricultural and Commercial Bank attempted, but failed, to get further assistance from the Bank of Ireland: F. G. Hall, *History of the Bank of Ireland,* pp. 162–3. It also applied to the Bank of England for a loan of £1 million, mainly on the security of local bills. This, not surprisingly, was rejected. See Michael Collins, *The Bank of England*

and the Liverpool Money Market 1825–50, unpublished PhD thesis, University of London, 1972, p. 127.

60 Barrow, *Emergence,* p. 152.

61 (Mountifort Longfield), 'Banking and currency', *Dublin University Magazine,* XVI, 1841, p. 380.

62 Thus of some twenty joint-stock banks with £10 shares in 1837, seventeen had been founded in 1836 and were concentrated almost exclusively in the Midlands, north-west and north-east of England. *S.C. on Joint Stocks Banks 1837,* Appendix I, nos. 7, 9, 10, 17, 24, 27, 32, 41, 47, 60, 65, 74, 79, 80, 91, 94, 100.

63 S. Evelyn Thomas, 'The first English provincial banks', *Economic History,* II, 1934, p. 138. It is likely that the Ulster Bank experienced such benefits during the 1836 crisis when 'their friends . . . abstained as much as possible from asking (for) discounts'. UBCM, 5 December 1836.

64 For example, the Western Bank of Scotland, which failed in 1857, had shares of £50.

65 'The Agricultural Bank of Ireland', *Bankers' Magazine,* III, 1845, pp. 200–6; *ibid.,* IV, 1845, pp. 280–5.

66 Mountifort Longfield, 'Banking and currency', p.382.

67 *S.C. on Joint Stock Banks 1837,* QQ. 3811 ff.

68 *Ibid.,* Q. 3820.

69 *Ibid.,* Q. 3868. Mahony stressed that this defect applied not merely to banks but to joint-stock enterprises throughout the United Kingdom.

70 *Belfast Newsletter,* 7 February 1837.

71 Pierce Mahony, *Confidential Letter to the Rt Hon Thomas Spring Rice, Chancellor of the Exchequer M.P.,* London, 19 June 1837, *passim.*

72 *Ibid.,* Appendix I.

73 *Ibid.,* p. 16. The prospectus of the Provident Bank of Ireland is reprinted in the *S.C. on Joint Stock Banks 1838,* pp. 45–7.

74 *Cork Constitution,* quoted in the *Belfast Newsletter,* 3 October, 1837. The Southern Bank of Ireland seems to have survived only about two months: W. P. Coyne ed., *Ireland Industrial and Agricultural,* (Dublin, 1902), p. 124; Pierce Mahony, *Confidential Letter,* pp. 12–15. On the Southern and the Provident banks, Mahony commented: 'The only hope I have about them is that they must die instantly, and before inflicting much evil. The danger would be their lingering on, and when breaking up, their inducing 'a run' upon other establishments'. *Ibid.,* p. 18.

75 *Secret Committee of the House of Lords on Commercial Distress, 1848,* Q. 7242.

76 'The present state of banking in Ireland', *Bankers' Magazine,* I, 1844, p. 290.

77 *Deed of Settlement of the National Bank of Ireland,* London, 1835, pp. 74–5.

78 *Decades of the Ulster Bank,* Belfast, 1965, p. 12.

79 *Belfast Commercial Chronicle,* 27 February 1836.

80 John Heron was a provision trader and shipowner, Robert Grimshaw a drysalter and associated with Thomas Grimshaw and Company, calico printers and dyers. Both Heron and Curell sold their businesses on becoming Ulster Bank directors. John Curell ran a substantial bleaching business in Ballymena and James Steen was a Belfast provisions trader and pork curer. See *Decades of the Ulster Bank,* pp. 18–21.

81 *List of Proprietors of the Northern Banking Company,* Belfast, 24 September 1824; Grimshaw was a member of the Northern Bank advisory committee from which he was obliged to resign as a result of his taking shares in the Ulster Bank. NBCM, 30 November 1835. Another serving member of the Northern's committee, William McCance, had to resign for the same reason.

82 Ulster Banking Company Deed of Co-partnership, PRONI D.A. 177/24, p. 13, clause X.

83 UBCM, 7 August 1837; 3 February, 6 March 1840.

84 Ulster Bank Half Yearly Balances, Vol. I, 1836–53. For more details on overdraft trends see Chapter Three.

85 Ulster Banking Company Deed of Co-partnership, p. 28, clause XXVIII.

86 UBCM, 5 December 1836. The run was described as 'smart', but the Ulster Bank's customers assisted by refraining from asking for discounts and no customers were lost as a result of the crisis.

87 *Belfast Commercial Chronicle,* 12 November 1836. The paper added that the signatures had been 'spontaneously attached' within an hour and could have been 'augmented ten fold' if time had permitted. The offending report which provoked this response was carried in the *Dublin Evening Mail* of 9 November 1836, a report which went so far as to cast doubt on the solvency of the Belfast Bank.

88 BBSM, 5 December 1836.

89 *Decades of the Ulster Bank,* p. 22. The first branch opened at Enniskillen on 3 August 1836, followed by Armagh five days later: *Belfast Commercial Chronicle,* 8 August 1836.

90 *Derry Journal,* quoted in the *Belfast Newsletter,* 23 March 1838. Belfast Bank *Annual Report,* 1838.

91 BBSM, 27 August 1838.

92 *Belfast Commercial Chronicle,* 27 February 1836. It is not known whether the Agricultural and Commercial Bank participated in inter-bank discussion. Although there is no reference to discussion with this bank in the records of the Belfast banks, it is possible, though unlikely, that discussion took place.

93 P. L. Cottrell, 'Commercial enterprise', in Roy Church ed., *The Dynamics of Victorian Business,* London, 1980, p. 241; Frank R. Kent, *The Story of Alexander Brown and Sons,* Baltimore, 1925, pp. 133–8. For a

Notes to pp. 50–54

thorough analysis of the 1837 crisis and subsequent depression see Ralph W. Hidy, *The House of Baring in American Trade and Finance,* Cambridge, Mass., 1943, pp. 205–302.

94 According to Clapham, Brown's applied to the Bank of England for help in June 1837 because the firm was 'loaded up with bills on exports to America that had not been paid for'; and pointed out to the Bank that if they were allowed to fail others would be dragged down. The Bank of England supported Brown's with assistance of almost £2 million. Clapham, *The Bank of England 1797–1914,* p. 158.

95 NBCM, 14 June 1837.

96 UBCM, 13 June 1837.

97 J. Wales to J. A. Simpson, Assistant General Manager, Bank of Liverpool, 25 November 1901. Belfast Bank Secretary's Letter Book 1884–1924.

98 See Kent, *Story of Alexander Brown,* pp. 25–48; J. R. Killick, 'Risk, specialisation and profit in the mercantile sector of the nineteenth century cotton trade: Alexander Brown and Sons 1820–80', *Business History,* XVI, 1974; Aytoun Ellis, *Heir of Adventure,* London, 1960.

99 Ulster Bank Share Register No. 1.

100 Note for instance the comments of four recent researchers into restrictive practices in British industry since the mid-1950s: Dennis Swann, Denis O'Brien, W. P. J. Maunder and W. Stewart Howe, *Competition in British Industry,* London, 1974, esp. pp. 169–70.

101 NBCM, 11 December 1865, 29 October, 16 November 1866. This is discussed in more detail in Chapter Four. It has recently been suggested that a merger of the Belfast Bank and Northern Bank was first proposed in 1866: Noel Simpson, *The Belfast Bank 1827–1970,* Belfast, 1975, p. 92; but this is not so.

102 BBSM, 18 March 1839.

103 The use of this type of terminology became common in the later nineteenth century. A useful survey of restrictions on competition in British banking is L. S. Pressnell, 'Cartels and competition in British banking: a background study', *Banca Nazionale Del Lavoro Quarterly Review,* 23, 1970, esp. pp. 386–9.

104 M. A. Utton, *Industrial Concentration,* London, 1970, pp. 100–1.

105 Northern Bank *Annual Report,* 1839.

106 NBCM, 29 June 1840. The branch opened on 16 July 1840 and was 'going on satisfactorily' shortly after; *ibid.,* 27 June 1840.

107 BBSM, 23 August 1841.

108 Provincial Bank 'Procedure Book', 30 September 1843.

109 *Belfast Mercantile Register,* 7 January 1843.

110 *Ibid.,* 4 January 1842; N. S. Buck, *The Development of The Organisation of Anglo-American Trade 1800–1850,* New Haven, 1925, pp. 93–7, 157–9.

111 R. C. O. Matthews, *A Study in Trade Cycle History, 1833–42*, Cambridge, 1954, has a clinical dissection of this depression. Note also Hobsbawm's comment that 'no subsequent cyclical depression was even faintly as catastrophic as the slump of 1841–2'. E. J. Hobsbawm, *Industry and Empire*, 1969, p. 94.

112 *Belfast Mercantile Register*, 5 July 1842. Longfield was rather more forthright, describing a five year 'circle' to which trade was subject. This circle comprised the following stages: caution – confidence – liveliness – overtrading – great apparent prosperity – sudden cessation – paralysis – distrust – panic – bankruptcies – caution. 'Banking and currency', *Dublin University Magazine*, XV, p. 223.

113 Mark Blaug, *Ricardian Economics. A Historical Study*, New Haven, 1958, pp. 98–100.

114 Ulster Bank Circular to Branches 15 April 1840, 18 July 1843.

115 Belfast Bank *Annual Report*, 1843.

116 *Ibid.*, and Ulster Bank Circular to Branches, 29 March 1844.

117 Ulster Bank *Annual Report* 1842, UBCM, 8 September 1843.

118 UBCM, 5 September 1842. The first reduction in dividend was announced after the bank suffered bad debts to the tune of £9,455 which virtually wiped out the reserve fund. This was the Ulster Bank's worst single year for bad debts until well into the second half of the nineteenth century.

119 Royal Bank *Annual Report*, 1840.

120 Ulster Bank *Annual Report*, 1843.

121 UBCM, 9 September 1844.

122 *Belfast Mercantile Register*, 7 February 1843.

123 NBCM, 12 September 1845. See also BBSM, 18 August 1845 and Ulster Bank *Annual Report*, 1845.

124 Leland H. Jenks, *The Migration of British Capital to 1875*, 1927, p. 128; J. H. Clapham, *Economic History of Modern Britain*, I, 1930, pp. 526–7; E. V. Morgan, 'Railway investment, Bank of England policy and interest rates 1844–48', *Economic History*, IV, 1940.

125 See the report of a public meeting of Belfast merchants, traders and bankers to consider the extension of communications in Ulster, *Belfast Mercantile Register*, 10 December 1844.

126 *Ibid.*, 7 January 1845.

127 *Ibid.*, 29 October 1844. By August the following year it was predicted that although the people of Belfast had abstained from 'gambling pursuits' in railway shares, such pursuits 'must lead to the ruin of thousands of innocent individuals' in Britain. *Ibid.*, 5 August 1845. Clearly, by the mid-1840s, financial crises were becoming easier to forecast.

128 This is not meant to imply that the relationship between money supply and economic activity has since been completely clarified!

129 F. W. Fetter, 'Economic controversy in the British reviews

Notes to pp. 56–60

1802–50', *Economica,* XXXII, 1965, pp. 424–37.

130   Michael Collins, 'The Langton papers: banking and banking policy in the 1830s', *ibid.*, XXXIX, 1972, pp. 47–59.

131   This brief outline owes much to the excellent articles by Marian Daugherty, 'The currency-banking controversy', *Southern Economic Journal,* VIII, 1942–3.

132   The exchange took place between 1854 and 1856, but added little in the way of ideas. J. E. Cairnes, echoing the Banking School's position, published his 'An examination into the principles of currency involved in the Bank Charter Act of 1844', *Journal of the Dublin Statistical Society,* III, 1854, pp. 40–78. He was opposed by W. Neilson Hancock, whose paper 'Sir Robert Peel's Bank Act of 1844 explained and defended', *ibid.,* V, 1856, pp. 261–76, as is evident from its title, was written very much along Currency School lines. A further contribution by S. M. Greer, 'On the Bank Charter Act of 1844', *ibid.,* pp. 335–50, was a lucid restatement of the Banking School's ideas in the 1850s.

133   R. D. C. Black, *Economic Thought and the Irish Question 1817–70,* Cambridge, 1960, p. 150.

134   8 and 9 Vic c. 37.

135   8 and 9 Vic c. 38.

136   BBSM, 18 August 1845; NBCM, 10 September 1845.

137   *Secret Committee of the House of Lords on Commercial Distress 1848,* Q. 4244, evidence of Robert Murray of the Provincial.

138   F. W. Fetter, *The Development of British Monetary Orthodoxy 1797–1875,* Cambridge, Mass., 1965, pp. 221–2.

139   *Circular to Bankers,* 862, 5 July 1844, p. 5. The explanation for this outburst probably lies in the fact that the *Circular* did not attach much importance to the issue of small notes, and considered their suppression 'a comparatively small measure'; *ibid.,* 831, 22 December 1843, p. 209.

140   'Scotch and Irish banking', *Bankers' Magazine,* II, 1844–5, p. 126. See also *ibid.,* pp. 379–84, for further justification of small notes in Ireland and Scotland.

141   '. . . all the working classes are now more above want and altogether in better condition than ever we remember them'. *Belfast Mercantile Register,* 20 May 1845. The general trend of circulation can be seen from the average monthly circulation of all Irish banks between 1839 and 1845. In March 1839 this was £6,290,000, March 1843, £5,105,000, and by March 1845 it reached an unprecedented peak of £7,052,000. *S.C. on the Bank Acts 1857,* BPP, 1857, X, Appendix 15.

142   Northern Bank *Annual Report,* 1846.

143   E. V. Morgan, *The Theory and Practice of Central Banking 1797–1913,* Cambridge, 1943, chapter 7.

144   D. P. O'Brien, *The Classical Economists,* Oxford, 1975, p. 157.

145   *Secret Committee of the House of Lords on Commercial Distress*

Notes to pp. 60–63

1848, Q. 7248, evidence of J. Bristow.
146   *Ibid.,* QQ. 7251–4. See also next section.
147   *Ibid.,* Q. 7267, Q. 4279, evidence of Robert Murray. Irish banks were required to pay notes at the branch of issue by the Payment of Bank Notes (Ireland) Act of 1828, 9. Geo. IV, c. 81. Although not obliged to do so, banks of issue in Ireland paid their notes at any of their branches.
148   Ulster Bank Circular to Branches, 1 December 1845.
149   J. W. Gilbart, 'On the laws of currency in Ireland', p. 320. On changes in the organisation of the linen industry see Ollerenshaw, 'Industry 1820–1914', pp. 71–2.
150   *Ibid.*
151   *Belfast Mercantile Register,* 10 June 1845.
152   Gilbart, 'On the laws of currency in Ireland', p. 320.
153   The circulation of small notes in Ulster continued to be greater than elsewhere in Ireland until late in the nineteenth century: *S.C. on Banks of Issue 1875,* Q. 2441.
154   Ulster Bank Circular to Branches, 30 October 1845. The extra exchange began on November 1 1845. This circular emphasised that its purpose was to 'lessen the apparent circulation in the returns required under the new Banking Law', and said that the Bank of Ireland was to be invited to join in the arrangement, which it subsequently did.
155   Barrow, *Emergence,* pp. 183–5, has the most detailed account of the early operation of the Dublin clearing house.
156   'The Irish clearing system', *Journal of the Institute of Bankers,* II, 1881–2, p. 270. *Secret Committee of the House of Lords on Commercial Distress 1848,* Q. 7313.
157   Letter from Gibbons and Williams to the Directors of the Northern Banking Company 16 October 1834. NBCM, 9 February 1835, 25 May 1846.
158   Solomon Watson had in fact been Dublin agent for Batt's Bank prior to the formation of the Belfast Banking Company in 1827. The Hibernian Bank also undertook agency work for the Belfast Bank for a short period but the latter transferred this after the Hibernian's behaviour during the crisis of 1836.
159   *The Parliamentary Gazetteer of Ireland,* Dublin, London and Edinburgh, 1844, p. xcvii. The six branches were Newry (opened in 1825), Carlow (1834), Drogheda (1834), Dundalk (1836), Mountmellick (1836) and Tullamore (1836).
160   Barrow, *Emergence,* p. 181.
161   This is not to say that the Famine should be given exclusive responsibility for causing a slow rate of branch expansion in the 1850s and 1860s as it is by implication in Joseph Lee, 'The dual economy in Ireland, 1800–1850', in T. Desmond Williams, *Historical Studies VIII,* 1971, p. 193.
162   Edward Nevin and E. W. Davis, *The London Clearing Banks,*

London, 1970, p. 64. The Irish bank which complained most about its inability to issue was the Hibernian which, because it operated from Dublin, was denied this power. One of its directors, Ignatius Callaghan, argued in 1838 that when the bank was formed in 1825 the directors had received an assurance from the Government that the Bank of Ireland's charter would not be renewed and so the Hibernian would then be able to issue notes. Indeed, Callaghan asserted that if the Hibernian's promoters had known that the power of issue would continue to be denied them, the bank would never have been founded in the first place: *S.C. on Joint Stock Banks 1838*, QQ. 1179 ff, esp. Q. 1185.

163 Letter from Charles Copland, Manager of the Royal, to the Chancellor of the Exchequer, 15 May 1837, in *S.C. on Joint Stock Banks 1837*, Appendix IV, no. 9.

164 See, for example, Ulster Bank *Annual Report* 1845. By 1856, deposits were acknowledged to be 'the chief source of profit': BBSM, 28 August 1856.

165 Thus the Northern, while welcoming the abolition of the Bank of Ireland's territorial privilege, which would 'enlarge the field for their operations' considered that 'the accompanying restrictions may make it doubtful how far such extension may be advantageous'. NBCM, 15 September 1845.

166 J. W. Bristow of the Northern Bank to William Kirk of Annvale, Keady, Armagh, 14 May 1845. Letter Book of William Kirk, PRONI D. 1185, Box 1.

167 *Belfast Mercantile Register*, 24 June 1845.

168 Contrast the optimistic report on the state of crops in the *Belfast Mercantile Register*, 2 September 1845 with the dejected one of 30 September 1845.

169 Clive Emsley, 'The Home Office and its sources of information and investigation 1791–1801', *English Historical Review*, XCIV, 1979, p. 537.

170 PBHO to Henry Goulburn 2, 6–11, 13 October 1845; to John Young 3 September 1846; to C. E. Trevelyan 8 March 1847, 12 July 1848. Provincial Bank Secret Letter Book 1844–53.

171 William Wilde, 'The food of the Irish', *Dublin University Magazine*, XLIII, 1854, p. 128; K. H. Connell, *The Population of Ireland 1750–1845*, Oxford, 1950, pp. 138–9. I am indebted to Dr E. M. Crawford of Queen's University, Belfast, for these references.

172 See G. L. Barrow, 'The use of money in mid-nineteenth century Ireland', *Studies*, LIX, 1970, pp. 83, 85–6.

173 *Secret Committee of the House of Lords on Commercial Distress 1848*, Q. 7330.

174 *Northern Whig*, 12 January 1826.

175 'The Cork Savings Bank 1817–1917', *Journal of the Cork Historical and Archaeological Society*, 2nd series, XXIII, 1917, p. 183. See also W. E.

Notes to pp. 67–72

Tyrrell, *A History of the Belfast Savings Bank,* Belfast, 1946, pp. 44–5.

176   *Secret Committee of the House of Lords on Commercial Distress 1848,* Q. 4247, evidence of Robert Murray.

177   *The Economist,* 19 January 1850, pp. 66–7; 5 July 1851, p. 736.

178   *Secret Committee of the House of Lords on Commercial Distress 1848,* Q. 7188.

179   Bank rate was raised from three and a half to four per cent on 21 January and to five per cent on 8 April 1847. Clapham, *Bank of England 1797–1914,* p. 429. See also G. L. Rees, *Britain's Commodity Markets,* London, 1972, p. 126.

180   BBSM, 28 August 1848.

181   PBHO to Robert Murray, 17 August 1847. Provincial Bank Confidential Letter Book 1836–61. For the warnings about the decline of creditworthiness in the grain trade see PBHO to branch managers at Sligo, 5 August; Cork, Limerick and Galway, 6 August; Derry and Waterford 7 August 1847. *ibid.*

182   Ulster Bank *Annual Reports,* 1847–50 *passim.*

183   *Secret Committee of the House of Lords on Commercial Distress 1848,* QQ. 7201, 7271, 7298; BBSM, 16 August 1847.

184   See C. N. Ward Perkins, 'The commercial crisis of 1847', *Oxford Economic Papers,* II, 1950, reprinted in E. M. Carus Wilson ed., *Essays in Economic History,* vol. 3, London, 1962 pp. 263–79. A. D. Gayer, W. W. Rostow and A. J. Schwartz, *The Growth and Fluctuation of the British Economy 1790–1850,* Vol. I, Oxford, 1953, p. 332.

185   *Secret Committee of the House of Lords on Commercial Distress 1848,* Q. 7262–3.

186   Northern Bank *Annual Report,* 1847.

187   Clapham, *Bank of England 1797–1914,* pp. 208–11; Ward-Perkins, 'Commercial crisis', p. 266.

188   *Secret Committee of the House of Lords on Commercial Distress 1848,* Q. 7209.

189   L. M. Cullen, *An Economic History of Ireland Since 1660,* London, 1972, pp. 138, 150. For a similar view see James S. Donnelly Jr, *The Land and People of Nineteenth Century Cork,* London, 1975, p. 377.

190   See, for example, Lester V. Chandler, *The Economics of Money and Banking,* sixth edition, New York, 1973, pp. 128–9.

191   *Secret Committee of the House of Lords on Commercial Distress 1848,* Q. 7220.

192   Donnelly, *Land and People,* pp. 87–91.

193   Letter from 'A working banker', 'Prospects for banking in Ireland and suggestions for Irish bankers', *Bankers' Magazine,* VII, 1847, p. 18.

194   The only known closure of a branch of any of the Belfast banks in the 1840s was the Belfast Bank of Lurgan which, as noted above, was replaced by an agency. For details of some other branch closures see L. M.

Cullen, 'Germination and growth', in Bernard Share ed., *Root and Branch: Allied Irish Banks Yesterday, Today, Tomorrow,* Dublin, 1979, p. 33.
195 BBSM, 25 August 1851.
196 *S.C. on Banks of Issue 1875,* Q. 3576.
197 Cullen, 'Germination and growth', p. 50.
198 'Annual report of the National Bank of Ireland', *Bankers' Magazine,* XV, 1855, p. 395.
199 Northern Bank *Annual Reports* 1849, 1850, 1852; Ulster Bank *Annual Report* 1850.
200 Clapham, *Bank of England 1797–1914,* pp. 429–32.
201 UBCM, 27 September 1852.
202 BBSM, 23 August 1852.
203 Ulster Bank Circular to Branches, 1 July 1852.
204 'Annual report of the Provincial Bank of Ireland', *Bankers' Magazine,* X, 1850, p. 390.
205 BBSM, 21 August 1854.
206 Ulster Bank *Annual Report,* 1850.
207 R. G. Morton, *Standard Gauge Railways of The North of Ireland,* Belfast, 1962, pp. 11–20. Railway mileage open in Ireland increased from 537 in 1850 to 1,364 in 1860. See B. R. Mitchell and Phyllis Deane, *Abstract of British Historical Statistics,* Cambridge, 1962, p. 228.
208 This paragraph is based on Leland H. Jenks, *The Migration of British Capital to 1875,* pp. 190–2; Clapham, *Economic History of Modern Britain,* II, pp. 368–71. A good general discussion of the crisis is J. R. T. Hughes, 'The commercial crisis of 1857', *Oxford Economic Papers,* VIII, 1956.
209 *Belfast Linen Trade Circular,* 301, 30 November 1857. On Liverpool see Cottrell, 'Commercial enterprise', pp. 237–8, 247–9; on Glasgow see R. H Campbell, 'Edinburgh bankers and the Western Bank of Scotland', *Scottish Journal of Political Economy,* II, 1955, pp. 133–48.
210 *Report of the S.C. on the Bank Acts 1858,* p. xvi.
211 *S.C. on The Bank Acts 1858,* QQ. 5166–8, evidence of James Bristow. Bristow considered that as a result of the crisis in America, 'trade was very much reduced in point of amount, but as regards panic or distrust, it did not occur with us until about the beginning of November, previous to that time trade had been in rather a dull state'.
212 Provincial Bank Circular to Branches, 16 October 1857.
213 *Ibid.,* 10 November 1857.
214 A. E. Feavearyear, *The Pound Sterling,* Oxford, 1931, pp. 273–6.
215 Clapham, *Bank of England,* 1797–1914, p. 232.
216 The same was true in Britain. See J. R. T. Hughes, *Fluctuations in Industry, Trade and Finance,* Oxford, 1960, pp. 63–4.
217 *Report of the S.C. on the Bank Acts 1858,* p. xvi.
218 *S.C. on the Bank Acts 1858,* Q. 5267.

219 *The Irish Banker*, 1, 1876, p. 6.
220 Barrow, *Emergence*, pp. 160–3, J. B. O'Brien, 'Sadleir's Bank', *Journal of the Cork Historical and Archaeological Society*, LXXXII, 1977, pp. 33–8. See also Malcolm Dillon, *The History and Development of Banking in Ireland from the Earliest Times to The Present Day*, Dublin and London, 1889, pp. 80–1, 84.
221 D. Morier Evans, *Facts, Failures and Frauds: Revelations, Financial, Mercantile, Criminal*, London, 1859, p. 228.
222 *S.C. on the Bank Acts 1858*, Q. 4093, evidence of Charles Halliday. Even before the 1857 crisis developed, the failure of the Tipperary Bank precipitated a run on the National Bank and the Provincial Bank beginning in Tipperary and spreading to Cashel, Thurles, Clonmel and beyond. See 'Run on Irish banks', *Bankers' Magazine*, XVII, 1857, p. 17. Confidence in banks in Tipperary was still incomplete almost thirty years later when the depositors of the Bank of Ireland, 'by some occult process of reasoning', attributed the failure of the Munster Bank to the Bank of Ireland, demanded gold and lodged it with other banks: M. Dillon, 'Banks and bankers in Ireland', *Journal of the Institute of Bankers*, VII, 1886, p. 22. Dillon further observed that 'the county of Tipperary has an unenviable reputation as the scene of several panics'.
223 The same was true of note circulation in Scotland; J. R. T. Hughes, *Fluctuations in Industry, Trade and Finance*, p. 278.
224 *S.C. on Banks of Issue 1875*, QQ. 2778–84, evidence of Edward James Mills, Inspector and Joint Manager of the National Bank of Ireland. Mills recalled that the run was caused by the failure of the Western Bank of Scotland and the Borough Bank of Liverpool, and that the failure of the Tipperary Bank had 'added to the alarm'.
225 *Report of the S.C. on the Bank Acts 1858*, p. xvi.
226 Northern Bank *Annual Report*, 1858, Ulster Bank *Annual Report*, 1858.
227 BBSM, 31 February, 15 August 1859.

Chapter Three

1 *Secret Committee of the House of Lords on Commercial Distress 1848*, Q. 7340. Bristow spoke on behalf of the three Belfast banks which sent on witness to all subsequent parliamentary enquiries to which they were required to submit evidence.
2 See Philip Ollerenshaw, 'Aspects of bank lending in post-famine Ireland' in R. Mitchison and P. Roebuck eds, *Economy and Society in Scotland and Ireland 1500–1939*, forthcoming, 1987.
3 In 1852 Monaghan and Dungannon were both served by the Belfast and the Provincial Bank, while the Ulster Bank had a branch in Monaghan but not Dungannon. *Thom's Directory*, 1852, p. 473.
4 See below, p. 104.

Notes to pp. 83–88

5   *S.C. on the Bank Acts 1858,* Q. 5308, evidence of J. Bristow.
6   See for example W. G. Hoskins, 'Harvest fluctuations and English economic history 1620–1759', *Agricultural History Review,* XVI, 1968; W. A. Cole, 'Factors in demand 1700–80', in Roderick Floud and Donald McCloskey eds., *The Economic History of Britain since 1700,* Vol. 1, Cambridge 1981, esp. pp. 53–6.
7   *S.C. on Banks of Issue 1841,* Q. 905; T. E. Gregory, *The Westminster Bank Through a Century,* Oxford, 1936, pp. 16–17.
8   J. W. Gilbart, 'On the laws of the currency in Ireland', *Journal of the Statistical Society,* XVI, 1852, pp. 307–26.
9   *Belfast Mercantile Register,* 7 January 1843.
10 *Ibid.,* 1 October 1844.
11 *Ibid.,* 26 November 1844.
12 Robert Murray of the Provincial Bank of Ireland before the *S.C. on Banks of Issue 1841* quoted in Gilbart 'On the laws of currency', p. 318.
13 *Ibid.,* pp. 315–18.
14 *S.C. on Banks of Issue 1875,* QQ. 3448–9.
15 See Gilbart, *Treatise on Banking,* 1849, Vol 1, pp. 129–30; Leone Levi, *History of British Commerce,* pp. 289–90.
16 PBHO to Lords of HM Treasury, Whitehall, 25 October 1844, Provincial Bank *Secret Letter Book 1844–53.*
17 PBHO to Rt. Hon Sir Robert Peel, 1 March 1845, *ibid.*
18 Provincial Bank Circular to Branches 6 August 1852. See also circulars of 19 September 1854 and 18 October 1855 for further comment on shortage of silver coin.
19 See Hall, *Bank of Ireland,* Appendix D.
20 *Secret Committee of the House of Lords on Commercial Distress 1848,* Q. 4147 evidence of John McDonnell, Governor of the Bank of Ireland.
21 Belfast Bank Instructions for Managers and Accountants, 1848, p. 25.
22 Ulster Bank Circular to Branches, 8 January 1852.
23 Ulster Bank Branch Instructions and Orders from Head Office, 1840, p. 34; Belfast Bank Instructions for Managers and Accountants, 1848, p. 38.
24 Pressnell, *Country Banking,* pp. 318–21.
25 *Secret Committee of the House of Lords on Commercial Distress 1848,* QQ. 7205–6.
26 Belfast Bank Instructions for Managers and Accountants, 1848, pp. 43–4.
27 Provincial Bank Circular to Branches 10 September 1855. See also circulars of 12 August 1854, 13 April 1855, 12 October 1855. On the special treatment of four month bills in 'linen districts' see the circular of 25 October 1856.

28 PBCM, 4 September 1846.
29 C. W. Munn, *The Scottish Provincial Banking Companies*, pp. 121–6; Shizuya Nishimura, *The Decline of Inland Bills of Exchange in the London Money Market 1855–1913*, Cambridge, 1971, pp. 31–3.
30 Belfast Bank Instructions for Managers, 1848, p. 38.
31 See below, pp. 103, 121–2.
32 PBCM, 9 March 1847.
33 PBCM, 24 March 1848.
34 *Secret Committee of the House of Lords on Commercial Distress 1848*, Q. 4234, evidence of Robert Murray.
35 *S.C. on the Banks Act 1858*, Q. 5237.
36 Ulster Bank *Head Office Weekly Balances 1836–42*. This weekly series contains data on deposits in this period but data on current accounts in credit and overdrawn are netted until May 1838.
37 Michael Collins, 'The business of banking: English bank balance sheets, 1840–80', *Business History*, XXVI, 1984, pp. 45–6.
38 Calculated from Northern Bank Abstracts of Branch Balances 1873–84, 4 vols. on the basis of data drawn from last week in August or first week in September.
39 An instance of this is the Barbour Thread Company at Hilden, Lisburn, whose account was with the Ulster Bank in Belfast. For another example see PBCM, 29 October 1852.
40 See above, n.1.
41 M. Collins and P. Hudson, 'Provincial bank lending: Yorkshire and Merseyside 1826–60' *Bulletin of Economic Research*, 31, 1979, p. 75. A detailed survey of bank lending in a textile area is Pat Hudson, 'The role of banks in the finance of the West Yorkshire wool textile industry, *c.* 1780–1850', *Business History Review*, LV, 1981, pp. 379–402.
42 William Boyd to the Manager of the Provincial Bank in Belfast 15 August 1867. Blackstaff Flax Spinning Co Ltd Secretary's Letter Book PRONI D2120/1/1. A similar arrangement was made on several occasions: *ibid.*, 9 September 1866, 6 November 1873, 10 September 1875.
43 All details of Ulster Bank customers in this section are drawn from the half yearly balances, vols. 1 and 2.
44 See Ollerenshaw, 'Aspects of bank lending'.
45 PBCM, 8 August 1851; see also *ibid.*, 20 April 1849.
46 NBCM, 25 January 1852.
47 Another example of this was the advance of '£16,000 or such smaller sum as might be required to make the parliamentary deposit' for the proposed Athenry and Ennis Junction Railway. The Provincial made the advance by discount of a directors' promissory note up to nine months' date. Interest was charged at five per cent although there was provision for a rebate at four per cent if the advance was repaid early. PBCM, 23 December 1859.

48 PBCM, 4 November 1853.
49 Joseph Lee, 'The provision of capital for early Irish railways 1830–53', *Irish Historical Studies,* XVI, 1968.
50 *Ibid.,* pp. 51–2.
51 BBSM, 8 January 1855.
52 PBCM, 6 February 1863.
53 BBSM, 15 November 1852.
54 *Ibid.,* 30 May 1853.
55 *Ibid.,* 27 December 1852; UBCM, 3 January 1853. At this same meeting the Ulster Bank's directors were also authorised to buy up to fifty £25 shares in the Belfast and West of Ireland Junction Railway.
56 BBSM, 5 December 1859.
57 NBCM, 5 December 1859.
58 BBSM, 3 August 1857. The railway in question is referred to as 'Banbridge Rail' which presumably was that which ran from Scarva to Banbridge via Lenaderg. It has been described as one of a number of 'small lines which acted as feeders for the Ulster Railway'. See R. G. Morton, *Standard Gauge Railways of the North of Ireland,* p. 19. The line opened in 1859.
59 S.C. on the Bank Acts 1858, Q. 5274.
60 For more details of securities held for advances see Chapters Four and Five.
61 Provincial Bank Circular to Branches, 28 July 1856.
62 See R. F. Henderson, 'Bank credit' in Brian Tew and R. F. Henderson eds., *Studies in Company Finance,* Cambridge, 1959, esp. p. 77.

Chapter Four

1 H. A. Shannon, 'The coming of general limited liability', *Economic History Review,* II, 1931, reprinted in E. M. Carus-Wilson ed., *Essays in Economic History,* Vol. 1, London, 1954, p. 358.
2 James S. Donnelly Jr, 'The Irish agricultural depression of 1859–64', *Irish Economic and Social History,* III, 1976, pp. 33–54.
3 'Annual report of the Provincial Bank of Ireland', *Bankers' Magazine,* XX, 1860, p. 440.
4 Ulster Bank Circular to Branches, 22 August 1860.
5 'Annual report of the National Bank of Ireland', *Bankers' Magazine,* XXI, 1861, pp. 497, 499–50. The Provincial and the National differed in their judgments as to how badly Irish farmers had been affected by depression. In 1861 the former considered that the consequences of two unfavourable harvests had been offset by higher butter, cattle and corn prices, thus enabling the farmers to recoup 'a considerable portion of the loss arising from the deficiency of the grain crops'. The latter was rather less optimistic, and believed that 'in these days of free trade and quick access to and from foreign ports' food imports had 'deprived the farmers of the advantage

which they would otherwise have obtained from the high prices which must have ruled'. The evidence assembled by Donnelly tends to support the view of the National.

  6 Ulster Bank Circular to Branches, 18 September 1861.
  7 Ulster Bank Circular to Branches, 19 June 1862.
  8 Provincial Bank Circular to Branches, 16 June 1862.
  9 Donnelly, *The Land and People of Nineteenth Century Cork,* London, 1975, p. 148.
 10 Ulster Bank Circular to Branches, 28 January 1863.
 11 Cullen, *Economic History of Ireland,* pp. 137–8.
 12 J. W. Bristow of the Northern Bank to Lord Dufferin 31 December 1866. Dufferin and Ava Papers PRONI D. 1071 B/F. In 1879 the Ulster Bank judged that by far the largest percentage of liabilities in Irish banks 'is due to small farmers and others who have deposits of a comparatively small amount lodged with them'. UBHO to H. Billinghurst, London and Westminster Bank, 13 March 1879.
 13 *S.C. on Banks of Issue 1875,* QQ. 2827, 2844, evidence of Edward James Mills.
 14 *Belfast Linen Trade Circular,* 505, 6 January 1862. For more details on the background to this period see Ollerenshaw, thesis, pp. 174–82.
 15 See for example James Campbell to A. Ellerman, 6 August 1861. Private Letter Book of James Campbell, PRONI D. 2450/1/6.
 16 A useful concise survey of the impact of the Civil War is Elijah Helm, 'A review of the cotton trade of the United Kingdom during the seven years 1862–1868'. *Transactions of the Manchester Statistical Society,* 1868–9, pp. 67–94. A thorough study is O. N. Greeves, *The Effects of the American Civil War on the Linen and Wool Textile Industries of the U.K.,* unpublished PhD thesis, University of Bristol, 1968–9.
 17 Northern Bank *Annual Report* 1862, Ulster Bank *Annual Report* 1862.
 18 Ulster Bank *Annual Report,* 1863, 1866.
 19 UBHO to William Barbour and Sons, Hilden, Lisburn, 24 November 1863.
 20 UBHO to William Barbour and Sons, 6 September 1864.
 21 Ulster Bank Half-Yearly Balances, 1852–60.
 22 Robert McCrum to George Johnston (Bank of Ireland Manager at Armagh), 22 February 1865, Letter Book of McCrum, Watson and Mercer. PRONI D. 2518/1.
 23 See Appendix.
 24 PBCM, 9 September 1864.
 25 Balance Sheet of the York Street Flax Spinning Company Ltd., 31 December 1864, PRONI D. 978.
 26 PBCM, 1 September 1865, 17 April, 1 May 1868.
 27 Belfast Bank Miscellaneous Papers.

Notes to pp. 108–112

28   PBCM, 2 March 1866.
29   See for example PBCM, 26 June 1863.
30   For further discussion see section 4.5.
31   PBCM, 12 January 1866.
32   PBCM, 27 September 1867.
33   PBCM, 5 February 1864. Another instance of a substantial advance which 'owing to its temporary character' was unsecured was £68,182 (including an overdraft of £20,343) to the Edenderry Flax Spinning Company Ltd, in January 1869. The Provincial's Court of Directors ordered the overdraft to be cleared in the spring 'and no such amount to be again advanced without security'. PBCM, 22 January 1869.
34   PBCM, 15 November 1867.
35   PBCM, 18 December 1868.
36   See Appendix.
37   Crick and Wadsworth, *A Hundred Years of Joint Stock Banking*, pp. 149–53.
38   Northern Bank *Annual Report*, 1864.
39   *Linen Circular* 976, 16 January 1871; 1029, 22 January 1872; 1081, 20 January 1973. The downturn is noted in particular in *ibid*, 1185, 18 January 1875: 'In common with every other mercantile and manufacturing industry in the United Kingdom, the Irish Linen Trade suffered from the widespread depression which prevailed, not only at home but abroad, during the past year'. On the international boom and collapse see J. H. Clapham, *Economic History of Modern Britain*, II, Cambridge, 1932, pp. 379 ff.
40   BBSM, 21 September 1874. There is a good discussion of this unfortunate episode in Noel Simpson, *The Belfast Bank 1827–1970*, ch. 7.
41   This description of Lowry, Valentine and Kirk's affairs is based on discussions in PBCM, 9 October 1863, 7 and 21 February, 10 July, 18 December 1868; 29 January, 26 February, 28 May, 12 November 1869; 17 June, 16 December 1870; 15 August, 31 October 1873; 27 March, 24 July 1874.
42   See section 5.3.
43   John Wallace to Y. N. Burgess 6 June 1874, Killyleagh Flax Spinning Company Papers, PRONI D. 1594 Bundle 238.
44   PBCM, 28 August 1874.
45   PBCM, 20 October, 8 December 1876; 20 May, 4 November, 16 December 1881; 27 October 1882; 28 December 1883; 6 November 1891.
46   For a good example of these problems see the Directors' Minute Book of the Portadown Linen Company Ltd, PRONI D. 1252/35/8 Box 410.
47   NBCM, 18 May 1874.
48   'Annual report of the Provincial Bank of Ireland', *Bankers' Magazine*, XXXV, 1875, p. 571.

49 UBHO to UBB Ballymena, 15 May 1874; UBHO to UBB Portadown and UBB Lurgan, 16 May 1874.
50 Northern Bank *Annual Report,* 1874.
51 *Northern Whig,* 27 June 1876.
52 Northern Bank Circular to Branches, 27 June 1876.
53 NBCM, 18 September 1876.
54 Northern Bank *Annual Report,* 1879.
55 For a brief summary of these developments see D. L. Armstrong, 'Social and economic conditions in the Belfast linen industry 1850–1900', *Irish Historical Studies,* VII, 1951.
56 Although this depression has not received the detailed research it deserves there is much valuable information in Paul Bew, *Land and the National Question in Ireland 1858–82,* Dublin, 1979, Chs. 3–6; Samuel Clark, *Social Origins of the Irish Land War,* Princeton, 1979, ch. 7; Barbara Lewis Solow, *The Land Question and the Irish Economy 1870–1903,* Cambridge, Mass., 1971, esp. pp. 121–46.
57 B. R. Mitchell and Phyllis Deane, *Abstract of British Historical Statistics,* Cambridge 1962, p. 451.
58 Cullen, *Economic History of Ireland,* p. 150.
59 The financial year is here defined as 1 September to 31 August.
60 R. W. Kirkpatrick, 'Landed estates in mid-Ulster and the Irish Land War', *Irish Economic and Social History,* V, 1978, p. 73. See also the same author's 'Origins and development of the Land War in mid-Ulster 1879–85', in F. S. L. Lyons and R. A. J. Hawkins eds., *Ireland Under the Union: Varieties of Tension,* Oxford, 1980, esp. pp. 201–2, 213–15.
61 Joseph Lee, *The Modernisation of Irish Society,* Dublin, 1973, pp. 11–12. Lee suggests that there were 569 branches in Ireland in 1880. Although no source is given for this figure it is presumably taken from a table, reproduced later in the present chapter, in the *Report on Agricultural Credit* of 1914, p. 18, which shows that it refers to 1890.
62 *S.C. on Banks of Issue 1875,* QQ. 3250–1, evidence of Peter du Bedat. See also *The Irish Banker,* 1, 1876, p. 6.
63 See Table 29.
64 'The progress of banking in Great Britain and Ireland during 1877', *Bankers' Magazine,* XXXVIII, 1878, pp. 1–4; 'The progress of banking in Britain and Ireland during 1880', *ibid.,* XLI, 1881, pp. 79–80.
65 Ollerenshaw, thesis, pp. 197–8.
66 *The Irish Banker,* II, 1877, p. 139.
67 *Report on Agricultural Credit 1914,* pp. 21–2.
68 'Annual report of the Provincial Bank of Ireland', *Bankers' Magazine,* XL, 1880, p. 588.
69 NBCM, 13 September 1880.
70 'Bank of Ireland half-yearly meeting, December 1879', *Bankers' Magazine,* XL, 1880, p. 208.

71 UBHO to T. H. Burke Esq at Dublin Castle, 5 April, 6 June, 23 October 1877.
72 UBHO to UBB Longford 28 September 1880.
73 Clark, *Social Origins,* p. 232.
74 Northern Bank Circular to Branches, 12 November 1877.
75 Northern Bank Circular to Branches at Mohill, Bailieborough, Carndonagh, Carrick-on-Shannon, Oldcastle, Strokestown and Virginia, 19 October 1880. See also Provincial Bank Circulars to Branches, 5 January 1878, 15 January 1880 and 24 January 1882. This last circular, in addition to reiterating warnings about advances and discounts to farmers and shopkeepers added that 'the same applies to Landed Proprietors whose circumstances are so seriously altered by legislation'.
76 In some respects, the joint agreement between the Belfast banks was similar to that prevailing in Scotland where the General Manager's Committee controlled lending and borrowing rates. The Scottish agreement did not apply to London offices, and thus allowed 'the Scots to compete on London terms and also, on occasions, to escape from the constraints of the cartel by making loans through London'. See Checkland, *Scottish Banking,* p. 486. The Ulster Bank could use Dublin in the same way as Scottish banks used London to escape from the cartel.
77 UBHO to UBB Armagh, 20 January 1865.
78 UBHO to UBB Dublin, 26 January 1865.
79 See for example UBHO to UBB Dublin, 29 May 1872 UBHO to UBB Ballymena, 10 August 1877.
80 Ulster Bank Circular to Branches, 9 March1865. When the differential rate was first introduced there were two rates, one for sums of less than £5,000 and one for sums of £5,000 or more. Later in the nineteenth century more divisions were introduced.
81 NBCM, 11 December 1865. For a full account see Simpson, *The Belfast Bank.*
82 The text of the letter is in NBCM, 29 October 1866. The letter itself is dated 24 October which was the same day that the proposal was noted at a meeting of the Belfast Bank Board of Superintendence: BBSM, 24 October 1866.
83 NBCM, 29 October 1866.
84 NBCM, 16 November 1866.
85 Belfast Bank Circular to Shareholders, 24 October 1865, containing resolution of proprietors passed unanimously on 13 October 1865.
86 BBSM, 13 November 1865.
87 Nevin and Davis, *The London Clearing Banks,* p. 71; Hunt, *Development of the Business Corporation,* pp. 153–6.
88 NBCM, 26 December 1866.
89 *Ibid.*
90 NBCM, 4 March 1867.

91 The decision to sell these shares was taken on the recommendation of the directors in February 1870, and by September of that year they had all been sold. NBCM, 28 February 1870, Northern Bank *Annual Report,* 1870.

92 UBCM, 4 September 1871.

93 *Ibid.*

94 Ulster Bank *Annual Report,* 1871.

95 UBCM, 1 September 1876, Minutes of Special Committee Meeting 26 October 1876, *Annual Reports,* 1876 and 1877.

96 John Dun, 'On the analysis of joint stock banking in the United Kingdom', *Journal of the Statistical Society,* XXXIX, 1876, pp. 33–7.

97 For analysis of these in 1874 and 1875 see Dun 'On the analysis . . .' p. 59.

98 UBHO to UBB Cavan, 5 December 1865, UBHO to UBB Strabane, 5 December 1865.

99 UBHO, to Belfast Bank Bank Directors, 2 February 1866, 6 August 1877.

100 UBHO to UBB Dublin, 24 June 1872.

101 UBHO to Belfast and Northern Bank Directors, 24 June 1872.

102 UBHO to Belfast Bank Directors, 6 August 1873.

103 UBHO to Belfast Bank at Letterkenny, 8 August 1873.

104 UBHO to Belfast Bank Directors, 12 March 1877. Part of the Ulster Bank's evidence was that a customer in Coleraine had seen a letter from the Hibernian stating its intention to send an inspector to do so. This customer had told the Ulster's manager in nearby Ballymoney that if he (i.e. the customer) 'would join in the requisition the Hibernian would open within three days'.

105 UBHO to Belfast and Northern Bank Directors, 3 May 1877.

106 UBHO to Northern Bank Directors.

107 UBHO to UBB Cookstown, 16 May 1875. J. T. Bristow of the Northern Bank said that he had heard that in those places where the Hibernian met one or more of the Belfast banks it 'allowed people a higher rate in exceptional cases' although only where 'large deposits were involved': *S.C. on Banks of Issue 1875,* QQ. 3496–7.

108 Northern Bank Private Circular to Branches, 24 April 1877. The Ulster Bank had evidently been pressing for an agreement of this kind with the Belfast and the Northern for some time. In 1875, for example, the Ulster commented that it had 'more than once mooted the subject to them, (but) . . . they had always poured cold water on it': UBHO to UBB Cookstown, 16 May 1875. The change of heart by the Belfast and the Northern was probably due to the increased aggression of the Hibernian between 1875 and 1877.

109 Northern Bank Private Circular to Branches (where the Northern's branches operated near to those of the Hibernian), 14 January 1878.

Notes to pp. 138–142

110 UBHO to UBB Enniskillen, 7 December 1866.
111 UBHO to UBB Strabane, 28 September 1861.
112 UBHO to UBB Omagh, 28 September 1861.
113 See Chapter Five.
114 For a comprehensive survey see H. O. Horne, *A History of Savings Banks,* Oxford, 1947.
115 See the graph facing p. 22 of the *Report on Agricultural Credit in Ireland 1914.*
116 'Irish savings banks' in W. P. Coyne ed., *Ireland Industrial and Agricultural,* Dublin, 1902, p. 130.
117 On Scotland see Checkland, *Scottish Banking,* pp. 487–8.
118 See in particular UBHO to Sir John Lubbock MP, 3 June 1880.
119 UBHO to William Digges La Touche, Munster Bank, Dublin, 11 June 1880. La Touche was asked to seek the support of The Dublin Chamber of Commerce. No letter appears to have been sent to the Belfast Chamber of Commerce.
120 UBHO to William Shaw MP, 4 June 1880. This particular letter was scathing about the bill: 'If the Government be prepared to assume the functions of a very large Bank of Deposit are they also prepared to discharge the duty of using their deposits for the purpose of assisting commerce and of performing the work now devolving on the ordinary banks whose means of usefulness they are about to curtail?' In a letter of 10 June 1880, Shaw was asked to use his influence to get the Bank of Ireland, National, Provincial and Hibernian to support the petition.
121 William Langton, 'On recent savings bank legislation', *Transactions of the Manchester Statistical Society* 1880–1, p. 156. Langton quotes an estimate suggesting that after the City of Glasgow crash 'an amount little less than the balance due to the Savings Banks was withdrawn from the hands of bankers in the United Kingdom.'
122 George Rae to Robert (?), North of Scotland Bank, 18 April 1882. See also Rae to Waterhouse and Winterbotham (Secretary of the Association of English Country Bankers), Lincoln's Inn, 19 June 1882. Mr Rae's Private Letters on Banking Questions; Midland Bank Archives M. 222/1.
123 The most recent and comprehensive survey of company law in the nineteenth century is P. L. Cottrell, *Industrial Finance 1830–1914; The Finance and Organisation of English Manufacturing Industry,* London, 1980, ch. 3.
124 S.C. on the Bank Acts 1858, QQ. 3958–62, evidence of Charles Halliday of the Bank of Ireland; Crick and Wadsworth, *A Hundred Years of Joint-Stock Banking,* p. 31.
125 Clapham, *Economic History of Modern Britain,* II, p. 350.
126 21 and 22 Vict., c. 91. For a summary of this legislation and its wider context see Sheila Marriner 'Company financial statements as source

material for business historians', *Business History,* XXII, 1980, pp. 203–35, esp. 231–2.
127 Crick and Wadsworth, *A Hundred Years of Joint-Stock Banking,* p. 32.
128 25 and 26 Vict., c. 89.
129 Belfast Chamber of Commerce Special General Meeting 11 July 1855, PRONI D. 1857/1/5.
130 See Cottrell, *Industrial Finance,* pp. 50–1, 76, for opinion in several manufacturing districts in northern England.
131 BBSM, 15 September 1879.
132 NBCM, 3 September 1866.
133 UBHO to the London and Westminster Bank, 20 August 1867. Similar letters were sent to the Clydesdale Bank and the Manchester and Liverpool District Bank.
134 Ulster Bank *Annual Report,* 1867.
135 Cottrell, *Industrial Finance,* p. 54.
136 G. A. Fletcher, *The Discount Houses of London,* London, 1976, p. 24; Crick and Wadsworth, *A Hundred Years of Joint-Stock Banking,* pp. 302–6.
137 BBSM, 17 September 1866. This somewhat smug comment was perhaps premature in the light of the subsequent problems faced by many linen firms formed in the mid-1860s.
138 *S.C. on Banks of Issue 1875,* QQ. 2356–8, evidence of James Belton, General Manager of the Munster Bank.
139 Clapham, *Economic History of Modern Britain,* II, p. 351.
140 John Dun, 'On the analysis of joint-stock banking', p. 26.
141 Clapham, *Economic History,* p. 351.
142 R. H. Inglis Palgrave, 'Notes on banking in Great Britain and Ireland, Sweden, Denmark and Hamburg . . .', *Journal of the Statistical Society,* XXXVI, 1873, p. 49.
143 On this episode see Checkland, *Scottish Banking,* pp. 466, 469–77.
144 Northern Bank Circular to Branches, 3 October 1878. The following day branches were instructed to send City of Glasgow notes, as they were paid, every day, together with notes of any other Scottish banks. For a similar reaction see Provincial Bank Circular to Branches, 4 October 1878.
145 Northern Bank Circular to Branches, 11 October 1878. UBHO to UBB Ballymote and UBB Dublin, 7 October 1878.
146 UBHO to UBB Westport, 8 October 1878, and UBHO to UBB Sligo, 9 October 1878. These two branches were the only ones affected.
147 Northern Bank Circular to Branches, 12 December 1878; UBHO to all branches, 12 December 1878.
148 Northern Bank Circular to Branches, 14 December 1878.
149 See Chapter Five.
150 Northern Bank Circular to Branches, 16 June 1879.

151 Northern Bank Circular to Branches, 17 December 1878.
152 UBHO to W. A. Ross of Clonard, 19 December 1878.
153 UBHO to J. H. Moreland, 29 January 1879.
154 42 and 43 Vict., c. 79.
155 BBSM, 15 September 1879.
156 BBSM, 13 October 1882.
157 James Carr to R. J. Kennedy, National Bank of Ireland, Belfast Branch, 6 July 1881, Private Letter Book of James Carr, 1864–1909.
158 BBSM, 30 January 1882.
159 'The modernising of Irish banks', *Bankers' Magazine,* XLII, 1882, p. 881.
160 Dun, 'On the analysis of joint stock banking', p. 27.
161 BBSM, 13 October 1882.
162 BBSM, 12 October 1883.
163 NBCM, 11 September 1882, 9 April 1883, 26 August 1885, See also *The Northern Banking Company Ltd 1824–1924,* Belfast, 1925, pp. 254–5.
164 UBCM, 1, 25 September 1882.
165 Report of the annual meeting of the Belfast Chamber of Commerce, *Belfast Newsletter,* 17 February 1879.
166 Secretary of The Blackstaff Flax Spinning and Weaving Company Ltd to George Cochrane, Lower Broughton, Manchester 16 May 1867; Secretary's Letter Book, PRONI D. 2120/1/1/. See above, p. 108. The first mention of Blackstaff in the Provincial's records is PBCM, 2 March 1866.
167 Alexander Johns to John Browne of Cromac Mills, Belfast 22 October 1885. Belfast Bank Secretary's Letter Book.

Chapter Five
1 M. Dillon, 'Banks and bankers in Ireland', *Journal of the Institute of Bankers,* III, 1886, pp. 23–4.
2 NBCM, 11 June 1888, Northern Bank *Annual Report,* 1888.
3 S. A. Johnstone to Sir John Preston (Belfast Bank Chairman), 22 July 1890, BBSM.
4 P. L. Cottrell, *Industrial Finance 1830–1914,* London, 1980, pp. 195–8.
5 The only full study of the amalgamation movement is J. Sykes, *The Amalgamation Movement in English Banking 1825–1914,* London, 1924. For a critique and more reliable data after 1870 see Forrest Capie and Ghila Rodrik-Bali, 'Concentration in British banking 1870–1920', *Business History,* XXIV, 1982, pp. 280–92.
6 UBHO to UBB Dublin, 5 June 1886.
7 Letter on Irish joint stock banks signed by 'Amalgamation' and dated 7 October 1892, *Bankers' Magazine,* LIV, 1892, pp. 697–9.
8 See memorandum of agreement of 1 January 1886 in Ulster Bank 'Agreements with Local Banks', Vol. 1.

9 UBHO to Charles Chambers, Provincial Bank of Ireland, London, 27 November 1887, 2 and 21 February 1888.

10 Memorandum of agreement between the Belfast, Northern, Ulster and Provincial Banks in Northern Bank Private Circular to Branches, 14 April 1888.

11 Some regarded an all embracing cartel as inevitable. See O. C. Barry, 'The effects of competition amongst Irish banks', *Journal of the Institute of Bankers of Ireland,* IX, 1907, p. 48.

12 UBHO to Samuel Gordon, Provincial Bank of Ireland, 7 March 1885. Three years late the Ulster made the same suggestion in almost identical terms: UBHO to Charles Chambers, 15 March 1888.

13 Checkland, *Scottish Banking,* pp. 485–7. The practice of a uniform tariff on rates and charges was unknown in England in the late nineteenth century. F. W. Fetter, *The Development of British Monetary Orthodoxy 1797–1875,* Cambridge, Mass., 1965, pp. 222 ff. cited in Checkland, p. 486.

14 H. I. Johns to T. B. Swayne, Bank of Ireland, Dublin, 14 May 1906. Belfast Bank Sundry Letter Book.

15 UBHO to Bank of Ireland, 18 March 1914.

16 Ulster Bank Special Circular to Branches, 2 February 1886.

17 M. Wilson to Directors of Northern and Ulster Bank, 9 August 1897. Belfast Bank Secretary's Letter Book.

18 *Idem* to *idem,* 16 August 1897.

19 *Idem* to *idem,* 23 September 1897.

20 By 1902 the Northern Bank had four branches in Belfast (Falls Road, Royal Avenue, Shaftesbury Square and Wellington Place), the Belfast four (Central, East End, Western and Markets) and the Ulster five (Donegall Place, Carlisle Circus, Mountpottinger, Shankill Road and York Street). *Thom's Directory,* 1902, pp. 974–5.

21 M. Wilson to Directors of the Northern Bank, 9 April 1898. Belfast Bank Secretary's Letter Book.

22 H. I. Johns to Andrew Jamieson (Governor of the Bank of Ireland), 12 March 1898, *ibid.*

23 *Idem* to *idem,* 16 March 1898.

24 J. W. Scott to Ulster Bank Directors, 29 January 1898, *ibid.*

25 For sharp comment on the 'wretched Fenian bubble', see 'Half yearly meeting of the Union Bank of Ireland', *Bankers' Magazine,* XXVII, 1867, p. 264.

26 Provincial Bank Circulars to Branches, 11 June 1852; 20 March 1857; 21 April, 15 July 1859; 27 June 1865.

27 Henry Patterson, *Class Conflict and Sectarianism: The Protestant Working Class and the Belfast Labour Movement 1868–1920,* Belfast, 1980, p. 21. A lucid discussion of the Home Rule movement and its repercussions in Ulster is Nicholas Mansergh, *The Irish Question 1840–1921,* 3rd edition, London, 1975, Chapters 5 and 6.

28 *The Economist*, 22 May 1886, p. 644.
29 *Ibid.*, 18 March 1893, p. 316.
30 *Ibid.*, 17 June 1893, p. 727.
31 Deputations were also sent by the Belfast Harbour Commissioners and Linen Merchants' Association. See Thomas MacKnight, *Ulster As It Is*, II, London, 1896, pp. 321–6.
32 *Mr Gladstone and the Belfast Chamber of Commerce*, Belfast, 1893, p. 5.
33 *Ibid.*
34 'Ultonia', 'Irish banks and the Home Rule Bill', *Bankers' Magazine*, LVI, 1893, p. 182.
35 David McKee to Robert Slater, Union Bank of London, 9 March 1893. Belfast Bank Secretary's Letter Book.
36 *The Economist*, 14 February 1914, p. 332.
37 Ollerenshaw, thesis, p. 293.
38 Northern Bank Private Circular to Branches, 25 February 1893.
39 *Ibid.*, 13 March 1893.
40 *Ibid.*, 6 March 1893.
41 *Ibid.*, 20 May 1893.
42 David McKee to the Belfast Bank branch manager at Newry, 11 March 1893: £4,000 in gold was sent from Newry to Rathfriland branch, and £3,000 to Kilkeel. Belfast Bank Secretary's Letter Book. The Belfast Bank imported £60,000 of gold coin via the Bank of Liverpool, 'as a precautionary measure against Mr Gladstone's highly objectionable policy in reference to Ireland'. David McKee to Robert Slater, Union Bank of London, 7 March 1893. *Ibid.*
43 UBHO to UBB Monaghan, 10 March 1893.
44 Cullen, 'Germination and growth', p. 48.
45 Letter signed on behalf of directors of the Belfast, Northern and Ulster Banks to Colonel R. G. Sharman-Crawford, Crawfordsburn, County Down, 28 March 1913. Ulster Bank Records.
46 Gordon McMullan, 'The Irish bank 'strike', 1919' *Saothar*, V, 1979, p. 47, n. 3.
47 Ian Budge and Cornelius O'Leary, *Belfast: Approach to Crisis*, London, 1973, p. 107.
48 *Northern Banking Company, Centenary Volume 1824–1924*, Belfast, 1925, pp. 246–7.
49 By 1913 Sharman-Crawford had been a member of the Belfast Bank Board of Superintendence for over twenty years.
50 Patrick Buckland ed., *Irish Unionism 1885–1925: A Documentary History*, Belfast, 1973, p. 208.
51 Sir Wilson Hungerford in interview with staff of the Public Record Office of Northern Ireland, November 1965, reprinted in Patrick Buckland, *Irish Unionism*, p. 212. Hungerford was one of four political

secretaries to James Craig, Political Staff Officer in the UVF: A. T. Q. Stewart, *The Ulster Crisis,* London, 1967, p. 83.

52 A. G. Ford, 'The trade cycle in Britain 1860–1914', in Floud and McCloskey, *Economic History of Modern Britain,* II, p. 31.

53 Ollerenshaw, 'Industry 1820–1914', pp. 86–96.

54 Christine Shaw, 'The large manufacturing employers of 1907', *Business History,* XXV, 1983, p. 52.

55 William Mitchell to Messrs Gill and Fisher, 29 November 1883. Letter Book of William Mitchell 1883–8, PRONI D. 864 No. 2. In a letter six days earlier Mitchell noted that 'Belfast is also bad and some heavy losses there among millers etc. . . .', *idem to idem,* 23 November 1883.

56 PBCM, 15 March 1878.

57 UBHO to UBB Dublin, 30 April 1880.

58 'Annual report of the Provincial Bank of Ireland', *Bankers' Magazine,* XLIII, 1883, p. 916.

59 J. Wales to James Gallagher, 25 April 1884. Belfast Bank Secretary's Letter Book.

60 David McKee to James Gallagher, 8 June 1885, *ibid.*

61 Sir William Crawford, *Irish Linen and Some Features of its Production,* Belfast, 1910, p. 9.

62 Linen Merchants' Association Annual Report, 28 January 1879, p. 10, PRONI D. 2088/17.

63 UBHO to the Whiteabbey Bleaching Company, 31 July 1877.

64 UBHO to the County Down Flax Spinning and Weaving Company, 4 March 1878.

65 Thomas Gaffikin to John Johnston, Banbridge, 15 September 1879, Letter Book of Thomas Gaffikin and Co., PRONI D. 1796/1.

66 Linen Merchants' Association Annual Report, 29 January 1878, p. 9.

67 *Ibid.,* 30 January 1883, p. 19; 29 January 1884, p. 10.

68 Robert McCrum to A. H Barlow, 27 October 1883, Letter Book of McCrum Mercer and Watson, PRONI D. 2518/1.

69 Linen Merchants' Association Annual Report, 9 February 1886, p. 15.

70 *Ibid.*

71 *Northern Whig,* 1 January 1885, cited in Boyle, *Economic Development of the Linen Industry,* p. 123.

72 BBSM, 4 April, 21 October 1887.

73 Alexander Johns to the Ulster Spinning Company Ltd, 20 January 1887. Belfast Bank Secretary's Letter Book.

74 David McKee to the Ards Weaving Company Ltd, 7 April 1887. *Ibid.*

75 Linen Merchants' Association Annual Report, 31 January 1893, p. 21.

76   Belfast Chamber of Commerce Annual Meeting, 15 February 1895, PRONI D. 1857/1/5.
77   UBHO to John Campbell, 25, 26 January 1892.
78   A. J. MaCauley to York Street Flax Spinning Company Ltd, 6, 10, 15 and 22 February 1890. Belfast Bank Secretary's Letter Book.
79   William Boyd to Messrs Storey, Cowland and Hill, 3 September 1901. Blackstaff Flax Spinning and Weaving Company Ltd, Secretary's Letter Book. PRONI D. 2120/1/2.
80   *Idem* to R. A. McCrory, 5 June 1900. *Ibid.*
81   H. C. Lawlor, 'The genesis of the linen thread industry – 3'. *Fibres, Flax and Cordage,* March 1945, p. 99, PRONI D. 1286, Box 1. A parallel can be drawn here between the relations between banks and flaxspinners in Ulster on several occasions in the late nineteenth century and in South Yorkshire in the 1840s and 1850s. In the latter region the decline of linen in the 1840s led to repeated demands from linen manufacturers and traders for extensions of bank credit to finance their operations: Cottrell, *Industrial Finance 1830–1914,* p. 216. Cottrell points out, *inter alia,* that the finance of yarn stocks 'proved difficult without bank support'. The periodic difficulties of some of Ulster's spinning companies, and their demands for bank credit, suggest that a similar situation sometimes prevailed in Ulster at the end of the nineteenth century.
82   UBHO to S. A. Bell, 24 August 1897, UBHO to the Belfast Flax Spinning Co., 14 March 1898.
83   J. Wales to Durham Street Weaving Co. Ltd, 6 May 1898, Belfast Bank Secretary's Letter Book.
84   M. Wilson to Island Spinning Company, 23 April 1897. *Ibid.*
85   UBHO to Combe, Barbour, Combe, 5, 12, March 1883.
86   A. Johns to Victor Coates, 20 25 July 1887. Belfast Bank Secretary's Letter Book.
87   David McKee to the Secretary of the Belfast and Northern Counties Railway, 1 May 1886, *ibid.* For brief comment of the effect of the depression of the mid-1880s on the B and NCR, and the dividend paid, see J. R. L. Currie, *The Northern Counties Railway 1845–1903,* Newton Abbot, 1973, pp. 207, 283.
88   Sidney Pollard and Paul Robertson, *The British Shipbuilding Industry 1870–1914,* Cambridge, Mass., 1979, p. 105.
89   Bank of Ireland Applications for Advances from Agents 1864–77, 23 May 1868.
90   *Ibid.,* 1877–99, 17 July 1879.
91   *Ibid.,* 10, 26 April, 1 November 1888.
92   A. J. MaCauley to Harland and Wolff, 3 November 1891. Belfast Bank Secretary's Letter Book.
93   Bank of Ireland Applications for Advances from Agents, 1900–1914, 15 January 1903.

Notes to pp. 175–186

94 PBCM, 15 February 1884.
95 UBHO to Workman Clark, 27 June 1898.
96 Bank of Ireland Applications for Advances from Agents, 2 March, 2 June 1898, 17 November 1904.
97 Bank of Ireland Branch Inspector's Book, 1909.
98 D. S. Johnson, 'The Northern Ireland economy 1914–39' in Kennedy and Ollerenshaw eds., *Economic History of Ulster,* pp. 192–3.
99 UBHO to Edward Robinson, 1 August 1895.
100 UBHO to Peter Keegan, 16 February, 14 March 1898.
101 PBCM, 24 August 1883.
102 *Ibid.,* 10 November 1905.
103 UBHO to Jaffe Brothers, Belfast, 9 April 1878.
104 Details of Boyd's accounts taken from letters in the Belfast Bank Secretary's Letter Book, 19 January; 2, 3, 4 May; 26 June; 12 October; 13, 15 November 1893; 16, 17 April 1894.
105 Among many examples see UBHO to Robert Lepper, 14 October 1861; UBHO to A. R. Norton, 11 September 1865. See also *S.C. on the Bank Acts 1858,* Q. 5274.
106 UBHO to Charles Duffin, 29 March, 1 April 1878.
107 J. Wales to the Directors of the Brookfield Linen Company Ltd, 16 April 1884. Belfast Bank Secretary's Letter Book.
108 A. Johns to John Browne, 13 October 1885, *ibid.* Browne himself had been present at the meeting at which it was decided to secure guarantees from directors of limited companies.
109 Ollerenshaw, thesis, pp. 284–5.
110 UBHO to R. Lloyd Patterson, 17 April 1878; UBHO to Belfast Bank Directors, 26 April 1878.
111 W. P. Kennedy, 'Institutional reponse to economic growth: capital markets in Britain to 1914', in Leslie Hannah ed., *Management Strategy and Business Development,* London, 1976, p. 160.
112 Hall, *Bank of Ireland,* p. 272.
113 Cullen, 'Germination and growth', p. 50.
114 Checkland, *Scottish Banking,* pp. 743–5, Nishimura, *Decline of Inland Bills,* pp. 105–10.
115 See *The Economist* Banking Supplements.
116 UBHO to H. Billinghurst, London and Westminster Bank Ltd, 12 August 1885.
117 R. C. Michie, 'The London stock exchange and the British securities market, 1850–1914', *Economic History Review,* XXXVIII, 1985, p. 62.
118 Cullen, 'Germination and growth', 42.
119 Joseph Lee, 'Capital in the Irish economy' in Cullen ed., *Formation of the Irish Economy,* pp. 59–60.
120 Ollerenshaw, thesis, p. 289, Nishimura, *Decline of Inland Bills,* pp.

Notes to pp. 186–197

105–10.
121 *Report on Agricultural Credit 1914*, p. 20.

Conclusion

1 S. G. Checkland, 'Banking history and economic development: seven systems', *Scottish Journal of Political Economy*, XV, 1968, p. 145.
2 Cottrell, *Industrial Finance*, p. 16.
3 Figures for England and Wales are taken from Shizuya Nishimura, *Decline of Inland Bills of Exchange*, pp. 80–1. Figures for Ireland are taken from the *Report of the Departmental Committee on Agricultural Credit* of 1914, p. 18.
4 Nishimura, *Decline of Inland Bills*, pp. 9–10.
5 Pressnell, *Country Banking*, p. 128.
6 *S.C. on Banks of Issue* 1875, QQ. 3459–60.
7 George O'Brien, *The Economic History of Ireland From the Union to the Famine*, London, 1921, reprinted Clifton, New Jersey, 1972, p. 544.
8 See, for example, R. D. C. Black, *Economic Thought and the Irish Question 1817–70*, Cambridge, 1960, p. 152; F. S. L. Lyons, *Ireland Since the Famine*, London, 1971, p. 59; Joseph Lee, *The Modernisation of Irish Society 1848–1918*, Dublin, 1973, p. 20.
9 UBHO to UBB Dublin, 22 October 1885.
10 J. Wales to the branch managers at Enniskillen and Belfast Markets, 6 June 1896. Belfast Bank Secretary's Letter Book. The Ulster Bank adopted a similar policy; UBHO to UBB Enniskillen, 24 December 1889.
11 Northern Bank Circular to Branches, 23 March 1888.
12 Ulster Bank Circular to Branches, 9 July 1863.
13 (G. L. Smyth), *Remarks on the Proposed Renewal of the Charter of the Bank of Ireland*, London, 1838, p. 23.
14 *S.C. on the Banks Acts 1858*, QQ. 3731–4, 3762, evidence of Charles Halliday.
15 Hall, *Bank of Ireland*, p. 401.
16 M. Wilson to Ulster Bank Directors, 10 January 1901. Belfast Bank Sundry Letter Book.
17 Joseph Lee, *Modernisation of Irish Society*, p. 20
18 R. H. Campbell, 'Edinburgh bankers and the Western Bank of Scotland', *Scottish Journal of Political Economy*, II, 1955; S. G. Checkland, *Scottish Banking: A History 1695–1973*, pp. 325–63; T. R. Gourvish, 'The Bank of Scotland 1830–45', *Scottish Journal of Political Economy*, XVI, 1969, esp. pp. 296–7.
19 Lee, *Modernisation of Irish Society*, p. 11, and the same author's 'Capital in the Irish economy' in L. M. Cullen ed., *The Formation of the Irish Economy*, Cork, 1969, p. 53.
20 Cornelius Dennehy, 'The industrial resources and banking systems of Ireland', *Irish Times*, 13 May 1864. The distinction between the Belfast

banks and other Irish banks was presumably the reason why Dennehy uses the plural 'systems' rather than the singular in the title of this letter.

21   *S.C. on Irish Industries 1885,* Q. 5878, evidence of Colonel O'Hara, chairman of the Galway Town and Harbour Commissioners; QQ. 10256–7, evidence of Peter McDonald, Dublin wine merchant and distiller, *ibid. Report of the Sub-Committee,* Part 2, p. 793.

22   *Ibid.,* Q. 4347, evidence of W. J. Lane, Cork butter merchant.

23   *Ibid.,* QQ. 1228–31, evidence of W. K. Sullivan, President of Queen's College Cork; *ibid.* Report of the Sub-Committee, pp. 784 ff.

24   L. M. Cullen, 'Germination and growth'.

25   *Royal Commission on the Purchase of Land (Ireland) Act,* BPP 1887, XXVI, Paper no. 3 sent in by Gilbert de Willis, Secretary to the Grand Jury of County Kildare, p. 977. I am grateful to Dr W. E. Vaughan of Trinity College Dublin for this reference. See also *S.C. on Irish Industries 1885,* QQ. 3440–2, evidence of Henry Parkinson, Dublin barrister and magistrate.

26   Lee, *Modernisation of Irish Society,* p. 19.

27   See, for example, C. P. Kindleberger, *Economic Response: Comparative Studies in Trade, Finance and Growth,* Cambridge, Mass., and London, 1978, pp. 70 ff. and the literature cited there.

28   For a survey of literature on this theme see Peter Mathias, 'Capital credit and enterprise in the Industrial Revolution', *Journal of European Economic History,* II, 1973.

29   David S. Landes, *The Unbound Prometheus,* Cambridge, 1969, p. 208.

30   A. Milward and S. B. Saul, *The Development of the Economies of Continental Europe 1850–1914,* London, 1977, pp. 527–8.

31   Gearóid Ó Tuathaigh, *Ireland Before the Famine 1798–1848,* Dublin, 1972, p. 144.

32   Cottrell, *Industrial Finance,* p. 239.

33   Landes *Unbound Prometheus,* p. 209; J. R. T. Hughes, *Industrialisation and Economic History,* New York, 1970, p. 87; Rondo Cameron, *France and the Economic Development of Europe 1800–1914,* Princeton, 1961, pp. 145 ff.

34   Cottrell, *Industrial Finance,* p. 244.

35   Raymond Goldsmith, *Financial Structure and Economic Development,* New Haven, 1969, p. 47; Rondo Cameron, 'Conclusion', in Cameron ed., *Banking in the Early Stages of Industrialisation,* p. 292.

36   Cameron, *Banking in the Early Stages of Industrialisation,* p. 295.

37   Lee, *Modernisation of Irish Society,* p. 14; See also J. M. Goldstrom, 'The industrialisation of the north-east', in Cullen ed., *Formation of the Irish Economy*; E. R. R. Green, 'Belfast entrepreneurship in the nineteenth century', in L. M. Cullen and F. Butel eds., *Négoce et Industrie en France et en Irlande aux XVIIIe et XIXe Siècles.*

Notes to p. 202

38 A recent excellent study which shows Belfast entrepreneurs in a more objective light is Alan Caskey, *Entrepreneurs and Industrial Development in Ulster 1850–1914: A Study in Business History,* unpublished MPhil thesis, New University of Ulster, 1983.

APPENDIX: TRENDS IN PROFITABILITY

Net profit as a percentage of capital employed

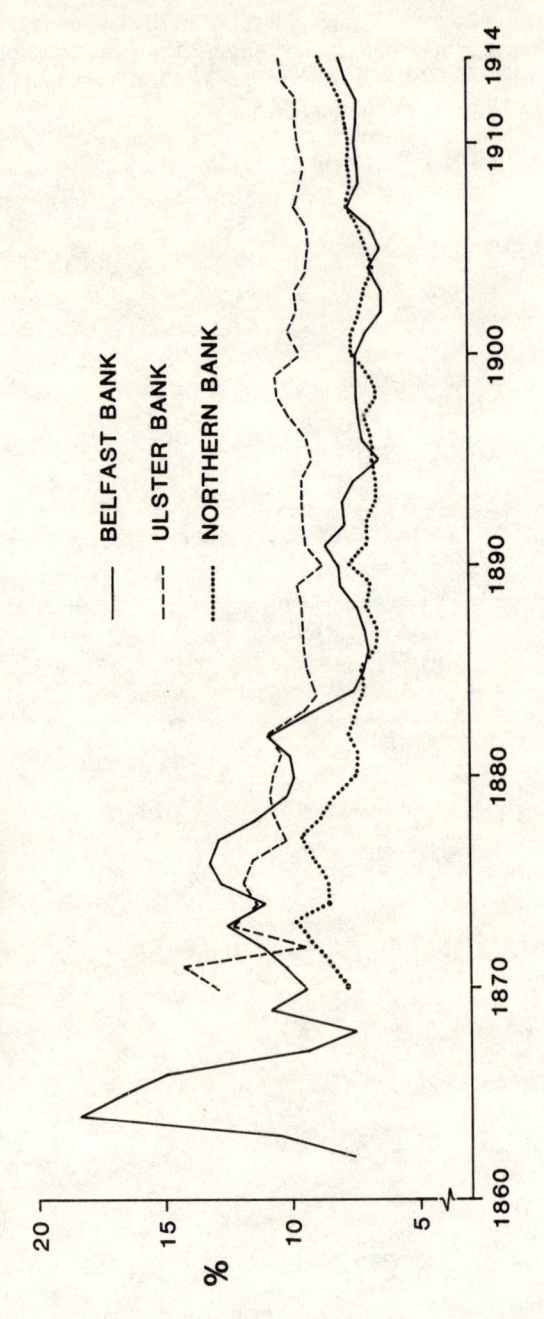

— BELFAST BANK
--- ULSTER BANK
⋯ NORTHERN BANK

Sources: Belfast Bank Miscellaneous Papers; Northern Bank Annual Reports; UBCM.

Note: Net profit = gross profit − (interest paid + working expenses) capital employed = paid up capital + reserve fund.

BIBLIOGRAPHY

Synopsis:
(a) Bank records
(b) Business records
(c) Periodicals and journals
(d) Parliamentary papers
(e) Printed works (pre-1914)
(f) Secondary sources (post-1914)
(g) Unpublished theses

(a) **Bank records**
Northern Bank (PRONI)
Deed of Co-partnership
Annual Reports, 1825–1914
Committee Minutes, 1824–1914
List of Proprietors (24 September 1824)
Circulars to Branches, 1870–1903
Abstracts of Branch Balances, 1856–60, 1873–84

Belfast Bank (PRONI unless otherwise stated)
Deed of Co-partnership (Northern Bank Head Office, Belfast)
List of Proprietors (1 August 1827) (Northern Bank Head Office)
Board of Superintendence Minutes, 1827–92
Annual Reports, 1828–1913
Note Circulation Book, 1839–45
Secretary's Letter Books, 1884–1906
Branch Letter Book, 1892–1912
Sundry Letter Book
Instructions for Managers and Accountants, 1848
Miscellaneous papers

Ulster Bank (PRONI)
Deed of Co-partnership
Stock Register, Vol. 1
Commitee Minutes, 1836–1913
Annual Reports, 1837–1914

Bibliography

Head Office Weekly Balances, 1836–42
Half-Yearly Balances, 1836–64
Notebook of P. Mackintosh
Circulars to Branches, 1840–71
Agreements with Local Banks, Vol. 1
Head Office Out-letter Books, 1861–1914
Private Letter Book of James Carr, 1864–1909
Branch Records (Aughnacloy, Downpatrick, Lurgan)

Provincial Bank of Ireland (*Allied Irish Banks, Foster Place, Dublin*)
Court of Directors' Minute Books, 1846–1914
Circulars to Branches, 1850–1914
Confidential Letter Book, 1834–61
Secret Letter Books, 1844–62
Procedure Book

Royal Bank of Ireland (*Allied Irish Banks, Foster Place, Dublin*)
Annual Report, 1840

Bank of Ireland (*College Green, Dublin*)
Applications for Advances from Agents, 1864–1915
Branch Inspector's Report Book, 1909
Acceptance Book, 1908–10

Midland Bank (*Poultry, London*)
Mr Rae's Private Letters on Banking Questions, 1880–93

(b) **Business Records (*PRONI*)**
Belfast Chamber of Commerce Papers, 1821–1900, D. 1857
Linen Merchants' Association, Minute Books and Annual Reports, D. 2088
Blackstaff Flax Spinning and Weaving Company, Reports and Notices to Shareholders, 1861–1901, D. 2120/6/6, D. 2120/1/1–2
James Boomer Letter Book, 1826–30, D. 2450/2/1
James Campbell Letter Book, 1860–5, D. 2450/1/6
Thomas Gaffikin Letter Book, 1879–1907, D. 1796/1
Killyleagh Flax Spinning Company Papers, D. 1594 Bundle 238
William Kirk Letter Book, 1832–53, D. 1185 Box 1
William Mitchell Letter Book, 1883–8, D. 864 No. 2
McCrum, Mercer and Watson Letter Books, 1863–1916, D. 2518/1–2
Beck Manuscripts, D. 1286 Box 1
Portadown Linen Company, Directors' Minute Book, 1873–77, D. 1252/35/8 Box 410
York Street Flax Spinning Company Balance Sheet, 1864, D. 978

Bibliography

(c) **Periodicals and Journals**
Bankers' Magazine
Belfast Commercial Chronicle
Belfast Linen Trade Circular
Belfast Mercantile Register
Belfast Newsletter
Circular to Bankers
Dublin University Magazine
Economist
Irish Banker
Irish Times
Journal of the Dublin Statistical Society
Journal of the Institute of Bankers
Journal of the Institute of Bankers of Ireland
Journal of the Statistical Society
Northern Whig
Transactions of the Manchester Statistical Society
Pigot's Directory 1824
Thom's Directory

(d) **Parliamentary papers**
Select Committee on the House of Commons to inquire into the state of the circulation of promissory notes under the value of £5 in Scotland and Ireland 1826, BPP, 1826, III
Select Committee of the House of Lords on promissory notes under the value of £5, 1826, BPP, 1826–7, VI
Select Committee of the House of Commons to inquire into the operation of the acts permitting the establishment of joint stock banks in England and Ireland 1837, BPP, 1837, XIV
Select Committee of the House of Commons appointed the following session to consider the same subject 1838, BPP, 1837–8, VII
Select Committee of the House of Commons to inquire into the effects produced on the circulation of the country by the various banking establishments issuing notes payable on demand 1841, BPP, 1841, V
Secret Committee of the House of Lords on commercial distress 1848, BPP, 1847–8, VIII
Select Committee of the House of Commons to inquire into the operation of the bank act of 1844 . . . and the bank act of 1845 . . . 1857, BPP, 1857, X
Select Committee of the House of Commons appointed the following session to consider the same subject 1858, BPP, 1857–8, V
Select Committee of the House of Commons upon the restrictions imposed and the privileges conferred by law on bankers authorised to make and issue notes in England, Scotland and Ireland 1875, BPP,

Bibliography

1875, IX
Select Committee on industries (Ireland) 1885, BPP, 1884–5, IX
Departmental Committee on agricultural credit in Ireland 1914, BPP, 1914, XIII
An Account of the number of banks, private and joint stock, registered in Ireland in each year 1820–44, BPP, 1844, XXXII
An Account of joint stock banking existing in January 1840, BPP, 1844, XXXII
Return of the number of applications made to the Bank of Ireland for the establishment of a branch, BPP, 1844, XXXII

(e) **Printed works (*pre-1914*)**

George Benn, *The History of the Town of Belfast,* Belfast, 1823
W. P. Coyne, ed., *Ireland Industrial and Agricultural,* Dublin, 1902
William Crawford, *Irish Linen and Some Features of its Production,* Belfast, 1910.
M. Dillon, *The History and Development of Banking in Ireland,* London, 1889
D. Morier Evans, *Facts, Failures, Frauds,* London, 1859
J. W. Gilbart, *Treatise on Banking,* London, 1849
Mr Gladstone and the Belfast Chamber of Commerce, Belfast, 1893
W. Neilson Hancock, *Report on Deposits in Joint Stock Banks in Ireland 1840–65,* Dublin, 1866
Thomas Joplin, *An Essay on the General Principles and Present Practice of Banking in England and Scotland,* 5th edition, London, 1826
S. Leoni Levi, *History of British Commerce,* London, 1890
Loyal National Repeal Association, *Report on Joint Stock Banking in Ireland,* Dublin, 1844
Thomas MacKnight, *Ulster As It Is,* London, 1896
Pierce Mahony, *Confidential Letter to the Rt. Hon. Thomas Spring Rice Chancellor of the Exchequer,* London, 1837
James Marshall, *Report to the Directors of the Provincial Bank of Ireland Suggesting a Plan for Commencing and Conducting the Business of Said Bank,* London, 1825
National Bank of Ireland Deed of Settlement, London, 1835
Origin and Progress of the Agricultural and Commercial Bank of Ireland, Dublin, 1835
F. W. Smith, *The Irish Linen Trade Handbook and Directory,* Belfast, 1876
(G. L. Smyth), *Remarks on the Proposed Renewal of the Bank of Ireland Charter,* London, 1838
Thomas Tooke, *An Enquiry into the Currency Principle,* London, 1844
Edward Wakefield, *An Account of Ireland Statistical and Political,* Vol. II, London, 1812

Bibliography

(f) **Secondary sources (*post-1914*)**

B. L. Anderson and P. L. Cottrell, 'Another Victorian capital market: A study of banking and bank investors in Merseyside', *Economic History Review*, XXVIII, 1975

D. L. Armstrong, 'Social and economic conditions in the Belfast linen industry 1850–1900', *Irish Historical Studies,* VII, 1951

T. S. Ashton and R. S. Sayers eds., *Papers in English Monetary History,* Oxford, 1953

Thomas Balogh, *Studies in Financial Organisation,* Cambridge, 1950

G. L. Barrow, The use of money in mid-nineteenth century Ireland, *Studies,* LIX, 1970

——, *The Emergence of the Irish Banking System 1820–45,* Dublin, 1974

Paul Bew, *Land and the National Question in Ireland 1858–82,* Dublin, 1979

R. D. C. Black, *Economic Thought and the Irish Question 1817–70,* Cambridge, 1960

Mark Blaug, *Ricardian Economics. A Historical Study,* New Haven, 1958

P. M. A. Bourke, 'The Irish grain trade 1839–48', *Irish Historical Studies,* XX, 1979

N. S. Buck, *The Development of the Organisation of Anglo-American Trade 1800–1850,* New Haven, 1925

Patrick Buckland, ed., *Irish Unionism 1885–1923: A Documentary History,* Belfast, 1973

Ian Budge and Cornelius O'Leary, *Belfast: Approach to Crisis. A Study of Belfast Politics 1613–1970,* London, 1973

Rondo Cameron, *France and the Economic Development of Continental Europe 1800–1914,* Princeton, NJ, 1961

—— ed., *Banking in the Early Stages of Industrialisation,* Oxford, 1967

—— ed., *Banking and Economic Development,* Oxford, 1972

R. H. Campbell, 'Edinburgh bankers and the Western Bank of Scotland', *Scottish Journal of Political Economy,* II, 1955

Forrest Capie and Ghila Rodrik-Bali, 'Concentration in British banking 1870–1920', *Business History,* XXIV, 1982

Lester V. Chandler, *The Economics of Money and Banking,* 6th edition, New York, 1973

S. D. Chapman, 'Financial restraints on the growth of firms in the cotton industry 1790–1850', *Economic History Review,* XXXII, 1979

S. G. Checkland, 'The Lancashire bill system and its Liverpool protagonists 1810–27', *Economica,* XXI, 1954

——, 'Banking history and economic development: seven systems', *Scottish Journal of Political Economy,* XV, 1968

——, *Scottish Banking. A History 1695–1973,* London, 1975

Bibliography

R. A. Church ed., *The Dynamics of Victorian Business: Problems and Perspectives to the 1870s,* London, 1980

J. H. Clapham, *An Economic History of Modern Britain,* Vols. I and II, Cambridge 1930 and 1932

——, *The Bank of England 1797–1914,* Cambridge, 1944

Samuel Clark, *Social Origins of the Irish Land War,* Princeton, NJ, 1979

M. Collins, 'The Langton papers: banking and banking policy in the 1830s', *Economica,* XXXIX, 1972.

——, 'The business of banking: English bank balance sheets 1840–80', *Business History,* XXVI, 1984

—— and P. Hudson, 'Provincial bank lending: Yorkshire and Merseyside 1825–50', *University of Leeds School of Economic Studies Discussion Paper No. 51,* March, 1977

——, 'Provincial bank lending: Yorkshire and Merseyside 1826–60', *Bulletin of Economic Research,* XXXI, 1979

P. L. Cottrell, *Industrial Finance 1830–1914: The Organisation and Finance of English Manufacturing Industry,* London, 1980

W. F. Crick and J. E. Wadsworth, *A Hundred Years of Joint-Stock Banking,* London, 1936

Andrew Crockett, *Money: Theory, Policy and Institutions,* London, 1973

François Crouzet ed., *Capital Formation in the Industrial Revolution,* London, 1972

L. M. Cullen, *An Economic History of Ireland Since 1660,* London, 1972

——'Landlords, bankers and merchants: the early Irish banking world, 1700–1820', *Hermathena,* 135, 1982–3

—— ed., *The Formation of the Irish Economy,* Cork, 1969

—— and P. Butel eds., *Négoce et Industrie en France et en Irlande aux XVIIIe et XIXe Siècles,* Paris, 1980

J. R. L. Currie, *The Northern Counties Railway 1845–1903,* Newton Abbot, 1973

Marian Daugherty, 'The currency banking controversy', *Southern Economic Journal,* VIII, 1942–3

Decades of the Ulster Bank, Belfast, 1965

James S. Donnelly Jr, *The Land and People of Nineteenth Century Cork,* London, 1975

——, 'The Irish agricultural depression of 1859–64', *Irish Economic and Social History,* III, 1976

R. D. Edwards and T. D. Williams eds., The Great Famine: Studies in Irish History 1846–52, Dublin, 1956

W. Aytoun Ellis, *Heir of Adventure. The Story of Brown, Shipley and Co.,* London, 1960

Bibliography

Clive Emsley, 'The Home Office and its sources of information and investigation 1791–1801', *English Historical Review,* XCIV, 1979
A. E. Feavearyear, *The Pound Sterling,* Oxford, 1931
F. W. Fetter, 'Legal tender during the English and Irish bank restrictions', *Journal of Political Economy,* LVIII, 1950
——, 'Economic controversy in the British reviews 1802–50', *Economica,* XXXII, 1965
——, *The Development of British Monetary Orthodoxy 1797–1875,* Cambridge, Mass., 1965
—— ed., *The Irish Pound 1797–1826,* London, 1955
David Fitzpatrick, 'The disappearance of the Irish agricultural labourer 1841–1912', *Irish Economic and Social History,* VII, 1980
G. A. Fletcher, *The Discount Houses in London,* London, 1976
R. Floud and D. N. McCloskey, *The Economic History of Britain since 1700,* 2 vols., Cambridge, 1981
N. E. Gamble, 'The business community and trade of Belfast 1767–1800', *Irish Economic and Social History,* VII, 1980
A. D. Gayer, Anna Jacobson and Isaiah Finkelstein, 'British share prices 1811–50', *Review of Economic Statistics,* XXII, 1940
——, W. W. Rostow and Anna J. Schwartz, *The growth and Fluctuation of the British Economy 1790–1850,* Vol. I, Oxford, 1953
Conrad Gill, *The Rise of the Irish Linen Industry,* Oxford, 1925
R. W. Goldsmith, *Financial Structure and Economic Development,* New Haven, 1969
T. R. Gourvish, 'The Bank of Scotland 1830–45', *Scottish Journal of Political Economy,* XVI, 1969
E. R. R. Green, *The Lagan Valley 1800–50. A Local Study of the Industrial Revolution,* London, 1949
T. E. Gregory, *The Westminster Bank Through a Century,* 2 vols., Oxford, 1936
F. G. Hall, *History of the Bank of Ireland,* Dublin and Oxford, 1949
Leslie Hannah ed., *Management Strategy and Business Development,* London, 1976
Ralph Hidy, *The House of Baring in American Trade and Finance,* Cambridge, Mass., 1943
E. J. Hobsbawm, *Industry and Empire,* London, 1969
H. O. Horne, *A History of Savings Banks,* Oxford, 1947
W. G. Hoskins, 'Harvest fluctuations and English economic history 1620–1759', *Agricultural History Review,* XVI, 1968
Pat Hudson, 'The role of banks in the finance of the West Yorkshire wool textile industry, *c.* 1780–1850', *Business History Review,* LV, 1981
J. R. T. Hughes, 'The commercial crisis of 1857', *Oxford Economic Papers* VIII, 1956

Bibliography

——, *Fluctuations in Industry, Trade, and Finance*, Oxford, 1960
——, *Industrialisation and Economic History. Theses and Conjectures*, New York, 1970
Bishop C. Hunt, 'The joint-stock company in England 1830–44', *Journal of Political Economy*, XLIII, 1935
——, *The Development of the Business Corporation in England 1800–67*, Cambridge, Mass., 1936
Leland H. Jenks, *The Migration of British Capital to 1875*, New York, 1927
F. Stuart Jones, 'The collapse of instant banking', *Bankers' Magazine*, CXXVII, 1971
——, 'The cotton industry and joint stock banking in Manchester 1825–50', *Business History*, XXI, 1979
Liam Kennedy and Philip Ollerenshaw eds., *An Economic History of Ulster 1820–1939*, Manchester, 1985
Frank R. Kent, *The Story of Alexander Brown and Sons*, Baltimore, 1925
J. R. Killick, 'Risk, specialisation and profit in the mercantile sector of the nineteenth century cotton trade: Alexander Brown and Sons 1820–80', *Business History*, XVI, 1974
C. P. Kindleberger, *Economic Response. Comparative Studies in Finance, Trade and Growth*, Cambridge, Mass., 1978
——, *A Financial History of Western Europe*, London, 1984
R. W. Kirkpatrick, 'Landed estates in mid-Ulster and the Irish Land War 1879–85', *Irish Economic and Social History*, V, 1978
David S. Landes, *The Unbound Prometheus*, Cambridge, 1969
Joseph Lee, 'The provision of capital for early Irish railways, 1830–53', *Irish Historical Studies*, XVI, 1968
——, *The Modernisation of Irish Society 1848–1918*, Dublin, 1973
F. S. L. Lyons, *Ireland Since the Famine*, London, 1971
—— and R. A. J. Hawkins eds., *Ireland Under the Union*, Oxford, 1980
W. A. Maguire, *The Downshire Estates in Ireland 1801–1845*, Oxford, 1972
Nicholas Mansergh, *The Irish Question 1840–1921*, 3rd edition, London, 1975
Sheila Marriner, 'Company financial statements as source material for business historians', *Business History*, XXII, 1980
Peter Mathias, 'Capital, credit and enterprise in the Industrial Revolution', *Journal of European Economic History*, II, 1973
R. C. O. Matthews, *A Study in Trade Cycle History*, Cambridge, 1954
Gordon McMullan, 'The Irish bank 'strike' of 1919', *Saothar*, 5, 1979
R. C. Michie, 'The transfer of shares in Scotland 1700–1820, *Business History*, XX, 1978

Bibliography

——, 'The British securities market 1850–1914', *Economic History Review*, XXXVIII, 1985

M. Miles, 'The money market in the early Industrial Revolution: the evidence from West Riding attorneys c 1750–1800', *Business History*, XXIII, 1981

A. Milward and S. B. Saul, *The Development of the Economies of Continental Europe 1850–1914*, London, 1977

B. R. Mitchell and Phyllis Deane, *Abstract of British Historical Statistics*, Cambridge, 1962

T. W. Moody and J. C. Beckett eds., *Ulster Since 1800*, London, 1954, 1957

E. V. Morgan, 'Railway investment, Bank of England policy and interest rates 1844–48', *Economic History*, IV, 1940

——, *The Theory and Practice of Central Banking 1797–1913*, Cambridge, 1943

R. G. Morton, *Standard Gauge Railways of the North of Ireland*, Belfast, 1962

C. W. Munn, *The Scottish Provincial Banking Companies 1747–1864*, Edinburgh, 1981

——, 'The coming of joint-stock banking in Scotland and Ireland c. 1820–45', in T. M. Devine and David Dickson eds., *Scotland and Ireland*, Edinburgh, 1983

——, 'The emergence of central banking in Ireland: The Bank of Ireland 1814–50', *Irish Economic and Social History*, X, 1983

E. T. Nevin and E. W. Davis, *The London Clearing Banks*, London, 1970

Shizuya Nishimura, *The Decline of Inland Bills of Exchange in the London Money Market 1855–1913*, Cambridge, 1971

Northern Banking Company Ltd Centenary Volume 1824–1924, Belfast, 1925

D. P. O'Brien, *The Classical Economists*, Oxford, 1975

George O'Brien, 'The last years of the Irish currency', *Economic History*, II, 1927

——, *An Economic History of Ireland from the Union to the Famine*, London, 1921, reprinted New York, 1971

J. B. O'Brien, 'Sadleir's bank', *Journal of the Cork Historical and Archaeological Society*, LXXXII, 1977

Gearóid Ó Tuathaigh, *Ireland Before the Famine 1798–1848*, Dublin, 1972

Henry Patterson, *Class Conflict and Sectarianism*, Belfast, 1980

L. S. Pressnell, *Country Banking in the Industrial Revolution*, Oxford, 1956

——, 'Cartels and competition in British banking: a background study, *Banca Nazionale Del Lavoro Quarterly Review*, XXIII, 1970

Bibliography

G. L. Rees, *Britain's Commodity Markets,* London, 1972
R. S. Sayers, *Lloyds Bank in the History of English Banking,* Oxford, 1957
W. M. Scott ed., *A Hundred Years A-Milling,* Belfast, 1951
Bernard Share ed., *Root and Branch. Allied Irish Banks Yesterday, Today, Tomorrow,* Dublin, 1979
Christine Shaw, 'The large manufacturing employers of 1907', *Business History,* XXV, 1983
Noel Simpson, *The Belfast Bank 1827–1970,* Belfast, 1975
A. Slaven, *The Development of the West of Scotland 1750–1960,* London, 1975
W. Smart, *Economic Annals of the Nineteenth Century, 1821–30,* London, 1917
B. L. Solow, *The Land Question and the Irish Economy 1870–1903,* Cambridge, Mass., 1971
A. T. Q. Stewart, *The Ulster Crisis,* London, 1967
Dennis Swann, D. P. O'Brien, W. P. J. Maunder, W. S. Howe, *Competition in British Industry,* London, 1974
J. Sykes, *The Amalgamation Movement in English Banking 1825–1914,* London, 1926
B. Tew and R. F. Henderson eds., *Studies in Company Finance,* Cambridge, 1959
S. E. Thomas, 'The first English provincial banks', *Economic History,* II, 1934
——, *The Rise and Growth of Joint Stock Banking,* London, 1934
W. Tyrrell, *A History of the Belfast Savings Bank,* Belfast, 1946
M. A. Utton, *Industrial Concentration,* London, 1970
C. R. Whittlesey and J. S. G. Wilson eds., *Essays in Money and Banking,* Oxford, 1968
T. Desmond Williams ed., *Historical Studies,* VIII, Dublin, 1971
E. M. Carus Wilson ed., *Essays in Economic History,* I, London, 1954
——, *Essays in Economic History,* III, London, 1962

(g) **Unpublished theses**

E. J. Boyle, *The Economic Development of the Irish Linen Industry 1825–1913,* PhD, Queen's University of Belfast, 1979
Alan Caskey, *Entrepreneurs and Industrial Development in Ulster 1850–1914,* MPhil, New University of Ulster, 1983
M. Collins, *The Bank of England and the Liverpool Money Market 1825–50,* PhD, University of London, 1972
O. N. Greeves, *The Impact of the American Civil War on the UK Textile Industries,* PhD, University of Bristol, 1968–9
J. J. Monaghan, *The Social and Economic History of Belfast 1801–25,* PhD, Queen's University of Belfast, 1940

Bibliography

P. G. Ollerenshaw, *The Belfast Banks 1820–1900: Aspects of Banking in Nineteenth Century Ireland,* PhD, University of Sheffield, 1982

INDEX

accommodation bills, 118, 148
Agricultural and Commercial Bank
  of Ireland, 57
  Belfast branch, 41, 42
  branch network, 39–40, 53
  capital structure, 39
  established, 31, 33
  failure, 43–5, 78, 92, 188, 189
  insolvency, 41–2
  resumption, 43
agriculture, 53, 54, 64–8, 70–2,
  81–4, 93, 190, 198
  depression of, 1859–64, 102–5
  depression of, late 1870s, 114–22,
  147
Agriculture and Technical
  Instruction, Department of,
  120
Allan, Charles, 175
Anti-Corn Law League, 159
Antrim
  county of, 8, 65
  town of, 49
Ardglass, 119
Ards Weaving Co., 170
Armagh,
  city of, 15, 16, 25, 26, 35, 49, 107,
  125
  county of, 8, 25, 26, 49, 65, 107,
  118
attorneys, economic role of, 4, 5–6,
  16–17
Aughnacloy, 81–2
Australia, 74

Bailieborough, 122
Balbriggan, 118
Ballinamore, 122
Ballybay, 64, 118
Ballybofey, 122
Ballymena, 15, 47, 49, 113
Ballymena, Ballymoney, Coleraine
  and Portrush Junction
  Railway, 99
Ballymoney, 49, 77
Baltimore, 51, 165
Banbridge, 49, 88, 99, 117, 177
Bank Acts (1844–5), 56–64, 69–70,
  76, 79–80, 84, 193
Bank of England, 22–3, 50, 56,
  59–60, 73, 75–6, 84, 87
Bank of Ireland, 43, 57, 63, 84, 120,
  132, 152, 153, 155, 183
  branch network, 18–20, 21, 35–6,
  157
  charter modified, 9–10
  competitiveness, 92, 194–6
  deposits, 92, 118–9
  discount rates, 41, 87
  established, 7
  lending, 107, 157, 174–6, 195
  note issue, 19, 62
  supports other banks, 9, 11, 43,
  195
Bank of Liverpool, 50
Bank notes
  exchange of, 21–2, 60, 62
  fiduciary limits, 57–9, 60, 79, 84
  fractional, 24, 61, 84

256

Index

importance of, 24–7, 32, 64, 84, 201
loss of confidence in, 27, 48, 77–9
seasonal fluctuation of, 81, 82–7, 94, 114
under £5, 23–7, 61, 67, 77, 84
Barbour, William & Sons, thread manufacturers, 106, 147
Barrow, G. L., 63
Belfast and Ballymena Railway, 98
Belfast and Northern Counties Railway, 157, 174
Belfast Annuity Co., 6
Belfast Banking Company, 32, 39, 42, 47, 49, 50, 62, 92, 101, 125, 126, 136, 139, 150, 155, 156, 157, 197
  advances, 98–9, 108, 151, 166, 168–9, 170–1, 172, 173–4, 177–9, 180–1, 193
  amalgamation talks, 126–8, 129
  assistance to W. and J. Brown, 50
  Board of Superintendence, 28–9, 99, 163, 168, 180
  branch network, 29, 36–9, 53, 72, 134, 135, 136, 152, 153, 156, 193, 200
  capital structure, 28, 128–9, 130, 149
  country agencies, 29, 200
  crisis of 1836, 49
  crisis of 1847, 68
  crisis of 1857, 77, 79–80
  deposits, 73, 77, 104, 105, 116, 137, 141
  discount policy, 87–8, 89
  dividend policy, 34, 54
  fraud in, 110–11, 191
  Home Rule politics and, 160
  incorporation, 143
  limited liability, 148, 149
  origins, 6, 7, 22, 27–30
  profits, 109, 203
  reserve fund, 80, 110
  share values, 32–3, 132
Belfast Chamber of Commerce, 2, 26, 142, 150, 159, 170
Belfast Chemical Works, 96–7
Belfast Flax and Jute Co., 147
Belfast Flax Spinning Co., 171
Belfast, Holywood and Bangor Railway, 98
Belfast Warehouse Co., 178–9
Belgium, 199
Bessbrook Spinning Co., 108
bills of exchange, 14, 15, 16, 22, 81, 87–90, 103, 108–9, 148, 185, 200
Blackstaff Flax Spinning Co., 94, 108, 150, 168, 171
Borough Bank of Liverpool, 74
Boyd, J. S., 177–9
Boyle, Low and Pim, private bankers, 63, 152
Bristow, J. T., 190
Bristow, J. W., 60, 66, 77, 81, 91, 94
British and Irish Fire Insurance Co., 19
Brookfield Linen Co., 171
Brown, W. and J. and Co., 50–1
Browne, John, 180–1
Brownlow, Charles, 14
building societies, 119, 139

Cameron, Rondo, 1, 201
Campbell, W. and J., provision merchants, 96
Carndonagh, 122
Carr, James, 148
Carrick-on-Shannon, 122
cash credit, 13–14, 33–4, 97–8
Castleblayney, 77
Cavan
  county of, 8, 118, 122
  town of, 97, 99
Checkland, S. G., 188
cheques, 61
City of Glasgow Bank, 145–6, 147,

Index

150, 182
City of Liverpool Steam Navigation Co., 174
Clady, 119
Clapham, Sir John, 77, 144
Clark, Samuel, 121
clearing house
  Dublin, 62
  Edinburgh, 62
Clones, 53, 99, 118
Coates, Victor and Co., engineers and boilermakers, 173–4
coin, 23–4, 25, 42, 84, 87
Coleraine, 9, 15, 35, 118, 136
Collins, Michael, 93
collusive agreements
  assessment of, 201
  in operation, 122–6, 134–40, 153–7
  in Scotland, 154–5
  signature of, 50–2, 122
Combe, James (Falls Foundry), 97, 172–3
Comber, 118
Commercial Bank, 6, 7, 8, 16, 21–2, 27
Cookstown, 98, 110
Cork
  city of, 45
  county of, 45, 103
Cork Savings Bank, 67
Cotton Famine, 102, 105
cotton industry, 8, 22, 69, 102, 109
Cottrell, P. L., 189
County Down Flax Spinning and Weaving Co., 167
Crawford, Sir William, 167
credit balances, 54, 90–3, 106, 116–9
Crédit Mobilier, 199
Crick, W. F., and Wadsworth, J. E., 142
Cullen, L. M., 4, 115, 118
Curell, John, 46–7, 49

Currency–Banking School controversy, 56–7, 58, 60

Dennehy, Cornelius, 196–7
deposits
  increasing importance of, 64, 137
  interest on, 19–20, 54, 136–7
  regional distribution, 91–3, 116–8, 190
  trends in, 70–2, 73, 77–9, 90–3, 104–5, 114–20, 183, 185, 196
Derry City, 7, 15, 25, 35, 36, 49, 93, 99, 118, 165
  see also Londonderry
Discount Office (Belfast), 4
distilling, 163, 175–6, 178–9
Dobbin, Leonard, 16, 26
Donegal, county of, 49, 102, 122
Donegall, Marquis of, 48
Donnelly, James S. Jr., 102, 103
Down, county of, 8, 17, 49, 65, 118
Downpatrick, 16, 17, 118
Drogheda, 72, 77
Dromore, 118
Dublin
  city of, 2, 3, 4, 5, 17, 19, 30, 31, 35, 42–3, 47–8, 54, 62–3, 123, 125, 152, 156, 165, 189, 192–3, 194, 197
  county of, 118
Dublin Stock Exchange, 145, 185
Duffin, Charles, 179–80
Duffin, Edmund Grimshaw, 179
Dun, John, 132, 148, 149
Dundalk, 9, 72, 77
Dundalk and Enniskillen Railway, 98
Dundas, George, 42
Dungannon, 7, 15, 77, 82
Dungiven, 118
Dunmurry, 165
Dunville and Co., distillers, 176
Durham Street Weaving Co., 172

Index

Edgeworthstown, 121
Edinburgh, 4, 17, 62, 196
Edwards, Revd. William, 176
Emerson, Arbuthnot, 40
Emerson, James, 40
engineering, 2, 163, 172–4
  see also shipbuilding
England and Wales
  banking in, 8–9, 10, 11, 12, 22, 23, 57, 58, 79, 93, 132, 144, 152, 159, 185, 189, 190, 199
  share speculation in 1836, 41
Enniskillen, 77, 193

Falls Foundry, 97, 173
Famine, the Great (late 1840s), 1, 31, 63–4, 65–9, 103, 138
Fenianism, 158
Ferguson's Bank, 7
Fermanagh, 118
Fintona, 118
Fivemiletown, 117
fluctuations, economic, 3, 9, 22–3, 41, 50, 52–6, 59, 67–70, 74–80, 81–90, 102–5, 109–10, 114–22, 142, 163–76, 191, 198–9
food processing, 2, 163
Fullarton, John, 56

Gaffikin, Thomas, 167
Gallagher, James, grain merchant, 166
Germany, 182, 199–200
Gibbons and Williams, bill brokers, 63
Gilbart, J. W., 12, 83
Gill and Fisher and Co., Baltimore, 165
Gladstone, W. E., 159, 162
Glasgow, 196
  see also City of Glasgow Bank
Goddard, James, 19
Goulburn, Henry, 66
grain trade, 68–9, 165–6

Greenhill, John, 159
Greeves, J. T. and M., flax spinners, 108
Grimshaw, Robert, 46–7, 49
Guinness, Mahon and Co., 152
Gunning and Campbell, flax spinners, 170

Haines, R. N., miller, 165
Hanington's Bank, 8
Harland and Wolff, 163, 174–6
Hayes, William and Son, flax spinners and weavers, 88
Hibernian Bank, 39, 64, 132, 161, 162
  branch network, 34, 123, 134–5, 136, 183
  competitiveness, 122–5, 132, 136–7, 154, 183, 194, 201
  crisis of 1836, 42–3, 47–8, 63
  dividends, 34
  established, 30
  precarious state, 153, 193
  share prices, 30
Higgin and Co., distillers, 176
Hillsborough, 118
Hind, John and Co. (Durham Street Mill), 168–9
Home Rule politics, 157–63
Houston, J. H., 25, 27
Heron, John, 46–7
Hughes, Thomas, 20

Inglis, H. D., 1
Irvinestown, 118
Island Spinning Co., 172

Jaffe Brothers, 177
Johns, Alexander, 127, 150
Joplin, Thomas, 17

Keady, 118
Keegan, Peter and Co., wine and spirit merchants, 175–6

259

Index

Kennedy, W. P., 182
Kildare, county of, 198
Killyleagh Flax Spinning Co., 111–2
Kindleberger, C. P., 1
Kirkpatrick, R. W., 118

Lancashire, 25, 69, 109
Land League, 120, 121
Land War, 102
Larne, 119, 163
Lee, J. J., 98, 99, 118, 186, 195, 199
Leitrim, county of, 122
Letterkenny, 99, 134–5, 136
Limavady, 77
limited liability for banks, 140–5, 147–50
linen industry, 2, 3, 54, 61, 67–8, 73, 74, 100, 102–3, 113–14, 129, 144, 163, 190
   finance for, 21, 88, 97, 100, 105–14, 147, 166–72
Linen Merchants' Association, 167, 168, 170
Lisburn, 106, 134
Liverpool, 50–1, 74
London, 4, 23, 31, 41, 66, 76, 105, 197
London and Westminster Bank, 143, 185
Londonderry, county of, 8, 49, 53, 65, 118
   see also Derry City
Longfield, Mountifort, 43, 44, 45
Louisburgh, 121
Lowry, Valentine and Kirk and Co., 110–12, 177
Lurgan, 7, 14, 16, 53, 113
Lyle, Thomas, 19

McCance, John, 13
McCracken, John, 8
McCrum, Watson and Mercer and Co., linen manufacturers, 107, 168

McNeile, John, 11
Magherafelt, 15, 77
Mahony, Pierce, 44
Malcolmson's Bank, 7, 9
Marshall, James, 17
Mayo, 120
Meath, 122
Merseyside, 2
   see also Liverpool
Mill, John Stuart, 56
milling industry, 165–6
Mitchell, William, grain merchant, 165
Mohill, 122
Monaghan
   county of, 8, 49, 118
   town of, 15, 77, 82
Moncrieff, William, 20
Moneymore, 53
Monkstown Spinning Co., 97
Montgomery, Hugh, 11
Moore Brothers and Killen, railway contractors, 97
Moore, Foxalle and McCann (Newry Bank), 7, 9
Moy, 125
Munster and Leinster Bank, 152, 155, 183, 185
Munster Bank, 31, 123, 130, 144, 152, 188, 189, 198

National Bank, 132, 183, 197
   branch network, 62, 73, 123, 125, 132
   competitiveness, 123, 125, 137, 194, 201
   crisis of 1857, 79
   deposits, 104–5
   established, 46
   limited liability, 148
   losses in the leather trade, 103
Navan, 72, 77
Newcastle-upon-Tyne, 79
Newport (County Mayo), 121

Index

Newry, 7, 9, 15, 35, 36, 118
Newry Navigation Co., 97
Newtownards, 134
New York, 74, 165
Nishimura, Shizuya, 190
Northern and Central Bank of
   England, 39, 40, 41
Northern Banking Company, 28,
   32, 33, 39, 47, 49, 58, 62, 63, 66,
   69, 77, 92, 100, 106, 125, 126,
   134, 135, 136, 139, 155, 197
   amalgamation talks, 126–8
   assistance to W. and J. Brown, 50
   branch network, 29, 36–9, 53, 64,
      91, 93, 119, 134, 153, 156, 201
   capital structure, 11, 53, 129–30,
      131, 149
   controversies with local banks,
      21–2
   converts from private bank, 9–17
   country agencies, 15–16, 18, 25,
      30, 201
   crisis of 1826, 23
   deposits, 20, 21, 70–1, 91, 92,
      115–18, 137, 141
   dividend policy, 54
   incorporation, 143
   lending, 97, 98, 99, 112, 113,
      121–2, 146, 194, 195, 198
   origins, 6, 7
   partners, 11–12
   profits, 109, 120, 203
   secret code, use of, 145–6, 160–1
   share prices, 30
   'small' notes, 24, 25, 62
   takeover of Ball's Bank, 152

O'Brien, George, 192
Old Bushmills Distillery, 178–9
Oldcastle, 122
Omagh, 99, 138
Oriental Steam Navigation Co., 175
Orr, James, 11, 13, 14, 15, 25
Ó Tuathaigh, Gearóid, 199

Overend, Gurney and Co., 129, 143

Parnell, Sir Henry, 10
Portadown, 113
Post Office, 66
   Savings Banks, 66, 138, 160
Pressnell, L. S., 190
Preston Banking Co., 109
Provident Bank of Ireland, 45, 53
Provincial Bank of Ireland, 30, 32,
   39, 44, 45, 49, 58, 62, 84, 87, 92,
   103, 120, 150, 155, 161, 183,
   197
   branch network, 17–20, 22, 34–5,
      36–7, 39, 53, 62, 64, 201
   crisis of 1847, 69
   crisis of 1857, 75
   discounts, 88, 89–90
   dividends, 34
   established, 17–18
   Great Famine and, 66
   joins collusive agreement, 154–5
   lending, 75, 97–8, 100, 103,
      111–13, 150, 165–6, 182, 197–8
   share prices, 30, 133
   'small' notes, 26, 84
provisions trade, 69
   finance of, 94, 96, 100

Rae, George, 140
railways
   construction of, 55, 74, 120, 199
   finance for, 74, 97–9, 174
   investment in, 55–6, 59
   share values, 120, 159–60, 174
Ramelton, 122
Raphoe, 122
Redesdale, Lord, 127
reserve liability, 148, 149
Richardson family, 108
Robinson and Cleaver, retail store,
   175
ropemaking, 163
Roscommon, county of, 118, 122

Index

Ross, W. A., flax spinner, 147
Royal Bank of Ireland, 54, 63, 64, 123, 132, 189, 197
Royal Bank of Scotland, 13

Sadleir, James, 78
Sadleir, John, 78–9
St Louis, 165
savings banks, 66–7, 120, 138–40, 160
Scotland
    banking in, 8, 12, 13, 17, 22, 23, 26, 74–5, 139, 145, 196–7
    banknotes in, 23, 25–6, 58, 60
    bank officers from, 18, 20, 200
    bank share premiums, 132
    General Managers' Committee, 154–5
Seapatrick, 88
Shannon, H. A., 102
Sharman-Crawford, Colonel R. G., 162
Shaw, William, 140
shipbuilding, 2, 163, 174–5, 195
Sinclair, John, 20
Sinclair, Thomas, 162
Sinton, Thomas, 177
Sloane, John, 20
Smithfield Flax Spinning and Weaving Co., 108
Southern Bank of Ireland, 45, 53
Spotten, William and Co., 110, 113
Steen, James, 47
Stewart, Alexander, 20
Strabane, 138
Strokestown, 118, 122

Tandragee, 113, 177
Taylor, John, 73
Tipperary Joint-Stock Banking, 31, 78, 79, 188, 189
tobacco industry, 163
Trustee Savings Banks, 138, 160
Tyrone, 8, 49, 118, 125

Ulster Banking Company, 43, 58, 62, 73, 100, 128, 137, 145, 154–5, 165, 185, 197
    account holders, 82
    assistance to W. and J. Brown, 50–1
    branch network, 49, 92, 121, 123–6, 134–6, 138, 153, 156, 183
    capital structure, 46–7, 130–1, 149
    competitiveness, 123, 125
    crisis of 1836, 43, 47–8, 49
    deposits, 73, 91–2, 104, 105, 106, 115, 116
    discounts, 89–90, 103, 106, 113
    dividend policy, 54
    established, 31, 33
    incorporation, 143–4
    lending, 94–7, 99, 100, 103, 106, 112–3, 147, 150, 167, 170, 171, 173–4, 175–6, 177, 179–80, 181–2, 192–3, 194, 195
    limited liability, 148
    organisation, 46–7
    profits, 183, 203
    share denomination, 44
Ulster Defence Union, 159
Ulster Railway, 98
Ulster Spinning Co., 169
Ulster Unionism, 162–3
Ulster Unionist Council, 163
Union Bank of London, 110
Unionist Defence Fund, 163
United States, 53, 55, 74–5, 105, 165
United Trust Co., 175
Usury Laws, 26

Virginia (County Cavan), 118, 122

Wallace, Hugh, 16–17
Watson, Solomon, bill broker, 8, 47, 63
Western Bank of Scotland, 74–5, 79

Index

Westport, 120
Whiteabbey Bleaching Co., 167
Whiteabbey Flax Spinning Co., 111, 112
Workman Clark and Co., 163, 175–6

York Street Flax Spinning Co., 107, 108, 151, 170–1
Yorkshire, 94